A YEAR AMONG THE NATURAL WONDERS OF HEARD ISLAND

Unique &

Unspoilt

To Glyn

Bernadette Hince

THE 1953 JOURNALS OF JOHN BÉCHERVAISE

EDITED BY BERNADETTE HINCE

Dedication

This book is dedicated to Fred Elliott and
Jack Ward, two fine men.

Contents

Glossary

aiguille	a sharp needle or pinnacle of rock. The most conspicuous ones on Heard Island are on Mount Olsen on the Laurens Peninsula.
ANARE	Australian National Antarctic Research Expedition(s)
anorak	a hooded parka or waterproof overjacket
azorella	the robust-looking cushion-forming perennial plant *Azorella selago*, designed to endure the bitter winds of the subantarctic. It forms dense spreading bright-green mounds that can be quite hard to the touch. In 1949, biologist Les Gibbney described how easily the foot can sink into azorella, as if 'into a thick Turkish carpet'. Visitors to Heard Island are now asked to avoid walking on the azorella, which recovers very slowly from trampling and can be eroded by cold wind if damaged.
bergschrund	a crevasse or fissure between a mountain and the top of a glacier
brash	broken fragments of ice
Chippy's (or Chippy's church)	the high-gabled hut at Atlas Cove used for storing equipment
crampons	a set of metal spikes fitted to boots for ice climbing
crevasse	a chasm in a glacier, often bridged (sometimes precariously) by snow
Dines (anemometer)	a device to measure wind strength (named after its inventor, English meteorologist William Henry Dines)
ding	a party or celebration, with alcohol issued
diver	a diving petrel. These birds nest in burrows; two species breed on Heard Island.
dog-line	a place where dogs (huskies) are tethered. The dogs on Heard Island in 1953 were being trained for use in Antarctica.
dogmobile	an oversized 'billycart' with rubber tyres built on an old Jeep frame pulled by dogs. When snow conditions were right, the dogs pulled a sledge instead.

elephant	an elephant seal. On Heard Island this is the southern hemisphere *Mirounga leonina. Also called* sea elephant.
ETA	expected time of arrival
Furphy	a cast-iron water tank (from the name of the firm J. Furphy and Sons Pty Ltd, Shepparton, Victoria, manufacturers of the tanks)
gash	waste, garbage (originally naval slang)
giant petrel	one of the largest seabirds except for the albatrosses. Until the 1960s all giant petrels (*Macronectes*) were one species; now northern and southern giant petrels are separate species. *Also called* GP, glutton, nelly or stinker.
japara	a (cotton) cloth rendered waterproof by oiling or waxing, used for clothing and tents
Kerguelen cabbage	the perennial plant *Pringlea antiscorbutica,* which has edible fleshy leaves and an edible root. In the absence of other more palatable plants, it has been used as a source of fresh greens.
leopard seal	the seal *Hydrurga leptonyx*. More leopard seals come ashore on Heard Island in winter than on any of the other subantarctic islands, but they breed in Antarctica's pack ice, not on the island. *Also called* sea leopard.
macaroni (penguin)	the penguin *Eudyptes chrysolophus*. It has yellow 'eyebrows' and is larger than the rockhopper.
nelly (or nellie)	a giant petrel
névé	hardened snow
Nullarbor	the flat unvegetated land south of the station between Atlas Cove, Corinthian Bay and Mount Drygalski. *Sometimes spelt* Nullabor.
obs	observations
OIC	officer in charge
onazote	the proprietary name for a rigid rubber foam whose air cells are insulated from each other
porkie (or porky)	a young fattened or rapidly fattening elephant seal
radiosonde	a unit which records and transmits weather details such as temperature, wind speed and direction. Radiosondes were attached to hydrogen-filled balloons which expand as they rise into increasingly low-pressure air, eventually bursting and falling back to earth or sea. Observers at Antarctic stations today still make daily releases of weather balloons.

rawin	a unit which records and then transmits data on upper-atmosphere winds. The rawin hut on Heard Island in 1953 was a hexagonal insulated plywood building, prefabricated like other huts there. *From* 'radio' + 'wind'.
road	a stretch of sheltered water where a ship can ride at anchor nearshore. The Atlas Roads of Atlas Cove offered such a possibility only in good weather. *Also called* roadstead.
rockhopper (penguin)	the smallest crested penguin, *Eudyptes chrysocome*. Like the macaroni penguin, it has yellow 'eyebrows'.
RTA	return(ed) to Australia
sago snow	small, round, hard and dry pellets of snow
sastrugi	wind-hardened ridges of snow
skeds (or scheds)	schedules, usually referring to scheduled radio contact times
slushy	a person rostered to help with domestic chores such as cleaning and washing up. Everyone on Heard Island had regular 'slushy' duty, and took turns as cook on Sundays to give the cook, Dick McNair, a day off. One additional duty was to wake everyone except those who were entitled to sleep in.
sonde	*see* radiosonde
ventile	an outer garment made from a closely woven English cotton fabric. Ventiles provide good protection from wind but not rain.
whizzer	a coded telegram

Introduction

When I opened my first box of John Béchervaise's papers in the National Library of Australia, the first thing I noticed was the musty smell. Though it took a minute to realise why, I immediately felt at home. It was the smell of old papers and books, of course. I grew up in a house full of old books, and my father has run a second-hand bookshop for almost all my life.

I reached into the box and pulled out a typed bound loose-leaf diary, whose pages were carefully numbered. From the age of 16 or 17, Béchervaise kept a 'daybook' like the one I was holding. Not only did he document his life systematically, but he typed up his diary every day or few days with carbon paper to make multiple copies of the daybooks, and later deposited them in various libraries. It was hard to avoid thinking, as I began to read, that he had meant them for publication one day.

It is impossible to imagine anywhere more spectacular than Heard Island, a remote ice-covered volcano in the Southern Ocean at 53°S, 73°E. It is Australian territory, much closer to Antarctica than it is to Australia or Africa. Today no-one lives on Heard Island—and for most of its history no-one has lived there. But from December 1947 to March 1955 a small Australian base operated on the island. The officer in charge during 1953 was John Béchervaise, an adventurer and climber who led the first ascent of Federation Peak, south-western Tasmania, in 1949. Heard is a small island, but its 2745 metre volcanic cone rises dramatically from sea level. It is covered in ice and ringed by almost permanent cloud. Its peak is often clear above the clouds and visible from the sea, but not from the island itself. Steam sometimes rises from fumaroles on its slopes. The sight and thought of the colossal mountain dominated the lives of the Australians who went to live there. When Béchervaise arrived in February 1953, this spectacular peak was unclimbed. Though he was there for the sheer excitement of a year on the island, his main aim was to climb the mountain. On a storm-ridden island like Heard, his greatest obstacle was the weather.

An American, not an Australian, discovered Heard Island. On 25 November 1853, Captain John Heard of the freight ship *Oriental* and his wife Fidelia were enjoying their first clear weather in 20 days of sailing the Southern Ocean. At half past eight in the morning they saw land at latitude 53°10′S. None was shown on the ship's charts, and at first John Heard took the sighting for icebergs. But when the clouds and haze around it cleared, the island with its high peak became plain.[1] It was remarkable that Heard Island should have stayed hidden for as long as it did. Only a few days' sailing to its north, the archipelago of Îles Kerguelen had been discovered three generations earlier, in 1772. Both islands are exposed parts of the largely submerged Kerguelen plateau, one of the largest submarine plateaus in the world, which rises up to 3000 metres above the surrounding seafloor. Captain James Cook sailed close to Heard Island in February 1773 but did not see it.[2]

Heard urged the US government to claim the island. In 1854, oceanographer Matthew Fontaine Maury wrote to the US Secretary of the Navy:

> Capt H. sent me a sketch of the island, which in the exercise of rights which usage gives to discoverers, he claims for the United States, and calls Heard's Island.[3]

At the time of Heard's discovery, shipowners had just begun to direct vessels along a newly adopted great circle route from the Cape of Good Hope to Australia and New Zealand. The faster passage took them further south-east in the Indian Ocean than formerly. For a few years after the island became known, sealing ships were drawn to Heard—the *Corinthian*, the *Atlas*, the *Laurens*. There were few fur seals (there is an ambiguous record of 500 skins being taken there). The sealers killed fur seals when they found them, but their main targets were the elephant seals—the largest seal of all. These huge beasts can be fast, but on land they move their great bulk in a cumbersome way and are close to defenceless when surprised. At sea they can stay submerged for hours. They dive to great depths in cold polar seas, protected by a thick layer of fat ('blubber'). This blubber yields a pure and stable oil, an item of commercial value in the nineteenth century. In the first six years after Heard Island's discovery the sealing was so intensive that, by 1859, there were few elephant seals to be had. Sealing became patchy for the next couple of decades and then more or less ceased.

Subantarctic islands are windy, cold and wet. Their climates are often described as 'vile'—on Heard Island there can be a gale, on average, on one day in every five. After the first burst of sealing, few people visited the island. Occasional voyages of science and exploration such as the British *Challenger* oceanographic expedition of the 1870s called there. Because of its icy coastline, wretched climate and lack of safe anchorages, Heard held little beauty for some. The *Challenger*'s chief scientist Sir Wyville Thomson wrote:

> We dredged a number of specimens at a depth of 75 fathoms, at the entrance of Corinthian Harbour ... in Heard Island (so far as I am aware the most desolate spot on God's earth).[4]

During the heroic era of the early twentieth century, the race to be first at the South Pole led to feverish activity. Explorers—among them Drygalski, Nordenskjöld, Scott, Bruce, Shackleton, Amundsen and Mawson—scrambled to finance expeditions to the unknown and perilous icy continent. After World War II, possession of the handful of tiny islands around Antarctica briefly became desirable. German ships had used some of these unoccupied subantarctic islands as refuges in two world wars, and Britain urged Australia and South Africa to claim and occupy those islands nearest to them. This would give Britain and her allies access to possible shipping or (they optimistically thought) to air bases in the southern Indian Ocean, and might prevent future use of the islands by other nations. The solidity of British ownership of Heard Island was (privately) in some doubt, and the transferral of its sovereignty was done as quietly as possible. The Australian government wanted to take 'all possible precautions against appearance in press of details of ceremony of Heard Island and especially wording of declaration'.[5] The South African government claimed subantarctic Marion and Prince Edward islands at the same time, in similar secrecy.

As historian Tim Bowden put it, 'The Australian Government developed Antarctic stations from 1948 with one aim firmly in mind—to establish Australia's claim on its Antarctic territories'.[6] To reinforce their territorial claim to Heard Island, a small base at Atlas Cove was built and manned—and all of the 86 sent there during that time *were* men—from 26 December 1947 (the day of the claim) until March 1955.[7] Though we cannot be sure what happened in sealing times, this mid-twentieth century presence was almost certainly the longest continuous occupation the island has ever seen. It was the first step since World War II towards Australia's eventual presence in Antarctica—and it was good practice at being cold.

The men on Heard Island in 1953 waited eagerly from the beginning of their year for news of the Australian expedition to Antarctica. They expected that some of them would be asked to help set up the first continental base. Five of them (Brooks, Dalziel, Elliott, Gwynn and Shaw) did go south to Antarctica to do so, early in 1954. The station on Heard Island ceased operation in March 1955, when Mawson station had been operating for a year. Few people have visited it since then— some scientists and their colleagues, and a handful of mountaineers, sailors and tourists. The island was occupied for a year by a US Coast and Geodetic Survey expedition in 1969–1970 and for a summer by a French expedition in 1971 (both expeditions included Australians). There have been shorter Australian National Antarctic Research Expedition (ANARE) visits and one year-long occupation in 1992 at The Spit, in the island's east.

During the summer months of 2000–2001, the Australian Antarctic Division sent 55 people to live and work on the island at Atlas Cove, Spit Bay and Brown Glacier.[8] At Atlas Cove they dismantled almost all that remained of the derelict huts once used by Béchervaise and his companions. Not long after, in November 2002, I visited the island, landing on the anniversary of John Heard's discovery 149 years earlier. I had not heard about the recent clean-up. Walking up the black sand beach of the cove to the rise where the old station had been, I was shocked to discover that almost nothing of it remained.

John Mayston Béchervaise (11 May 1910 – 13 July 1998)

John Béchervaise was an observer of nature and a writer. Time on Heard Island represented a chance for him to think and write in a bleakly beautiful place. A month before he left home in Belmont, Victoria, he wrote to friends. 'You might wonder why anyone should want to go to a place like Heard Island,' he said. 'For a year money, the post office, telephones, lectures, broadcasts, motor-cars, railways, trams, newspapers, feminine society, even time itself ceases to have much significance.' In 1953 Béchervaise had a wife and four young children. Yet he continued this letter, 'I do not expect to be lonely ... It will be rather pleasant to be circumscribed by the sea on an island barely twenty miles long.'[9]

Béchervaise was born in Melbourne. After teaching in England for six years during World War II, he returned to Australia and taught at Geelong College in Victoria, where he had been a teacher during the 1930s. He encouraged his students to explore the wilder parts of their country, leading expeditions to central Australia and to Rodondo Island off Wilson's Promontory in Victoria. One of the students he inspired by his adventurousness, Fred Elliott, was with Béchervaise in the first ascent of Federation Peak, and became a meteorological observer to join the 1953 Heard Island party.

In the late 1940s Béchervaise worked for the Australian Geographical Society as assistant editor on the magazine *Walkabout*. In December 1949 he wrote a story for the magazine about Macquarie Island, halfway between Tasmania and Antarctica, noting in his daybook that it was his first Antarctic publication. Through *Walkabout* he met the head of the Australian Antarctic Division (physicist Dr Phillip Law), and John King Davis who introduced him to Douglas Mawson. These events were the beginning of his long involvement with the South Polar regions.[10] Two years later, *Walkabout* published an article by a Tasmanian historian about another Australian subantarctic island, Heard Island.[11] Within a year, Béchervaise had accepted the job of officer in charge there.[12] In February 1953, the day after he boarded a ship taking him to the island for a year, the Australian government approved plans to occupy the Antarctic continent itself.

The officer in charge on Australia's subantarctic stations on Heard and Macquarie islands was responsible for the health and safety of the men living there. It was a difficult job. The year before Béchervaise's time, two ANARE men had died on Heard Island. They lost their footing when caught by high waves on a narrow beach between icy cliffs and the sea. One man was swept away and drowned. The second man froze to death as he struggled to return across a glacier for help.

Life on the Island

The annual ANARE parties to Heard Island consisted of nine to 15 men (there were 13 in 1953). Every year they arrived by ship, which unloaded a year's supplies and then returned to Melbourne with the men from the previous year's occupation. There was no schedule for the ship to call at any other time.

It is difficult to describe just how different a life the men led in the isolation that followed the ship's departure. There were gales, snowstorms, the thud of surf, and 'inexhaustible acres of angular black grit' blown around by the strong winds. There were no women, no families, no children or old people, no shops, no trees, and no human inhabitants other than those occupying the station. The view from the station, wrote the leader of the 1954 party, was one of 'baleful magnificence'.[13] The only ways of travelling (apart from local use of the tractor) were on foot, skis or by dog sledge, or at sea by small boat—an extremely risky venture in a region where 15 metre waves are not uncommon and a rescue boat is seldom available.

For company the men had each other, the dogs and the radio, with its extended blackouts. The average temperature was just above zero, but windchill made it uncomfortably and often dangerously cold outside. The station had 38 huts, mostly at Atlas Cove. There were magnetic huts two kilometres (1¼ miles) to the west, one for absolute measurements and one for variometric, and a seismic hut 800 metres (half a mile) to the east.[14] One of the most remarkable of the old huts was Admiralty Hut, built in 1929 by the crew of the whaling ship *Kildalkey* and used for shelter by Douglas Mawson's British, Australian and New Zealand Research Expedition later the same year.

The men ate well. Their supplies included extra stocks in case resupply was delayed, and there were always stocks left over from previous expeditions. The main indication of a change in season was not a change in the consistently grim weather, but the arrival of seabirds, penguins and seals to breed. In summer wildlife was plentiful, and it was shot for man and dog food. Sydney's *Daily Telegraph* reported in 1947 that 'the men will live on fish, tinned eggs, and meat', a completely untrue but no doubt desirably dramatic picture of the grimness of life there. They had a slow-combustion Aga stove, and an astonishingly varied larder (though its contents were irreplaceable once used, until the following year's provisions arrived on the next ship)—everything from angelica and arrowroot to Worcestershire sauce.

Expeditioners were encouraged to eat the wildlife—penguin, skua, seal— and brought their own frozen meat and fresh mutton.[15] When sheep from the ship were released, they took off immediately. It was impossible to catch them, and they survived on the island's vegetation until they were hunted and shot, or were lost in blizzards. The island's most common and distinctive plants are its cushion plant *Azorella selago*, tussock grasses (*Poa cookii* and *P. kerguelensis)*, the grass *Deschampsia antarctica* and Kerguelen cabbage (*Pringlea antiscorbutica*). 'There was abundant evidence of the grazing of our sheep; in some selected places the poa grasses were cropped almost away,' Béchervaise wrote.[16]

Evening meals could be remarkably good, even by today's standards. On special occasions the men might have had:

A good vintage hock with pea soup, lobster entrée, roast lamb w vegetables, cherries and custard, black coffee, apricot liqueurs and cigars: 'good fellowship, good food, good wine and fine, fat cigars'.[17]

The men took any possible chance to celebrate—birthdays, Midwinter and other celebrations. They made special menu cards and did not stint on food. Most of them were young, and vigorous outdoor activities in cold weather gave them big appetites.

They devised apt names for dishes. Edinburgh pudding and Phillip sauce were dubbed for the occasion of the special coronation menu. Other dishes were given Heard Island names even though the connection was tenuous—Big Ben cigars, for example, after the lazily smoking volcano behind the base, and azorella olives (from the name of a cushion plant which had nothing at all to do with olives). Some things on the menu were genuine local produce—the native Kerguelen cabbage, for example, whose cabbagy rosettes of leaves when raw taste like tough salad rocket. Penguin breast (as we know from explorers' journals) is perfectly palatable, and penguin liver 'superb', according to 1953 expeditioner Fred Elliott. The 'Drygalski mutton' was semi-indigenous, being a freshly killed sheep from those released near the camp. Like other groups who lived on the island, Béchervaise and his men observed certain standards for meals and communal life: generally, they dressed for dinner (sensible after a day of mucky work) and avoided what they considered bad language.[18] Despite the bracing—or, more accurately, inescapable—wind, supplies included air freshener ('Airwick'), which sat on special little shelves in the latrines.[19]

The mechanic turned the diesel-generated power off at 11.30 at night, and on at 6 in the morning. In the ice-covered landscape, free water usually froze and there was no ready supply of running water. The men built a snow-melter which could burn seal blubber to melt snow for drinking water. They disposed of rubbish and sewage in the icy waters of a nearby beach. Outdoor work required layers of clothing—two or three pullovers, a waterproof canvas 'submarine suit', a wind-proof jacket and trousers ('ventiles'), gloves. Clothing was unsophisticated;

some verged on inadequate. Like much of the other equipment, and the huts themselves, it was a result of post-war shortages and economical innovation. For climbing trips, men nailed tricounis (serrated nails) to their boots and made their own over-gloves.

Routine work included building and maintaining the huts; 24-hour meteorological watches; seismological and magnetic observations; regular radiosonde balloon releases; radio communication; biological censuses; post-mortems of penguins, seabirds, elephant seals and leopard seals; branding of seals and banding of seabirds; feeding and caring for themselves and the dogs; and 'gash' (rubbish) runs, all of which left very little time for expeditions or 'jollies'. Whenever an aurora could be observed, that is, when the clouds allowed it to be clearly seen, its progress was documented. There were many aurorally active nights, but few when clear skies allowed anything to be observed (in the first two months, the men saw and recorded only one of 35 known auroras).

In 1950 ANARE brought Labrador and Greenland huskies to Heard Island, to breed dogs for future Antarctic operations. They were usually chained, and were kept at Atlas Cove. Feeding the 50 or more sledge-dogs in 1953 was part of the daily rhythm of life. Every few days, the men killed a seal for the dogs. The dogs ate well—fresh elephant seal and leopard seal meat. On 18 October 1953 dogman Leon Fox took out his 'shag whag' (a dog-driven sled—his name referred both to its wagon function and to the local Heard Island blue-eyed shags or cormorants, which the men ate) and brought in 'a ton of quivering meat'.

Life on a small base on a subantarctic island was isolated but far from private. On Heard Island in 1953, the men built two-bunk partitions within the sleeping rooms. As officer in charge, Béchervaise saw all private radio messages before they were sent. He rarely recorded irritation with his companions, or disagreements among them. It is a notable absence, and confirms for me that he had an eye to a future audience. Letters to his wife (letters which would return to Australia on the same ship he would be boarding himself) show his occasional annoyance with others. The general absence of disharmony can also be attributed to Béchervaise's good leadership in trying circumstances.

As a counterpoise to the lack of personal revelations, a few moments— such as those on excreting as a public activity—are almost too frank.[20] But what is most striking about the men's days, to anyone familiar with life in Antarctica today, is the compellingly communal nature of life then, something which has changed greatly on modern stations (as it has elsewhere) with internet connections and access to modern media.

The Climbs

In June 1953, Béchervaise was slithering about on the roof of the mess hut erecting a flag for the coronation of Elizabeth II. Behind him rose the still-unclimbed snowy peak of Big Ben. Suddenly Fred Elliott appeared over a snowdrift. 'They've climbed Everest!' he shouted up to Béchervaise. While Everest had remained unclimbed, Béchervaise had held a faint and private hope of being in its summit party. 'What is now the greatest physical adventure lying ahead of man?' he wrote that night. 'There will be many who will also feel a sense of sadness, almost of desecration.'[21] It did not stop him from continuing to plan his own first ascent of Heard Island's peak.

John Béchervaise, Fred Elliott and Peter Shaw made two attempts to climb Big Ben, once in August and a longer attempt in November. Both failed. On the first, Béchervaise and Shaw were almost overcome by carbon monoxide poisoning. On the second, after reaching about 1500 metres (5000 feet), the men were trapped in camp by dreadful weather for much longer than they had ever imagined possible. Supplies dwindled to alarmingly low levels, and they were forced to retreat in dangerously poor visibility. They had spent 18 days on the mountain. The weather did not clear enough to see Big Ben until 20 days after their return to the Atlas Cove station.[22]

The Diaries

The man who emerges from the Heard Island diaries was an adventurer who enjoyed trying to understand the world, and who had an iron determination to document his life, as well as the ability to do so. He left for us his own picture of himself. On Heard Island he typed on black wet nights. When the lights went out in the biology hut he worked by lamplight. He wrote close to 1000 words a day over 13 months, a consistently astonishing effort after days of cold, wind, work and sole responsibility for his 12 companions.

There is little doubt that his daybooks were meant as a public record as well as a personal one. Not only was he exceptionally articulate, but he was assiduous in keeping a diary. He typed each day's entry (with carbon copies) on his Remington typewriter. As well as those held by the National Library of Australia, there are copies in the State Library of Victoria.

In keeping with the times in which he wrote, Heard Island expeditioners were advised to keep themselves busy, avoid self-pity, and refrain from discussing their personal affairs with others. Béchervaise's writing was restrained and—probably even at the time—rather old-fashioned. It does not give away much of the man himself, beyond his own ambitions, but it is a remarkably polished and thorough record. Today, we take the computer's ability to add and delete text for granted. Béchervaise had no such liberty, but his daybooks are almost free of revisions (and there are precious few typos).

The National Library of Australia holds 77 boxes of his papers—diaries, travel journals, press clippings, manuscripts of papers, poems and an unpublished novel. Béchervaise kept everything: theatre programs, receipts, menus, tickets from weighing machines, copies of letters, an astonishing volume of paper altogether.

His name is commemorated by Béchervaise Island (the largest island in the Flat Island group near Mawson station, Antarctica), Mount Béchervaise (2360 metres, in the Prince Charles Mountains, Antarctica) and Bechervaise Plateau at the base of Federation Peak in south-western Tasmania.

YIKPO

A special ANARE version of the five-letter Bentley code (E.L. Bentley's *Complete Phrase Code* devised for telegrams, first published in 1909) was used for personal correspondence radioed in Morse from Heard or Macquarie islands (and later Antarctica). The use of a code minimised strain on busy radio operators.

Each ANARE code word stood for a commonly used phrase or sentence. One common code word, WYSSA ('All my/our love darling') gave its name to the 'whizzer' or telegram itself. Expeditioners had a monthly limit of 100 free words, and next of kin could use 75 free words a month. Families often devised their own meanings to add to those given in the code book, which included handy phrases such as:

YAURN   Snow is drifting through the station

YIHMO   I have grown a beard but think I'll shave it off before I return to Australia

YIKPO   This place gives you a pain at times

The message Béchervaise's wife Lorna and sister Mary sent on 5 March 1953:

WYUHM WYTAT WYTOY YAACS YAALC YAANF children WYTYO
WYVUB Lorna WYVOZ Mary

translated to:

'We are all thinking about you. We miss you more than we can
say, Darling. We think about you all the time. Have not heard
from you for what seems ages and hope you are getting along
alright. Hoping to hear from you shortly. How are you, darling?
The children send their love. Your loving wife Lorna, Your loving
sister Mary.'

Radio blackouts were common, and this message reflected the
frustrations of frequent inability to communicate.

Editorial Note

Making a short book from a long journal has been an interesting
experience. This book contains only a fraction (somewhat less
than one-sixth) of John Béchervaise's original diaries covering his
13 months on Heard Island in 1953–1954. He typed up some 550 pages
of daybook from the time of his departure from Melbourne in February
1953 until he finished the Heard Island journal on 15 March 1954.
Some of the practices I have adopted in handling the diary have
been dictated by the need to make the text fit comfortably into a
book of this size.

The book probably presents a misleading impression of the amount
of action in the men's daily life, and the frequency of journeys away
from the station. Though they lived in one of the most spectacular
settings on earth, the island's geography and climate made it almost
impossible to travel far from their huts. And there, the concerns of daily
life were—surprisingly—almost as repetitive and domestic as they are
anywhere else. (It is often the same in Antarctica.) The men's lives were
also typically very busy, first of all in making a base habitable for each
group of people and in keeping it so despite the weather, and then
in doing the work which took them there, whether this was cooking,
weather-reporting, seal biology or upper atmosphere physics. 'There
is a vast amount of work to be done,' wrote Béchervaise a fortnight after
his arrival, 'before I shall be very happy about the general appearance
of the camp. Everywhere there is junk of every description, half
buried in sand.'[23]

In selecting the highlights of his year, much of the humdrum detail has disappeared. Retaining a representative proportion of daily chores—or even of the many descriptions of the island's spectacularly bad weather—would have made dull reading.

I have tried to retain Béchervaise's voice, but inevitably the shorter version to some extent reflects my own style as well as the modern liking for short sentences. I have corrected obvious typos and idiosyncratic spellings, so that 'snwo', for example, now reads 'snow', and 'laundary' reads 'laundry'. Numbers over nine have generally been changed from a spelt-out form to numerals. I have occasionally (but not often) altered the wording of a phrase or sentence, or moved a line or two, to improve the flow of text. Béchervaise generally wrote Bernie Izabelle's name as 'Berni', which I have changed to 'Bernie'. Where Grahame Budd's first name was spelt incorrectly, I have amended this. Béchervaise spelt the McDonald Islands variously (as have many others); here the spelling is standardised as 'McDonald', following the recommended spelling for this Australian placename. He also consistently referred to the 'Baudissen' Glacier, a spelling used in maps of the time. I have amended this throughout to 'Baudissin', its accepted modern spelling.

The places where text was omitted are so numerous that they are not indicated by ellipses (…). For those who might want to compare this book with the text as it appears in the original diary, or for anyone wanting to use an electronic version of the text for their own purposes, I have deposited an electronic version of the fully transcribed, uncut text of Béchervaise's Heard Island journal in the National Library of Australia's Manuscripts Reading Room.

In Béchervaise's time the Antarctic Division required expeditioners to hand over all photographs taken on expedition. The result in Béchervaise's case has been that, while his papers are held in the National Library of Australia, his photographs now reside elsewhere, in the Antarctic Division in Kingston, Tasmania. This practice, though required, was not uniformly followed even in 1953. Béchervaise noted that Vic Cleland, one of the 1954 Heard Island men, 'expressed the opinion that I was an absolute fool, more or less, for "giving" all my pictures to the Antarctic Division. He reckons that he will hand over no negatives except those taken with the rather poor camera supplied and on films sent down by the Division.'[24]

Acknowledgments

I thank the National Library of Australia, especially Director-General Jan Fullerton, for the 2006 Harold White Fellowship which led to this book. I also thank Library staff members Margy Burn, Chris Mertin, Marie-Louise Ayers, and the staff of the Petherick Reading Room and its Manuscripts, Pictures, and Map collections. Publications and Production Manager Susan Hall, images editor Felicity Harmey, text editor Michaela Forster, book designer Lindsay Davidson and others involved in the production have done brilliant work on this publication.

I thank Tim Bowden for offering his transcript of an interview with John Béchervaise, Tim Ealey for providing copies of documents, and Stu Fitch for generously providing copies of his own Heard Island writings. I also thank the Rev. Frances Ward for comments and help with copyright issues and Tony Doyle for help with copyright permissions. For comments on the manuscript I thank Peter and Gwen Shaughnessy and Jennie Whinam. For sharing their first-hand knowledge of John Béchervaise and Heard Island, I thank Grahame Budd, Neilma Gantner, Ken and June Peake-Jones, and especially Fred Elliott (Heard Island, 1953) and Jack Ward (who spent a year at Mawson station in Antarctica in 1955, when Béchervaise was officer in charge). Fred and Jack have given invaluable help and encouragement in the preparation of this book.

Finally, thanks to the members of John Béchervaise's family for copyright permission.

Readers with queries are invited to contact me at coldwords@gmail.com.

Bernadette Hince
Canberra, April 2010

Endnotes

1   Anon., Remarks on passage of Bark *Oriental*, MS227–28. Cambridge: Scott Polar Research Institute.

2   P.D. Shaughnessy et al., 'Fur Seals at Heard Island: Recovery from Past Exploitation?', in M.L. Augee (ed.), *Marine Mammals of Australasia: Field Biology and Captive Management.* Sydney: Royal Zoological Society of New South Wales, 1988: 71–7.

3   Letter dated 12 June 1854, quoted in K.J. Bertrand, *Americans in Antarctica 1775–1948*, special publication 39. New York: American Geographical Society, 1971: 231.

4   Sir Wyville Thomson, *The Voyage of the 'Challenger'.* London: Macmillan and Co., 1877: 220.

5   Department of the Navy, Ceremony at Heard Island, Declaration, 8 January 1948. National Archives of Australia: MP1049/5/0, 1870/2/8.

6   Tim Bowden, *The Silence Calling: Australians in Antarctica 1947–97.* Sydney: Allen and Unwin, 1997: 259.

7   'Peter was standing in our room, a little drunk. "Why did I come down here? The only time I'm really relaxed is when I'm a little drunk or hearing Beethoven. Any civilized community would have 13 women."' (Béchervaise Papers, diary entry, 17 April 1953, National Library of Australia, MS7972, Box 5).

8   Dana Bergstrom and Paul Scott, 'Heard Island Uncovered: 2000–01 Summer ANARE', *Australian Antarctic Magazine*, vol.2, 2001: 30.

9   Béchervaise Papers, diary entry, 12 January 1953, National Library of Australia, MS7972, Box 5.

10   Béchervaise Papers, cutting of article, 1 December 1949, National Library of Australia, MS7972/3/4, Box 19, Folder 64; Tim Bowden, oral history interview with John Béchervaise, 3 December 1987, Geelong.

11   W.L. Crowther, 'Heard Island', *Walkabout*, vol.17, no.9, 1951: 44, 46, 48.

12   In discussing Heard Island with Béchervaise in 1952 Law said 'that if I would consider going with next years [sic] party he would put me in charge of the station' (Béchervaise Papers, note, 7 May 1952, National Library of Australia, MS7972, Box 5).

13   Grahame M. Budd, 'Exploration of Heard Island between 1947 and 1971', *Antarctic and Southern Ocean Law and Policy Occasional Paper*, vol.10, 2006: 11.

14   Béchervaise Papers, Heard Island general report 1953, National Library of Australia, MS7972, Box 5.

15   Australian National Antarctic Research Expedition, *Heard Island and Macquarie Island Operations Manual.* Melbourne: Antarctic Division, 1953: 51.

16   Béchervaise Papers, diary entry, 9 May 1953, National Library of Australia, MS7972, Box 5.

17   Béchervaise Papers, diary entry, 29 June 1953, National Library of Australia, MS7972, Box 5.

18   In 1952 the men were instructed by cable, 'All men to get up for breakfast and, in order to maintain high tone, foul language should be barred from the mess' (Leslie Gibbney, Heard Island diary, 10 May 1952, National Library of Australia, MS9392).

19   Béchervaise Papers, diary entry, 12 October 1953, National Library of Australia, MS7972, Box 6.

20   Béchervaise Papers, diary entry, 3 March 1953, National Library of Australia, MS7972, Box 5.

21   Béchervaise Papers, diary entry, 2 June 1953, National Library of Australia, MS7972, Box 5.

22   Béchervaise Papers, diary entries, 15 November 1953 ff., National Library of Australia, MS7972, Box 6, Folder 21; Grahame M. Budd, 'The ANARE 1963 Expedition to Heard Island', *ANARE Reports Series A*, vol.1, 1964: 4.

23   Béchervaise Papers, diary entry, 4 March 1953, National Library of Australia, MS7972, Box 5.

24   Béchervaise Papers, diary entry, 6 February 1954, National Library of Australia, MS7972, Box 6.

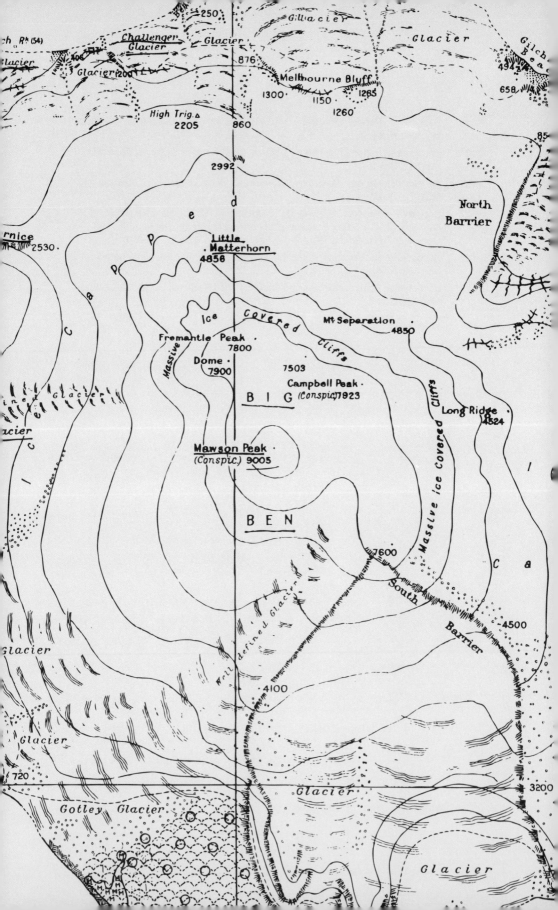

Dear Glyn

No letter from me, but
a couple of random ones
from others as packing.

Regards

John

6/5/11

The Men

John (J.M.) Béchervaise, officer in charge, aged 42 on arrival at
Heard Island

23 April 1953

*I can scarcely believe I am the same person who has sat in an office and
taught in dozens of dusty class-rooms. It is a curious sensation. Today
it occurred as I rolled a cigarette. 'Yes, they are your hands alright—but
what on earth are you doing out here, in the sub-Antarctic?'*

Jim (J.A.) Brooks, geophysicist, aged 23

8 July 1953

*These hard isolated days are toughest on the younger members of the
party. Jim Brooks, for instance, youthful, dynamic and most energetic
occasionally will suddenly collapse and become overwrought, irritable
and brusque. He realizes it and fights against it, underneath being on
the edge of tears.*

Ken (K.E.) Dalziel, radio supervisor

After he returned from Heard Island, Dalziel published a children's book
(*Penguin Road*, 1955), written originally for his own children, describing
the year on the island.

19 May 1953

*Ken is a forceful character who often only just manages to screen
impatience when things go wrong. He is also fairly mercurial in
temperament, working like a galley-slave at times and suddenly
becoming momentarily disheartened.*

Fred (F.W.) Elliott, weather observer, aged 24

Elliott had been taught by Béchervaise at Geelong College, and was in Béchervaise's first ascent of Federation Peak. He was as keen as Béchervaise to climb Heard Island's peak. On 1 June 1953 he wrote in his journal, 'I became a met observer in order to get down here to have a shot at Big Ben'.

8 July 1953

His attitude to the isolated life of Heard Island is quite exceptional. I have never known him to be less than cheerful. He loves every minute of life down on this sub-Antarctic island and his hopes for further expeditions should easily be fulfilled.

Leon (L.N.) Fox, dog attendant

20 April 1953

Leon is absorbed, heart and soul, in his work with the dogs. He loves the whole mob and describes them as the best set he has ever had. I like catching a glimpse of him in an old seal-blood stained submarine suit shuffling round his charges in pouring rain. Every now and then he will pause and a great husky stands up and pats both Leon's shoulders at once.

Arthur (A.M.) Gwynn, medical officer, aged 44

Irish-born Gwynn had the most experience of the subantarctic. He spent 1949 as the doctor and officer in charge on Macquarie Island, and spent the second half of 1950 on Heard Island after the emergency midwinter evacuation of the island's doctor (Serge Udovikov) on HMAS *Australia*.

9 April 1953

He is always following his own biological pursuits and works most industriously. One never quite knows where he will be. We seldom get much conversation from him outside his own subject. At the moment— nearly 11.30pm—he is away alone making a leopard seal count along Corinthian Bay, working on a broom-black night by torchlight. He has wisdom and I value his opinion.

Jack Hughes, diesel mechanic

9 April 1953

He is the problem of the party, I think. He can be most efficient and knows his work but he broods too much. There may be something intrinsic to engineering that causes a lone engineer to be a problem.

Bernie Izabelle, weather observer, aged 24

Frenchman Bernie Izabelle had Arctic experience with Paul-Emile Victor's *Expéditions polaires françaises* to central Greenland.

1 May 1953

Bernie is extremely thorough. Every detail of the bathroom drainage system has been overhauled by him. He betrayed at any distance his French origin as he heated his soldering irons over the coke of the small hand forge.

Dick (R.G.) McNair, cook

Both McNair and Parsons had served on RRS *Discovery II* missions.

3 March 1953

He is certainly an incomparable cook. In manner he combines a certain boyish shyness with a brusque, determined and forthright speech. He is developing a flaxen beard and is both virile and handsome in appearance.

Cec (C.F.) O'Brien, radio operator

4 April 1953

Cec is a cheerful larrikin with an extremely good nature. Sometimes he assumes a sort of boisterous coarseness. But he is keenly interested in all manner of worthwhile things, has read a lot. He has trimmed his beard to the chin and looks a somewhat dashing young pirate.

Ron (R.V.) Parsons, radio operator

Parsons had been a radio operator on Macquarie Island in 1951.

6 March 1953

Ron is a great and pleasant character, always cheerful and ready to take a lead.

4 December 1953

He's something of a dormant volcano and unpredictable, yet I hope we shall be able to finish the year in peace.

Peter (P.J.R.) Shaw, meteorologist

3 April 1953

Peter, a restless driving force, is improving, becoming much less dogmatic. He readily acknowledges an error of judgement and although he seems assertive is probably fundamentally modest.

Len (L.R.) Welch, weather observer

9 April 1953

Len is the perfect domestic. He is inordinately proud of his work in the sleeping hut; the actual quality is fair. He is completely single-minded and sometimes quite selfish. He is often garrulous, a complete extrovert. He is capable of becoming very excited but calms down pretty quickly.

Some Events in the Sporadic
History of Heard Island

25 November 1853	American sealing captain John J. Heard made the first documented sighting of the island which now bears his name.
15 February 1855	Erasmus Darwin Rogers of the *Corinthian* made the first recorded landing on Heard Island.
1850s – late 1870s	Sealers visited Heard Island, mainly taking elephant seals for their blubber.
1857	The American brig *Zoe* (Captain James H. Rogers) landed first mate Henry Rogers with a sealing gang of 25 men. They made the first recorded wintering on the island.
1861	Elephanting crew from the *Alert* were left on the island on 5 January. In September the ship returned and found that one of the men left at Saddle Point 'frose to death' on 12 or 13 August.
6 February 1874	Men from the British *Challenger* oceanographic expedition spent three hours ashore. They collected flowering plants, mosses and seaweeds before bad weather forced them to leave.
1880	The sealing ship *Trinity* was wrecked near Spit Bay; her crewmen were rescued after 15 months ashore.

February 1902	Baron Erich von Drygalski's German South Polar Expedition in the *Gauss* visited Heard Island, collecting animal and plant specimens and rocks at Atlas Cove.
1910	An option was granted to a Mr Bogen for an exclusive licence to occupy Heard Island for three years for whaling; this did not happen.
15–23 January 1929	E. Aubert de la Rue and his wife Andrée, left by the British–Norwegian whaling expedition *Kildalkey*, prospected for minerals, and collected plants and animals.
November–December 1929	Douglas Mawson's British, Australian and New Zealand Antarctic Research Expedition spent eight days on the island, leaving emergency rations and a Union Jack.
26 December 1947	Group Captain Stuart Campbell read the declaration of Australian possession on Heard Island.
December 1947 – March 1955	A small scientific base on Heard Island was manned by Australian National Antarctic Research Expeditions (ANARE) to reinforce Australia's possession of the island. This was the first lengthy period of occupation of the island since sealing times, and the longest documented occupation yet.
26 May 1952	Death of ANARE members Alistair Forbes and Richard Hoseason.
1953	The *Heard Island and McDonald Islands Act 1953* formalised the boundaries of Australia's sovereignty as 'all the islands and rocks lying within the area bounded by the parallels 52 degrees 30 minutes and 53 degrees 30 minutes south latitude and the meridians 72 degrees and 74 degrees 30 minutes east longitude'.

21 February 1953	John Béchervaise and other members of the 1953 ANARE landed at Heard Island.
15 March 1954	John Béchervaise and other members of the 1953 ANARE left Heard Island.
9 March 1955	The ANARE station at Atlas Cove was closed down.
January–March 1963	ANARE parties were landed at Atlas Cove and Long Beach from the *Nella Dan*, and a group led by Grahame Budd tried unsuccessfully to climb Big Ben.
25 January 1965	Southern Indian Ocean Expedition members Grahame Budd, John Crick, Warwick Deacock, Colin Putt and Philip Temple from the *Patanela* made the first ascent of Heard Island's 2745 metre ice-covered volcano Big Ben.
March 1969 – April 1970	US Coast and Geodetic Survey parties from the *Southwind* and *Columbia Hawk* occupied the island. As part of the expedition, three ANARE men made a brief visit ashore from the *Southwind* on 11–17 March 1969, and six Americans wintered there, with six others replacing them from November 1969 to April 1970.
25 January – 9 March 1971	A 14-man French–Australian expedition party in the *Gallieni* visited Heard Island. Two Australians from the party made a brief landing on McDonald Island on 27 January 1971 (by helicopter, the first recorded landing on the island). The *Nella Dan* rescued Australian Ian Holmes (with a broken leg) by helicopter.
19–21 January 1972	Jerome Poncet and Gerard Janichon in the French yacht *Damien* visited Heard Island en route to the Ross Sea.

March 1980	An Australian Division of National Mapping party surveyed around Heard and McDonald islands from the *Cape Pillar*.
1981	A brief landing was made by passengers aboard the *Lindblad Explorer.*
January–February 1983	Members of the *Anaconda II* party made the first recorded landing on Shag Island to the north of Heard Island on 26 January. They also made the second ascent of Big Ben.
5–17 February 1983	The Heard Island DX Association expedition aboard *Cheynes 2* visited Heard Island. A five-man expedition from the ship (four Austrians and one Australian) tried unsuccessfully to climb Big Ben; they encountered waterlogged conditions and thick fog.
March 1983	An ANARE party visited the island.
1 November 1983	Heard and McDonald islands were listed on Australia's Register of the National Estate.
October–November 1985	ANARE parties camped on the island at Atlas Cove and Spit Bay.
April 1986	Solo sailor Gerry Clark, aboard the *Totorore*, spent eight days of bad weather anchored at Heard Island, with only two chances to go ashore.
November 1986 – January 1987	An ANARE party visited the island.
September 1987 – March 1988	An ANARE party spent five and a half months on the island.
January 1989	During an ANARE marine science voyage, members of the party visited the island for two days.

January, May and June 1990	ANARE parties visited the island.
1991	An ANARE party visited the island for three days.
January–February 1992	An ANARE field party reported degeneration of French Arbec huts at Atlas Cove.
February 1992 – March 1993	Five ANARE men spent a year at Spit Bay in fibreglass huts.
31 January – 3 February 1994	The German yacht *Freydis* visited the island.
3 December 1997	The Territory of Heard Island and McDonald Islands was added to the World Heritage List for outstanding natural values.
1999–2000	Four members of the Australian Army Alpine Association made the third ascent of Big Ben.
February 2000	ANARE workers from a fisheries patrol vessel began initial clearing of derelict buildings at Atlas Cove, which continued the following summer.
November 2000 – March 2001	During an ANARE five-month summer expedition, a worker who patrolled four of Heard Island's beaches collected an estimated 1½–2 tonnes of marine debris, almost all of it plastics.
October 2002	Heard Island and McDonald Islands Marine Reserve was established under the Australian *Environment Protection and Biodiversity Conservation Act 1999*.
2003–2004	An ANARE scientific party occupied the island for two months in summer.
2010	Heard Island is unoccupied.

February 1953

Arrival

Tuesday 10 February 1953

It is not yet five days since we put to sea. Only now are the days becoming entities. There are plenty of people who are 'good' sailors, but far fewer who would be so certain if they were suddenly disgorged through the Rip on a black night in a 540 ton vessel bound on a great circle route for Heard Island. Not only land-bred were laid low but several of the Vikings including Captain Andersen.

It is still very difficult to believe in the reality of this venture. There were two short months of preparation for this voyage. Only two months between utter strangeness and near comradeship. We only came together on a few occasions; sometimes at tent-making, once or twice a week for a discussion or intensive physical training. The rest of the time we met as groups in passing. The 'met' men—Peter Shaw, Len Welsh, Bernie Izabelle and Fred Elliott—kept buzzing back and forth between the meteorological bureau and Tottenham where kind-hearted but torrid-voiced George Smith keeps stock of every commodity required on the far islands.

We'd all come trailing along from the 8.32 morning train; following the cinder-path to the big shadowy shed. George would already be on the job with packing cases, pots of paint and notebooks and a mighty stock of familiar oaths. Often Lem Macey would be there. He is the permanent radio and engineering man at Ant. Division Headquarters. All sorts of things were fabricated and repaired. The great, heavy black rubber pontoon that had been holed by the French (but which also belonged to the French) had to be patched. Like the sea elephants themselves, these pontoons bend to the waves and carry up to five tons.

Arthur Gwynn, bird-man and medical officer, seldom came out to Tottenham. He was forever checking drug-lists in Melbourne or trying to finish off a paper on seals or penguins. He is the only one of us who has already been on Heard, having relieved Udovikov. The special errand of mercy on the part of the *Australia* is said to have cost £50,000. Ken Dalziel was largely caught up on the rawin apparatus at Essendon but he came out to Tottenham whenever possible.

Jim Brooks, the geophysicist, was pretty constantly at work on the tents, except when he and I studied for a crowded week at the Royal Melbourne Hospital. The Royal Melbourne was an utter revelation. Within minutes of meeting the Director of Anaesthetics, Jim Brooks and I were garbed in gowns and masks and became part of the curiously anonymous retinue of the operating theatres. Jim's job was to learn the names and uses of the operating instruments; mine was to become familiar with at least the less complicated anaesthetics—essentially with 'open ether'.

I was astonished to discover, as I drifted silently between the theatres, that I was in no ways nauseated. In the utter depths of unconsciousness the patient becomes an object of infinite pity. While the surgeons are busy with their knives and forceps, the anaesthetist is intent only on preserving a sufficient depth of narcosis and on the fine indications of the patient's condition. What loss of blood and terrible indignities the human body can suffer short of death.

My work with Rex Irvin at the Bureau of Mineral Resources was star-distant from surgery and fascinated me even more. There was a tranquillity in a day I spent at the magnetic observatory on the Toolangi hilltop with Rex. Fine rain filled the forest like dewdrops in a cob-web; no-one except a good farm-wife with tea and scones disturbed our day.

One of the lighter aspects of preparation was my appointment as Postmaster, Heard Island. The *Tottan* carries and returns with the only mail for the year, but the necessary documents of appointment had to be inked over no less thoroughly than had I received a call to control Her Majesty's Mails in a provincial city.

A Medical Evacuation

Dr Serge Udovikov was evacuated with appendicitis in winter 1950 by the naval cruiser HMAS *Australia*, which brought two doctors to replace Udovikov—Arthur Gwynn (who stayed until February 1951) and Otto Rec.

Australian doctors sent to Antarctic and subantarctic bases are now, by policy, appendix-free.

Thursday 12 February 1953

It is a week since the *Tottan* left the Spencer Street berth. For all that time we have never had a moment's stillness. Every hanging thing sways perpetually. It has become very raw and cold. The sun seems obscured by a thin watery haze; it is a peaked landscape (or seascape) like the faces of cold ill-fed men. The sea is not really violent but every movement is transmitted through this little ship. The iron decks are washed by the unpredictable sea. Every time I start typing it has been the same; after half-an-hour or so of desultory effort, I can no longer concentrate. Then I ease myself along the passage and grip the companionways until I reach the captain's little stateroom where there is always a crowd.

Most of the last four days in Melbourne were centred at the *Tottan*. Lorries and trailers kept arriving. Crates and drums and larger single items were winched from the wharf to the holds. The wharfies were scarcely more interested in loading cases of scientific instruments than they would have been in wool bales. It was brazenly hot. There was a fairly determined effort to cause a crate or two of beer to disintegrate but this did not succeed. Occasionally some of them would be mildly curious about the *Tottan*'s destination. 'Gawd, you goin' darn there, mate? 'Ow much danger money d'yer get? Are there any natives darn there? Wot, no women? Wouldn't bloody well suit me. Wot's the purpose of the thing, anyway?'

In my *Walkabout* office Charles [Holmes, the editor] was rather terse and business-like and asked innumerable questions. His mind was weighted with a thousand trivialities. His ways are not mine. I suppose we are about equally sympathetic with each other.

The Careful Diarist

Béchervaise's journal was meticulously typed in multiple copies. On Heard Island, he would type up his scraps of notes in the evening, usually after a long working day. He sent or gave various pages of his daybook to family and friends.

Sunday 15 February 1953

Southern Ocean, Lat 53°S, Long 108°E

There is not generally much to distinguish day from day. All night
long I wedge myself in the little yellow-wood bunk. In the darkness
innumerable noises resolve themselves into the throb of the engines,
the racing of the screw, the whining of the wind. Last night no-one slept
for more than a few minutes at a time. It was necessary to be sufficiently
aware to remain in one's bunk. I reckoned I had everything pretty well
wedged but my typewriter, tangled in the legs of a chair, performed
a slow unceasing *danse macabre* round the drifting medical chest.
We have all become used to being sea-sick.

Just after lunch today out on the port bow appeared a great white streak
just above the horizon. We all crowded to the bridge. The berg resolved
itself out of the mist and became a scarcely believable island of ice,
perhaps 200 feet high and anything up to three or four square miles in
area. After an hour or so we were close enough to see the terrible ice-
cliffs, although we were never nearer than about three miles. The great
ice-berg receded to port. The radar-screen has been kept on in case
other bergs are about. To see such an enormous tabular ice-berg is most
unusual at this time of year.

Southern Ocean
Approx. Lat 52°S, Long 108°E
Sunday 15 February 1953

My dearest Lady Scarlet,

Tonight I am writing only for my beloved. Very constantly I have
thought of you during this restless voyage; thought of you and the
children with fathomless love and gratitude. You must know how deeply
the whole future is bound up with you. When I return we shall do so
many things together. I have a curious excitement looking forward to the
time when suddenly, miraculously, my ship will enter the bay and
we shall all be reunited.

There were very few left on the wet wharf when we actually sailed,
at about 5.30. We slid down the river and out to sea. As we gained
the Heads I saw a car's lights flashing and returned the flash with
an Aldous lamp. I could see you sitting there, only a short distance
away. You will never be any further away from me.

The birds of this Southern Ocean are nearly always visible. For several days we had the huge wandering albatrosses with wing-spans up to 11 feet. Now there are shearwaters and storm-petrels skimming the crests of the sea. For months they will remain at sea and only find their way to some lonely island to breed.

Monday 16 February 1953

We should reach Heard Island next Saturday or Sunday. At dawn this morning we passed another ice-berg. These southern ice-bergs are detached fragments of the great ice barrier, or shelf ice, of Antarctica. The one we saw yesterday resembled Mount Conner in Central Australia; it appeared as though it would be quite easy to land a plane on its great flat summit.

We are rolling along at about 10 knots, but in yesterday's storm our speed was reduced to three or four. Alan Spalding, the old Geelong Collegian who managed to get on the voyage at the last moment, is busy preparing his material for the *Age*. He is the typical journalist and was very unhappy when Jerry [Donovan, the voyage leader] wouldn't agree to him radio-ing a story back on our engine failure. He was envisaging all sorts of cosy headlines—'Expedition vessel wallows helplessly in mid-ocean'. Jerry suppressed the tale because of anxiety it might cause amongst men's families. Just as I typed the last sentence an extra big roll sent the remains of a cup of coffee flying over all my papers.

Tuesday 17 February 1953

Lat 54°15′S, Long 95°E

Today well south, only 200 miles from the great ice-barrier and in the strong easterly currents. Apparently by sailing so far south we move through quieter water but must be vigilant for ice. No party en route for Heard has ever encountered so much. The sea temperatures have dropped to within a degree or two of freezing and the air is almost as cold.

Late this afternoon a majestic ice-berg appeared over the horizon. We watched the pearly vastness approach, grey and eroded, towering over 350 feet from the sea. While still a long way off, a vast mass silently detached itself and flung spray to a height of 200 feet.

We gradually came abreast at a distance of about a mile. The sea was filled with floating ice-debris. It was our first great ice-berg at close quarters, and most impressive. Finally it passed astern. We thawed out frozen fingers but a few minutes later were again gaping from the bridge at a school of spouting whales. For hours afterwards in the long twilight the ice-berg was visible.

This morning Jerry and I dragged out the three big mail-bags for Heard. There are bundles of periodicals and magazines, letters with gay stamps from all over the world; several hundred envelopes to be post-marked HEARD ISLAND and returned to stamp-collectors everywhere.

Hoseason and Forbes

In May 1952 three men crossing a narrow beach under the ice-cliffs of the Nares Glacier were swept off their feet by high waves. Radio operator Richard (Dick) Hoseason drowned; carpenter and dog attendant Alistair (Jock) Forbes died of exposure while trying to get help. The survivor, weather observer Lawrence (Laurie) Atkinson, struggled into camp the next day with news of the tragedy. Forbes' body was recovered and buried in a grave marked by a cross near the station. Hoseason's body was not recovered at the time. The following January, remains found at Corinthian Bay were interred with Forbes. The men are commemorated by the names of features in the area where they died: Forbes Bluff and Hoseason Beach.

In the Great South Sea
on Wednesday 18th February 1953

My Dearest Little Judy-Pie,

I love you and love you and love you … and if I kept on going for the whole page, I would not be able to tell how much I love you (and Pixie and Anne and Billy and Mummie, too).

My dearest dearest Elizabeth,

It's a funny thing how fathers are not too good at saying how much they love their daughters BUT THEY DO nor at expressing how proud they are of them BUT THEY ARE.

I was relieved that there were no letters addressed to Forbes or Hoseason who died on the glacier; somehow, evidently, they were extracted and returned to relatives. We are now in radio communication with Heard Island. It's a grim thought that a smaller party will be returned than passed this way last year.

Saturday 21 February 1953

We should reach Heard Island before darkness falls. We are making nearly 10 knots and have only about 100 miles to go. For two or three days we have been in radio communication. On ship and land there is evident excitement. This morning's report from Heard stated that Big Ben was clear from base to summit; it was one of the best days for the entire year. We all stood on the bridge after breakfast in bright sunlight and scanned the horizon.

The last two days have been turbulent. In the mess large dishes of soup or stew leapt every obstacle and sprayed their contents over everything including the men. Clouds of sugar flew through the air. Every now and then men slid out of control from side to side, landing in disconcerted heaps on the floor. Yesterday was my day for cleaning in the galley. The floor was as slippery as ice. Clouds of steam rose from the spilt saucepans although every one was firmly held by high iron fiddles. I didn't manage to retain a single meal. Last night I tried to type but found it impossible. With the intense cold and rawness and movement, life became miserable. Soon I shall pack my typewriter. From the time we anchor until every operation is complete, sleep will be brief and work will proceed under bright lights.

I had scarcely finished writing when Freddie burst in to say Heard was in sight. We ran up to the bridge and for just a few brief moments, at about 11.30, before the grey wall of cloud obscured everything, we saw the island from a distance of 50 or 60 miles, rising as an enormous snow-white mountain from the sea. It was an awesome first impression. Mawson Peak [the island's highest point] showed as a defined dome above the vast mass of Big Ben. Everyone was silent at the sight.

It didn't last long. We were steaming forward into the featureless sea walled round with greyness. During the afternoon two of the largest wanderer albatrosses we had seen wheeled down to accompany us. We occasionally glimpsed Heard Island showing gloomily and uncertainly through grey rifted mist.

We approached from the east and fairly far south until the echo-sounder showed water shoaling from 70 fathoms to 20. Then the skipper turned the *Tottan* northwards and coasted cleanly between Shag Island and the prominent headlands and glaciers. We slid past Cape Bidlingmaier and Saddle Point, the grey pressure ridges of the Baudissin and Challenger glaciers—where Forbes and Hoseason perished last year.

We came to our final radio 'sched' with Heard Island as we drew level with Rogers Head. The voices came very clearly through the mist. Terribly excited. The loneliness of 12 months about to end. The 1st officer said, 'Tell them, we'll be in Atlas Cove in 20 minutes!'

The weather had turned to a half gale. Now the details of the Laurens Peninsula were visible, bare lava scree alternating with ice and waterfalls. On the basalt cliffs above the camp stood a solitary human figure.

I slipped down to the mess room for a bite of food but had scarcely eaten anything when Dick shouted, 'They're here; got the mail ready?' The little launch manned by three or four richly bearded Heard Islanders rose and fell to a high swell, moored fore and aft against the *Tottan*'s side. In a matter of minutes I was aboard, with Jerry, Dick and Lem Macey, and Ken Dalziel (who was appointed ashore at the last moment to assist with the overburdened radio schedules). We rode ashore over the crests of great bouncing waves, very cold and green, with rain in our faces.

I shall not forget my first-footing on Heard Island. A beach of black volcanic sand; the huge dismembered carcase of an elephant seal (killed that morning for the dogs), dozens of energetic black skuas flapping the air and wheeling round the flaccid red remains. The tractor drew us into the camp, a bewildering assortment of huts set between three great radio masts in the corded lava field and the black sand. The first sound of Heard Island is the moan of wind in wire and the howling of dogs. It seemed terribly complicated; a grey settlement below low clouds; occasional large tussocks of coarse grass and moss as bleak as any Hebridean outpost in mid-winter. I kept thinking in the back of my mind, how will this look in summer? But it *was* summer.

I had to find a *pied a terre* in a fully occupied camp. Gully [Les Gibbney], [1952] officer in charge and biologist, showed me round the camp and I chose the biologists' hut—for the time. It is warm and bright. I gathered together my gear and dumped it thankfully. Jerry set himself up in the hospital; the others found places. In the bright polygonal mess hut we found a grand meal prepared by Paul Thessier, the [1952] cook.

More than usual lights attracted the exquisite grey prions. They fluttered visibly against the black sky. Once they reached the earth they could only flutter helplessly, out of their cliff-top element. They shuffled into corners of black sand but the roaming husky bitches caught them up carelessly; lovely destroyers. All the dogs, and most of the bitches, are chained or enclosed—about 80 of them. Just a few loose, and a small perfectly white woolly puppy. The big dogs howled; some weigh 130 pounds.

I went to the biology hut, rolled out my old sleeping bag and without removing much clothing went to a hard and rather restless bed.

Sunday 22 February 1953

I was awakened by a shout from Lem. The *Tottan* was no longer at anchor. We walked up among the great mossy tussocks and over the extraordinary lava flows, which in places look as though they might have cooled last week, to the cliffs overlooking the cove. I found the landscape fascinating. A few shades of green cushion plant (there are about six or eight species of plants, mostly mosses, on the entire island) hardy enough to survive the deep winter snow growing in windswept arcs, the astonishing rope-like twisted lava, numerous sea elephant cows, quite torpid, a tribe or two of crested penguins on the cliff-top, and some utterly fearless cormorants. Some wonderful colour at our feet, greens and greys and black, and, whenever we lifted our eyes, endless contorted ice. No *Tottan*.

We returned to camp. Radio news had come through. Last night's blow (at about 3a.m.) had found the *Tottan* caught in a wind funnel from the Jacka Glacier, suddenly dragging her anchor. There was consternation. The engines failed to respond quickly from sleep. The vessel drifted to within 100 yards of the rocks. The anchor cable had to be cut (although it was buoyed), and in the nick of time the *Tottan* got away. The skipper said later today that he 'was the loneliest man in the world'. It would take a lot to disturb Andersen so.

Delays fret Jerry Donovan. He is an amazing character—bald, small, tight-featured and a little pinched. One might imagine him tough (and would be right) and perhaps humourless (and would be wrong). He is very quiet, slowly spoken, even hesitant, but he knows his mind. I admire his calmness and fairness. The *Tottan* costs £200 per day and Jerry would spare no-one in this relief operation to achieve maximum efficiency. Least of all, he would spare himself. He never hesitates to take a full share of crucial jobs.

I found tall, clear-eyed Peter Brown, this year's (last year's) dog-man (since the death of Forbes), storeman and auroral observer, a good companion. We went round the stores; had a long conversation on aurorae and a long session on the dogs. Apparently his dog-work has been excellent; he has some well-trained teams and uses them regularly for sealing expeditions. He must be quite young but his wispy flaxen beard and unkempt hair makes his age indeterminate.

Shortly after four the *Tottan* entered Atlas Cove. We put out in the cutter to the ship. It is a matter of limb-preservation to wait for the upward toss of an eight or nine foot swell before grabbing the short ship's ladder and clambering up the side. We opened the number 1 hold for some fresh foods. Another launch load returned; this time with M. Stahl and his gravimeters. He guards them like the Ark of the Covenant and will not let them leave his arms. They are very heavy and fragile. Lanusse helps but neither speaks much English, virtually nothing, and few of us are much better when it comes to technical French. The skipper, watching the weather, is not happy in the narrow, misty entrance to the cove.

By now the first pontoon is inflated and we shove her overboard. It's big—about 20 feet by eight. We are to take the ship's boat to haul the pontoon over the whitecaps. Lem Macey fights hard to start the motor and eventually it kicks over. We cast the lines aboard and are free. Immediately the engine of the ship's launch packs up and we are adrift without power, everyone lining the *Tottan*'s side splitting themselves with laughter. Just in time the inimitable Henry (one of the Norwegian crew) comes down to play with his engine. Eventually we are underway, coughing uncertainly. The island cutter comes alongside (and was I relieved!) and brings us ashore. All this time Ron Parsons and I sat aboard the great clumsy almost airborne pontoon, grinning and trying not to make it look feeble. The tractor dragged our craft up onto the beach; the pontoon was moored. We had a good meal. Apart from Cec O'Brien (who was on the *Tottan* to make sure nothing for Heard was left), my whole 1953 party was landed.

Monday 23 February 1953

I didn't hurry to rise. A leisurely move at about six. Breakfast and down to the beach. Loading and unloading, never-ending dumps— ordinary foods, luxury items, fresh foods, amenities, general cargo in 20 categories. Icy cold; heavy drooping showers of sleet and snow; sudden bursts of frozen sunlight; aching arms and lagging feet; mounting piles of crates—and at last such squalls that the *Tottan* puts to sea.

At dusk I changed from a glorious heavy submarine suit capable of dealing with weather. Then I put out an issue of wines—sherry, hermitage, claret, port. In a spontaneous way, the meal developed into a sort of party. We had chicken as the main course, chicken from 3000 miles away carried in the madly swaying refrigerator of the *Tottan*'s for'ard hold. Then at 8.30 we had a picture show in the rec room, accompanied by a vast crate of beer. There must have been 25 at least present. A crazy show—Mickey Rooney and Judy Garland, completely fatuous. Shouted comment, often extremely witty, and exceedingly bawdy. It was well on to midnight when I left to write this account; the party must have continued until three or four.

Claret and Hock

Partly as a result of changes in the industry itself, and also following Australia's wine agreements with the European Union, traditional wine names have changed considerably since I started drinking. Béchervaise's claret (in Australia meaning any red wine), burgundy (a lighter red), hermitage (shiraz) and hock (a white wine—among others, Penfold's Special Bin hock) have all been lost from general use. Sherry and port are going.

Tuesday 24 February 1953

By six we were battling with the keen air down on the beach, shoving in pontoons. Over the headland the mast of the *Tottan* swayed gently.

So started one of the toughest days I have ever experienced. We toiled without rest, except for a brief midday meal, until long after dark. It sleeted and rained and was bitterly cold. Pontoon after pontoon came in piled high with crates and drums. It must have been 70 tons borne ashore. Every crate and drum, weighing from 30 to 400 pounds had to be lifted onto a sledge or trailer and unloaded quickly. At times the pace was too hot to dump stores with any system; just a vast disorderly and unsorted pile. The pontoon men in their Mae-Wests came in clinging to the crates, four to each pontoon and two in each boat crew. Ceaselessly loading or unloading all day, until we were lifting automatically; trudging after the tractor, looking like walking kelp. When finally we finished we were all pretty well flayed and stumbling with fatigue.

Wednesday 25 February 1953

We all were down on the beach before seven; however it was too rough to continue unloading. There were constant snow-showers and rain and heavy winds from the west. Jerry arranged for drums to be brought up from the beach. After lunch unloading continued.

The day ended long after dark. One of the late, cold dusk jobs was endeavouring to anchor the rawin hut sections with big stones. By the end of the day, unloading had been accomplished.

Thursday 26 February 1953

Day of *Tottan*'s Departure

During the night the wind reached over 80 miles per hour in furious gusts. By now all the outgoing party were packing furiously.

I helped Peter to label outgoing cases. The sled finally conveyed everything to the beach. The weather was bad and appeared to be worsening. At about two we commenced farewelling men and loads. We were drenched and wading and working furiously, speeding the parting Heard Islanders. What seemed impossible gradually occurred. Jerry and Spalding were last to leave. Jerry thanked me for what I had done. Then the mists swallowed up the *Tottan* and we were very much alone.

> Heard Island
> 26 February 1953
>
> Dear Phil,
>
> From the first and so far only view of anything like a sizeable mass of Heard, I have been thrilled with my charge. I believe it offers everything I could have desired, a worthwhile year's project in everyway. Thank you for your confidence. We'll do our best.

Friday 27 February 1953

Breakfast at eight; then everyone was free to work as he liked. Arthur and I reorganized the sleeping quarters, making as much personal room as possible between the radially spaced bunks [in the 14-sided hut]. All the party found work to do; Leon slaved with his dogs. We scarcely touched stores. I typed the rosters; we were all mostly in bed by midnight. For the first time I slept in a bunk.

Saturday 28 February 1953

We are beginning to settle down to feeling the station as our charge. Arthur took Ron, Jack, Ken and Jim over to the glacier with a tractor and pickaxes to collect ice. They brought back half a ton and a sheep which had been injured and which they had killed. We are still working too hard but should be able to relax soon.

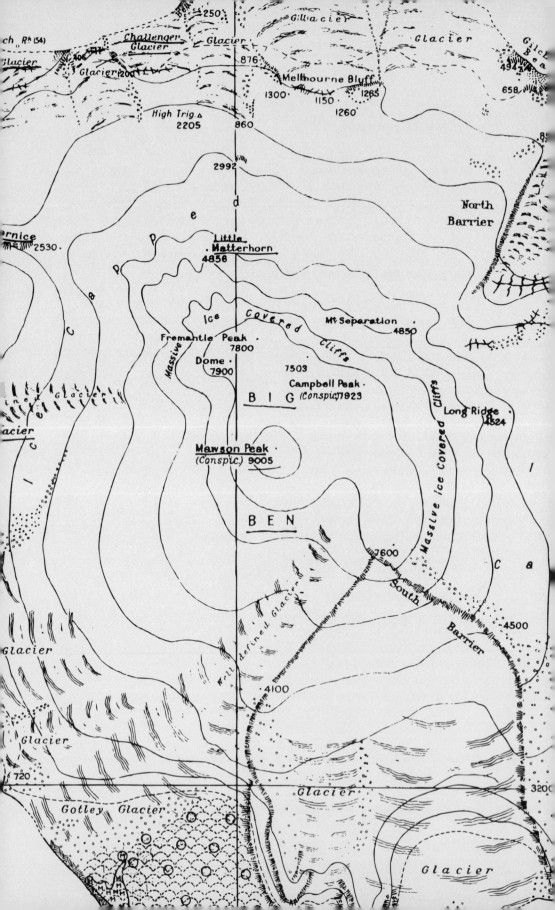

March 1953

French Lessons in the Mess

Sunday 1 March 1953

First Sunday on Heard Island, air temperature 31°F in the morning. Throughout the day there were sudden and violent snow showers. The mountain never cleared for a moment. It has brooded beneath cloud since we arrived.

Arthur and Leon went off to shoot a seal at West Bay. After lunch, Leon and Dick, amidst much cheering—and furious argument amongst the dogs—started off to collect the carcase. They were careering into the mist along the black shores of Atlas Cove. Dick came back with a sorry tale of the dogmobile being bogged at West Beach and all the dogs fighting and unruly.

Ken did us proud with a wonderful dinner; Jim Brooks typed menus in Bernie's best French. It was a fine occasion with claret and liqueurs, cheese, coffee, savourys. Before the films I read a couple of poems and said the Lord's Prayer for the Sabbath. The evening was a great success. I have come over to the biology hut, through thin dry snow, to record the first day of March.

Monday 2 March 1953

Heard Island is now our station. Often something sets the huskies howling. It seems incredible that they can lie in the open, when the dry snow fills the hollows and is plastered in thin ridges round the doors, a curious contrast with the black volcanic sand. Pale moonlight from an almost full moon filters through low misty cloud. Fine dry snow falls. How acclimatized we have become in a few days—we no longer dress as though it were midwinter.

The day brought minor troubles. Ron Parsons had his hand crushed when the gale caught the food store door; the first sonde flight was useless when the balloon burst on the hut wall; Arthur had a sheaf of papers blown away and failed to recover some, while the dogs ate the rest. The second balloon flight was successful but the sonde recorder broke down. Jack became ill with a sort of cramp. Bernie and Peter had trouble with hydrogen generation and Bernie managed to get a blast of caustic in his face.

The *Tottan* has left Kerguelen and is proceeding to Melbourne; apparently the McDonald Group was inaccessible under prevailing weather.

Jerry: 'McDonald Island now remains a nut for you to crack at next-relief.'

Weather 'Obs'

The 'Met people' made three-hourly weather observations ('obs'), day and night. If any weathermen were away on a field trip, the work had to be shared by the remaining observers.

The men released a hydrogen-filled balloon carrying a radiosonde (or 'sonde') at least once daily at 9 when possible, which transmitted air pressure, temperature and humidity readings back to them by radio. From late May 1953, the weathermen on Heard Island also attached a rawin device tracked with a radio theodolite (housed in a hut built without metal—even the bolts were wooden).

It was sometimes extremely hard to fill a large (1.5 metre diameter) balloon and release it in Heard Island's gusty winds. On at least one occasion, there were five attempts in a day, and only the last one was successful.

'Preparing the hydrogen alone is no sinecure. The ferrosilicon and caustic are placed in the cylinder; then hot water is admitted. The action is immediate but the open valve is screwed in and finally shutoff against a pressure that may rise within minutes to 2000 lb. per sq. in. When it cools the pressure drops away to 700 or 800' (John Béchervaise, diary entry, 17 March 1953).

Every day the observers made a synoptic chart from their observations and radioed the data to Australia whenever possible. They also punched observations onto Hollerith punch cards, which were packed in tin-lined cases, soldered shut and eventually sent to the Weather Bureau in Melbourne.

So ends our fourth day alone. Sitting here warm and comfortable, it is hard to imagine we are so far out in the Southern Ocean. Beyond these walls, only a mile away, is the eternal grey ice; a few hundred yards away are seals and penguins. Only the howling wind gives it all away; we never hear this lonely, powerful wind in the civilized parts of the world. It races up laden with the breath of the Antarctic Continent, dry and cold and merciless.

Tuesday 3 March 1953

Last night the lights went off at midnight. I went to the mess and found little Bernie playing the piano by torchlight—and outside the dogs howling like wolves.

Good black coffee was ammunition for the bitter morning. Some of us went down to help Len release the radiosonde balloon, a trying task in a high wind. It is a cold, bleak place, the radiosonde hut, where hydrogen is generated in icy cylinders and everyone must be alert at all times for fire and explosion. The sonde is attached to the great white balloon straining to be away. Two or three of us grasp it with outstretched arms and it is away, rising at a thousand feet a minute. Each balloon eventually comes to grief in the frigid upper air, anything up to 100,000 feet high, and many miles away over the lonely sea. Each flight is 30 or 40 pounds.

After that I visited our common place of relief. I don't remember ever having excreted in public before coming to Heard Island. There are four seats and we sit philosophizing and reading magazines. Not having had army experience I was at first repelled by the idea of communal excretion. Now it seems normal enough. I used to hold the idea that communal feeding was equally indecent.

Before dinner the mountain began to clear for the first time since our arrival. For brief minutes was the whole mountain clear, with a huge lenticular cloud to our south between the precipices and the rising gibbous moon. As the sunlight faded, shades of grey filled the vast valleys above the glaciers. Great avalanches thunder down to the Baudissin and Challenger glaciers. Whoever climbs Mawson Peak will tread 9000 feet of ice and snow. All the way he will be prepared for weather as violent as any nature offers.

We slipped out from dinner several times to watch the mountain, spellbound. Dinner was a gay meal. Dick had excelled himself with amazing gateaux covered with preserved banana and crystallized cherries.

Wednesday 4 March 1953

Last night Arthur, Peter, Fred and I started off over a light powdering of snow for Corinthian Bay. Along the dark beach Arthur counted 10 leopard seals. They sometimes reared their small carnivorous heads and looped away to sea. We followed round to the glacier ice and the swift, milky stream, then returned directly across the flat. We stumbled across the dehydrated carcase of a leopard, its teeth bared in a sort of static fury.

Finally Arthur and I strolled along the shore of Atlas Cove but only saw one leopard. Apparently the seal population of Atlas Cove and Corinthian Bay has decreased over the last few years, not solely by depredation of the dogmen. It seems that they have become sensitive and man-shy.

This morning I had my first go as slushy. Washing-up for 13 took me a long time. My last job for the day was to unpack tobacco and cigarette cases. The men are running short of the supply issued during the changeover.

Thursday 5 March 1953

A bleak, raw day. After breakfast Ken, Arthur, Jack and I commenced bolting together the base of the rawin hut. When we finished for the day the framework was complete, the floor fitted and the structure levelled with blocks of stone.

During the day there were glimpses of Big Ben, sunlit above the clouds. Another area of the island, quite low, out beyond Saddle Point, is frequently sunlit. Arthur calls it 'The Riviera'.

Our first radio contact with Sydney.

Friday 6 March 1953

There is no incentive to rise to Heard Island mornings. The brittle patter of sleet and the howling wind negate all resolution. This morning it was submarine suits—stiff clumsy garments that make one feel a cross between a robot and a scarecrow—and several hours on the rawin project, up on the snow and rain-swept basalt. We dug half a ton of sand or more from the spray-whipped beach and followed the grinding tractor up over the rises.

On the outskirt of the camp, Leon is attending his dogs. Beautiful quarrelsome dogs, every now and then attacking each other in more than mock combat, striving to bite each other's genitals. As we went up to lunch I discovered ill-feeling towards Peter on the part of Jack. Peter had apparently seemed superior when the steel sling drawing a huge load of wet black sand had broken—the almost inevitable mutual contempt of the theoretician and the practical man. I smoothed Jack and later had an opportunity to speak to Peter.

After lunch we mixed concrete. There was a welcome break for the Radio Australia Antarctic Session, then more concreting and afternoon tea. We continued working until we had made five supports fast and were very pleased with ourselves. What a contrast this life is with my desk life at *Walkabout*.

Dinner was merry. Someone suggested that the beautiful and carelessly draped girl on Jim's calendar was not in the right place. 'No,' said Ron Parsons, 'she ought to be on the top bunk in the next room!' Ron Parsons, Dick McNair and Jack Hughes are keen on rendering down blubber from the seals killed for dog-meat.

'Calling Antarctica'

Every Friday, Radio Australia broadcast 'Calling Antarctica' for the men on Heard and Macquarie islands (and later, on the Antarctic continent). Family members in the Melbourne studio could talk or send messages to the men.

Sunday 8 March 1953

We are reserving Sunday as a free day with the hope that every man who is able will get out. After breakfast Arthur, Peter and I set out for the west coast of the Laurens Peninsula. We reached West Bay and inspected the elephant seals, half-a-dozen great sluggish bulls and a good many pups and cows. Arthur discovered some brands. It was wonderful to be free. The cold surf pounded the stones until they raced and clattered. All along the beach lay great whips and snakes of green and yellow kelp, and the evidence of the sea-leopards' diet—hundreds of penguin skins and skeletons, all completely clean and empty.

We came upon a little parade of gentoo penguins. Further on a solitary chin-strap penguin, black eye and chin-strap, a rare bird on Heard. He has his usual haunts 3000 miles west in the Weddell Sea and South Georgia. While Arthur and I were ringing a paddy—the little white hens of Heard Island, and the only true land bird in the Antarctic—Peter passed unseen below us. We found him beyond a large macaroni [penguin] rookery. Below the terminal moraine of an un-named glacier is a penguin road, perfectly graded and appearing unbelievably man-made, down the side of the steep hill. A few little old men ambled up and down, following the pathway of many centuries. The distance these penguins waddle is incredible.

We rose onto the terminal moraine of the un-named glacier, one of the few on Heard Island that does not quite reach the sea. Enormous heaps of broken stone, every edge sharp and fresh, rising hundreds of feet into the air—countless millions of tons of stone moving slowly before the gigantic bull-dozer of the ice. On the moraine we found the nests of several pairs of Antarctic terns, graceful black-capped birds with grey and white bodies. Their nests are mere scoops marshalling a few fine stones against which the eggs are well camouflaged.

Penguin Roads

Penguin 'roads' are paths penguins have trodden by habitual use. They are often remarkably straight and appear well tended. Biologist Jeremy Smith described a penguin road on Heard Island: 'It looked just like a road cut by a grader across the slope,' he said. 'It was a breathtaking sight, mostly because it so uncannily resembled a man-made feature' (Jeremy Smith, *Specks in the Southern Ocean*, 1986: 68).

Wednesday 11 March 1953

Between us and the mountain is a great flat sandy wilderness, an isthmus between Corinthian Bay and Atlas Cove. It is waterlogged from rain and spray, a dismal but fascinating desert holding only a few elephant and leopard seal skeletons and a dozen half-buried fuel drums. The isthmus gripped Leon's dogmobile too firmly this afternoon when he and Arthur went to rescue a dying sheep. They had to carry the trembling creature back to camp. We made it as comfortable as possible but it died tonight. Ever since we arrived the weather has been bitter, with snow every day. Now we have lost four sheep including the one we killed. Eight continue to graze on the slopes of Drygalski but only the strongest will survive. I feel that the breed was wrong; perhaps Herdwick sheep would have acclimatized better.

There was a good deal of activity today in spite of the wild snow-showers. Len nearly crushed his foot when a hydrogen cylinder crashed from an insecure mounting. The general opinion is that the station was in very poor condition when we took over. Most of the personal living quarters and amenities were squalid. It is hard to judge, being such new brooms ourselves; and necessary to remember the tragedy last year, its effect being not only on the spirits of the survivors but throwing a big additional burden of work on everyone.

It is after midnight and the lights have gone off. The wind is shaking the hut and whistling in the aerials. It is a difficult sound to describe. It changes pitch with the gusts; a lonely, desolate sound; cold and emotionless.

Thursday 12 March 1953

A wild, bleak day with even the Laurens Peninsula shrouded with blizzardly cloud. Gusts well over 60 miles per hour. Arthur and Leon disposed of the sheep carcase, feeding it to the dogs after a post-mortem (lung cysts with pneumonia).

Friday 13 March 1953

Arthur has been catching dove prions and divers for banding, by the light of the searchlight beam. They seem to flock on these dull, drizzling nights. They are exquisite little grey blue birds with a fantail and complicated beak (like that of the shearwaters). They will be released in the morning, except one poor little bird, a diver of scientific interest.

Sunday 15 March 1953

We set off at 9.30 to have a look at the Vahsel Glacier. It is difficult on the flat leading to the moraine to avoid collapsing the innumerable divers' burrows that honeycomb the black sands. There is a curiously fantastic atmosphere about the azorella glens. Everything is extraordinarily clear-cut, perfect hummocks of brilliant green surrounded by black sands, and sometimes yellows from mosses.

Soon we reached the ice of the Vahsel. We roped and donned crampons. At first there were no serious crevasses, just snow-filled cracks. But as we moved westward the ice-scape became more rugged until we were in a field of great seracs, treading narrow ridges between immense blue gulfs, many of which showed no bottom. Higher up we found the crevasses narrower and snow-bridged. By 3 o'clock we were on the lower slopes of the Abbotsmith moraine. We left our packs and gear, and descended to the cliff-tops through broken rocks and azorella. The coastline is fringed with unsound volcanic screes. The weather suddenly changed to fierce north-west winds and rain. We had a brief snack and set off home. The deluge had covered the ice with unpleasant streams and quagmires of brash. We arrived home wet and tired at 6.30, finding the camp in a cheerful mood and a grand meal, complete with crepes suzettes, prepared by Bernie.

The rain had almost filled our tank. I re-lit the bath-heater. At 11.40 the lights were switched off by the tired engineer [Jack Hughes]. Arthur was caught in the bath. I fetched candles for his finishing operations; then lay at peace in a hot bath by candlelight and smoked two cigarettes in pure luxury.

Tuesday 17 March 1953

A wild bleak day with gusts carrying dry snow-stars and black grit in about equal proportions. Spiteful, frozen dust.

The Met people had a heartbreaking day. Two sonde balloons (roughly five feet in diameter) were torn away by the gale and burst in spite of the efforts of four or five men. The third flight was successful after lunch. I made a large sling with four corner cords from a sheet and it seemed to control the balloon better in the initial stages.

In between assisting with sonde flights I set out tins of chocolate and bottles of wine. Arthur was skinning his Kerguelen diver's little dusky body. To celebrate Saint Patrick's Day—as good a reason as any—we had planned a 'ding' celebration. I laid out some sherry, claret and port and about 20 bottles of beer. But everyone was too tired. We decided to postpone our beer, sat over our port for a while and drifted early to bed. We are all working too hard.

Dings

'Dings' or parties were held regularly, usually at the end of the week, and included a film (or two). Each week the officer in charge distributed a ration of cigarettes or pipe tobacco and chocolate. Alcohol was also issued by the officer in charge and was restricted to special occasions, such as dings.

Wednesday 18 March 1953

The long awaited calm day, with a breeze of only five to eight knots. After breakfast a large party commenced erecting the rawin walls. By lunchtime we had all the walls in position and bolted together.

After lunch everything went wrong. We tried to erect the centre strutting and it wouldn't fit. Ken and Jim bolted the sections of the metal scaffolding together and they twisted like lead. By tea-time it had turned very cold and the wind was rising. In an effort to dismantle the scaffolding, I nearly came to grief. The ladder broke and I fell beneath the large 4 x 6 beam and other debris, stunned but conscious. Fortunately beyond bruises and nausea there was no damage.

I have decided the 2a.m. Met men may sleep until 10.30, unless they are on slushy duties. Peter doesn't spare his men and probably he does not spare himself. He has a strange, argumentative manner and can easily rile Len, who is a dogged and experienced man. Peter often opens his mouth too wide, but he has the grace to admit errors.

Thursday 19 March 1953

Leon and Arthur set off in the dogmobile to dismantle the morning's seal kill. They returned in the late dusk. Although the dogs had been magnificent they had managed to stick in the sea at low tide about 400 yards from camp. Several of us donned parkas and gumboots and walked along the cold seashore to help. The jagged skylines of Mount Aubert de la Rue and Olsen were velvet against a pale and bitter sky. A wild and lonely atmosphere, more forlorn than the Outer Hebrides, only a quarter of a mile from camp.

At 1625 an aurora—a great pale glow stretching from east and west. Tonight is the first night that the sky has been clear enough even to see an aurora since we arrived.

Friday 20 March 1953

Our mountain showed himself for hours, a great dazzling white dome.

After lunch Peter and I walked to South West Bay. Looking at the mountain I had the feeling that a direct approach might be possible for a strong small party with bivouacs. The route might well be too exposed for tents. We returned to camp by the Andrée spur. At our feet the white rock was frost-riven and sharp as glass. We were intrigued with the sandblasted rocks. I recall Phil Law saying that these stones, some only weighing a few pounds, were the best souvenirs of Heard Island.

The camp looked particularly fair in the warmer light, its reds and greens soft and clear. We reached it in time for tea and the exciting news that Radio Australia had announced a Continental venture at the end of the year. The ship would come and spend Christmas here and leave the 1954 party. Then she would proceed to the Antarctic Continent, and pick the 1953 party up on her return. Several members of the party keenly debated their chances of joining the southward party for the trip.

Sunday 22 March 1953

Arthur, Leon, Len and Jim left this morning for the Laurens Peninsula. Arthur and Leon will camp at the 'ternery', where Antarctic terns are nesting on the moraine below Anzac Peak.

The morning's duty fully absorbs every minute. In the afternoons there is time to breathe. I employed it by doing the first wash since I left Melbourne—two kerosene tins and plenty of Persil. In the late afternoon, managed to get everything into the drying-room.

Washing Day

There was no drying room in earlier ANARE years, and washing clothes was a laborious duty. Les Gibbney described his efforts in 1950:

'Positively everything went wrong. For a start, it was a large wash and the only containers we have are kerosene tins. The idea is to boil them over a primus, and my first mistake was to put too many clothes into the bucket, with the result that I scorched two holes in one of my pillow slips. I then tried the oil-burning copper in the wash-house, but only succeeded in obtaining masses of oil fumes and very little heat. However the wash was eventually finished although I can't say that the clothes were very much cleaner than before and certainly my temper was volcanic. I did more swearing today than for many a long year. But in the evening, peace came to me as I relaxed in my easy chair, carefully avoiding the drips from the saturated underclothes that now festoon the hut' (Leslie Gibbney, diary entry, 26 April 1950).

'Did some washing, sheets + towels + managed to get them white. The water from the snow-melter smells very strongly of blubber so I put dettol [an antiseptic] in it but the combination was even worse' (Fred Elliott, diary entry, 21 June 1953).

The evening meal was in the grand manner. Peter had prepared mushroom soup, omelettes (over which he grew lyrical, and which were very good), a great mixed stew, rice pudding and apples. Not a man was left unsatisfied.

Monday 23 March 1953

Fred, Cec and I breakfasted by candlelight, leaving heavily laden in driving snow at 7.20. As we travelled a pale sun gave a glint to the seaward rocks. We passed up through the great squabbling macaroni rookery, far more crowded with moulting penguins than when we last passed that way, reached the shingle below the extraordinary penguin 'road' and followed up the alluvial flat to the base of the moraine. Here we found the tent looking very snug and Arthur and Leon busily packing.

The landscape is strange, unfriendly and yet vividly beautiful—black, green and yellow, with minute patches of brighter orange lichens. Below Mount Dixon we came upon a number of sooty albatross chicks all puffed up in grey down. While they venomously regurgitated and spat, Arthur ringed half-a-dozen. A few mother birds whirled round us, seeming smaller than their great fluffy offspring.

We dropped down to a little alluvial flat with several shining pools. Here we camped but were disappointed in not finding running water. The pools, which we drew on instead, were alive with small red and black crustacea.

Arthur and I went down to the little cove. There was a rookery on a slope of black sand. Several thousand macaronis stood in pairs (with just a few unmatched) in perfectly serried ranks, clucking and squawking regardless of the world. Bare earth, perhaps 15 feet in breadth, stretched all round the rookery, like a broad border to a living carpet. Round this edge strutted a few skuas and a solitary white giant petrel, on the look-out for the aged or infirm—or any straggler wounded by the marauding leopard seals which parade the shallows. Arthur captured a couple of lone penguins, being careful not to disturb the 10,000 obviously mated pairs. He expertly stunned them and cut their throats. From both sides of the sternum he obtained large dark steaks and also excavated for the livers and hearts. We worked by torchlight then tramped up the spongy azorella to camp.

Arthur, Leon and Cec cooked the evening meal. We crowded into one tent and fed to repletion. After clearing away the debris, we lay in our own tents, brewed more tea and listened to the curious 'morse-code' cry of the prions, nesting nearby in the azorella and flying wildly through the dark night.

Heard Island's Albatrosses

Two species of albatross breed on Heard Island, the black-browed albatross and the light-mantled sooty albatross. On 17 November 1953, news arrived that a black-browed albatross ringed on Heard Island as a chick in February 1951 had been recovered near Sydney.

Tuesday 24 March 1953

A perfect day with extraordinarily good weather. We climbed the rise south-east of the camp and entered a weird lava-flow landscape reminiscent of moonscape imaginings. The lava is thinly veiled with mosses and azorella, and there are numerous cones, craters and fumaroles. Much of the lava is as hard and brittle as glass. In one small crater we found mosses and small land-snails. The latter must have their origin in the older, greater land masses of the Antarctic and must have survived a great deal of volcanic activity.

We followed glacial streambeds through black ash and dirty ice-cliffs—a landscape devoid of life and strangely exciting—then mounted the tortuous lava field and picked a way through a maze of steel-hard spikes often beautifully hued with golden lichens. Behind us rose the icy mountains and out to sea the precipitous McDonald Group. Then Red Island showed below, a cone connected to the main peninsula by a low isthmus.

Fred and I left the others to inspect the fur seals (they saw 28) and returned to camp to cook. We had a contemplative journey across the lava. On the descent to camp we sat and gloried in the wide, lonely panorama. The air froze as we prepared the evening meal of penguin steak but it was so calm that I cooked in the open. A handkerchief used to strain the water froze in a few seconds. Soft cloud covered the moon. We brewed more tea in our own tents and were reluctant to let the day die.

Wednesday 25 March 1953

We awoke to purposeful rain. We had ample hot porridge, bacon and coffee, and it required an effort of will to leave the warmth and strike camp. Our packs were much heavier with wet tents. Close to the albatross rookery, we discovered a small fumarole cave and had an early lunch sheltered from the cold rain. Some stiff climbing followed and we were glad of another cave below a large loose moraine below Mount Dixon.

From there we were able to strike a good route over older lava. I prefer lava to azorella. The latter is so soft and yielding that it clogs the footsteps. Each step sinks deep into the soft green and occasionally the foot slips down into some hidden hollow. At least the lava is what it appears to be. Its chief difficulty lies in the numerous loose lumps and splinters requiring judgement for balanced traversing. Leon does not travel well on rock but is as game as one could wish. Arthur is agile and dogged; he often felt the weight of his pack but plugged on uncomplainingly. Fred was quite happy mostly. Cec O'Brien complained that he would never recover but kept a good sense of humour.

The spiky aiguilles of the Olsen cliffs came out of the mists. Fortunately the tide was very low, and we were able to make our way to West Bay without having to climb through the rookeries. The sea fought amongst the rattling boulders and shingle, and occasionally leapt up spitefully and tried to wet us more completely. Quite unconcerned innumerable penguins made their landfall along the coast, and set out to waddle to distant rookeries. Evidently they prefer the inconvenient and distant landing to further hazards of leopard seals.

Wet as shags and far more weary, we reached the magnetic huts. It had not been a quick journey, on account of our loads. The tents were too robust for such a trek. We carried three between us, somewhat unnecessarily, though they provided maximum camping comfort. The weight of a tent, dry, is about 15 pounds, duralumin poles and nylex sheets extra!

A good turn of speed brought us to Atlas Cove and we staggered in gratefully. There was a slight sense of anti-climax, for no-one could really know what a struggle the day had been. Naturally the men who had remained in camp were only mildly interested.

Thursday 26 March 1953

It was comforting to be home again and in a warm bunk, and to hear the wild morning wind. Under roofs the weather can sound terribly wild; out in the open, with just a frail tent, is different.

I spent the entire morning fixing a pane of windolite in the mess room. They all need mending but the one I replaced was letting sand and water in to the piano. We changed for the evening meal.

Friday 27 March 1953

There was the usual expectant gathering in the radio room but the programme was so blended with atmospheric disturbances that we caught only occasional words in a blather of exasperating cacophony. It is thwarting in these times of radio blackout. The 'weather' is sent by special arrangement via Kerguelen but no private messages or ordinary administrative traffic passes that way.

I chose some wines for dinner and prepared for the first French session. At 5.30 a few of us gathered in the mess room. The text of the first [Linguaphone] record and a rough sketch were written on the wall. Bernie was full of instruction and the hour passed quickly.

Kerguelen and the Other Subantarctic Islands

Scattered through the southern seas are about 20 cold, wet and windy subantarctic islands, lying between the inhabited southern continents and Antarctica. The islands, which are the territorial possessions of countries as far away as Norway and France, include Australia's Heard Island and its nearest neighbour Îles Kerguelen, 450 kilometres to the north-west. Most of France's southern Indian Ocean possessions (Îles Crozet, Amsterdam and Kerguelen), as well as the South African Marion Island and Australia's Macquarie Island, have been occupied since the 1950s, unlike Heard Island.

In the 1940s and 1950s, the Heard Island base was in touch with bases on Marion Island (nearly a thousand miles away), Îles Kerguelen and Amsterdam (where French military men were posted), and weather stations in Capetown, Pretoria and Madagascar, for scientific and social reasons (including long-distance chess games), as well as to relay communications.

Sunday 29 March 1953

Judith Mary was much in mind, it being her seventh birthday. With the blackout one feels somewhat isolated.

Arthur, whenever possible, drifts off to the beaches to count leopards. This afternoon he shot (and unfortunately lost) an Arctic tern. This is the season when the terns of both poles gather on Heard, an amazing yearly reunion.

I decided on a roast dinner, fussing round my pots and ovens like Mrs Beeton herself. The menu was onion soup with spices; roast leg of lamb with roast potatoes, roast carrots, onions and peas with brown gravy, plum pudding with custard and nutmeg, and coffee (made in a ferrosilicon bag!), with Hunter River hermitage.

Monday 30 March 1953

During the last few days there have been enormous ice avalanches from the mountain, some reaching Corinthian Bay. Mount Olsen is becoming bare ice and rock, and all the hanging glaciers are feeding splendid waterfalls.

Leon discovered a large elephant on the beach below the camp and promptly shot it for dog meat. He spent a good part of the day sloshing round in blood and Jack brought up sufficient meat on the sledge for five days.

At dinner we played some lovely Kathleen Ferrier records. Her voice is exquisite. The new gramophone arrangements in the mess are splendid.

Tuesday 31 March 1953

Much colder today. I flew the flag at half-mast for Queen Mary's death. Peter's forecast was vindicated and occasional snow-showers fell. As Len said, somewhat unkindly, 'the man cannot always be wrong!'

Dick, Arthur and Leon took the dogmobile over to Drygalski to inspect the sheep and leave some straw and fodder in their shelter cave. Leon has been requested to limit his dogs to about 50. It is sad but necessary. The dogs are already far too big a job, and many are useless for both breeding and sledging.

When I came across to the biology hut at about 10, the clouds rested lightly on Big Ben. At every opportunity I inspect the great dome. I am sure his ascent is a problem mainly of weather. There has not yet been time for relaxation, contemplation, reading, writing or organization of a personal life. Another month or so should see us really well established.

View over Atlas Cove (right foreground) and Corinthian Bay (background) from Mount Olsen, 1953. The ANARE station is almost indiscernible on the peninsula in the middle ground. It lies on the left shore of the small cove which is partly hidden behind Peter Shaw.

Béchervaise Papers, National Library of Australia, MS7972

The men of the 1953 party, Heard Island.

Front row, squatting (L to R): meteorologist Peter Shaw, cook Dick McNair, geophysicist Jim Brooks
Second row (L to R): weather observers Bernie Izabelle and Len Welch, radio operator Ron Parsons, weather observer Fred Elliott, diesel mechanic Jack Hughes, dog attendant Leon Fox, medic and biologist Arthur Gwynn, radio supervisor Ken Dalziel, radio operator Cec O'Brien, officer in charge John Béchervaise. The husky is either Frani or her sister Kari.

Photograph: John Béchervaise
Béchervaise Papers, National Library of Australia, MS7972

A pen and ink drawing of the ANARE station by Fred Elliott, 1953.

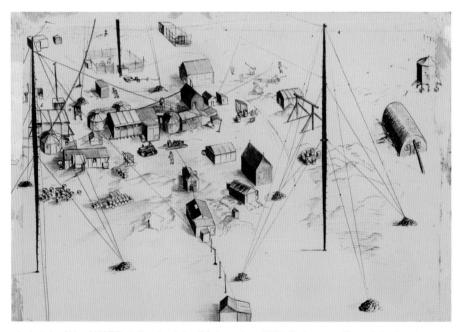

A sketch of the ANARE station by John Béchervaise, 1954. It shows radio aerials, the doggery (top left), the Met hut and round radio hut (centre left), two round sleeping huts behind the rec hut (left centre of sketch), and Chippy's church with a steeply pitched roof and crosses.

The ANARE station showing Big Ben in the background, 1953.
Photograph: Fred Elliott

Meteorological instruments with Mount Olsen in the background, 1953.

Photograph: Fred Elliott

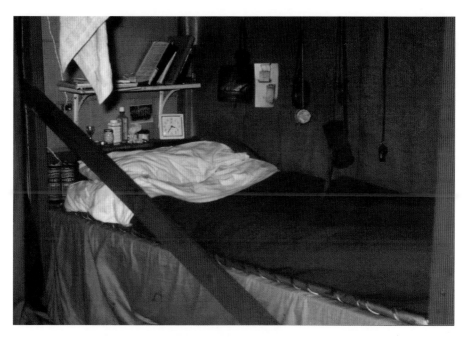

Fred Elliott's bunk in the sleeping quarters at Atlas Cove, 1953.

Photograph: Fred Elliott

Dick McNair, Leon Fox and Len Welch in the rec hut, 1953.
Photograph: Fred Elliott

Heard Island from the sea, 2002.

Photograph: Bernadette Hince

Souvenir Bastille Day menu, with signatures, doggerel and one of Fred Elliott's miniature French flags, 14 July 1953.

Reproduced by permission of Fred Elliott

John Béchervaise's Heard Island daybooks, 1953–1954.

Béchervaise Papers, National Library of Australia, MS7972

April 1953

The Only Life in Millions of Square Miles

Wednesday 1 April 1953

Jim and I walked round the beach to West Bay. A taut grey leopard seal lay stretched on the beach. Above him, near high watermark, lay a film of frozen sea. We soon reached the magnetometer hut and changed the trace, then hurried back into a freshening wind for breakfast. An hour or so later there was a long snow plume driving westward like a streamer.

Leon started his unhappy task of destroying the surplus dogs with a .22 rifle, well out of sight of the others. Later, in a hurricane of rain and cold, Jack tractored the carcases to the sea at Wharf Point.

At about 10, Ken and I walked up over the streaming basalt to inspect the rawin hut. Coming back through the wild, wet night to the lights of the main camp, there was a sudden, rather thrilling realization that our settlement, with perhaps that of Kerguelen, is the only life in millions of square miles of ocean.

> **Daily Jobs at West Bay**
>
> Someone had to walk to the magnetic hut at West Bay, a mile and a quarter west of Atlas Cove, every morning to check batteries, change the trace and replace the photographic paper.

Thursday 2 April 1953

Today Big Ben was frequently visible, silver and shadowed and extremely beautiful. Every job on Heard Island is within sight of the mountain. On a day like today everyone, now and then, just stops and gazes. It is wonderful to be working on some mundane job and, with a raising of the head, take the sight of the huge high snow buttresses.

Friday 3 April 1953

Good Friday

Ken, Dick, Len and Jack went fishing in the dinghy. Their catch consisted of a couple of 'rock-cod' and some extraordinary 'alligators', fish that seem all mouth and trail away absurdly. It would be quite easy to place one's clenched fist in the mouth of a foot-long 'alligator'.

After dinner Peter played all the records of the Bach *St Matthew Passion*, sung by members of Bach's own church, Saint Thomas Leipzig. Freddie, Bernie, Len (for a while), Peter and I sat by the light of seven candles in the mess. We entirely forgot we were marooned on a sub-Antarctic island thousands of miles from home.

Saturday 4 April 1953

Bernie achieved the highest sonde flight we have made so far, 75,000 feet.

The last day or two has revealed an atmosphere of overwork. Therefore there were wines and liqueurs for dinner, then films and beer. Outside was a foul night of gale and snow. Inside we sat through a film of war adventure in Brittany. We drank and smoked and passed dishes of nuts and sweets.

Sunday 5 April 1953

Easter Sunday

Finished the partition walls. Soon the whole party will have convenient 'two-man flats', each equipped with sufficient clothing space and with lights, tables and chairs.

I sent a cable of good wishes to the new party on Marion Island, 1400 miles away, staffed from South Africa. A very happy evening meal. It may have been imagination, but I fancied that two or three men might be in danger of losing their sense of humour.

Tuesday 7 April 1953

Blizzards of fine snow, eddying like smoke, bore over the frozen sand and piled in drifts. To move from hut to hut was to be encrusted with snow and the wind was breath-taking.

The Met people had a very bad morning with their sondes. The first was driven against the wall and ruptured; the second dragged and left part of the apparatus behind; a cold frustrating morning. In the afternoon, they managed to release their balloon in a brief lull between gusts reaching 60 miles per hour. The dogs huddled against the blizzard and seemed happy all flecked with ice, some curled, some standing facing the storm. Old Leon drifted round as usual, his blood-stained parka covered with snow. A solitary pup will remain after he has completed his melancholy destruction.

Friday 10 April 1953

Arthur, Ken and I set out at 9.30 into a stiff wet gale. By the time we turned north-west under Mount Aubert de la Rue the weather helped rather than stayed our progress and we began to delight in the rounded shore boulders and the sloping azorella, the silver misted sea and the kelp, laid flat in wavering patterns at low tide. The kelp is fascinating and terrible. Rooted just below high-tide level to the harsh, black rocks it streams out 15 or 20 feet in thick brown branches. It appears alive and malignant sometimes, as though desperately straining to be free. And free it often is in long dead strands, growing yellow and stinking in decay where it has been cast by the storms. It is gross and slimey to walk over. But at a distance, against the light on the water, it is Medusan hair on the half-submerged heads of giantesses.

The shore of Heard is colourful with many kinds of sea-weed. Delicately branched fronds in wine and crushed cherry red, olive green, yellow, warm and purplish browns, they provide as much wealth of colour and shape as the wild-flowers of warmer coasts. There are very few shell-fish or shells, except for a mauve limpet. Real beaches are rare, and then have black sand. Practically the whole coast of Heard is bounded by huge rounded stones, or high, inhospitable cliffs of ice or rock.

Today's journey was chiefly over endless slippery round boulders. On several occasions we glimpsed the camp across the water. We followed up a steep but stable scree to an azorella traverse between cliffs and sat well sheltered for lunch. Eight hundred feet, almost vertically below, was the sea. Elephant seals lay in the estuary of the Jacka streams, looking from our height like big fawn slugs. There was no horizon, just a perfect silver-grey blending of sea and cloud. We opened our '02' rations—packed 10 years ago by some girls probably, working a shift in a war factory, who could never have dreamed that they would be finally opened on a remote Antarctic island—and ate our biscuits in deep contentment.

02 Rations

02 ration tins were used by the Australian armed forces in World War II. A tin held three meals:

Meal 1

carrot biscuits	3 ounce packet
fruit and nut	3⅜ ounce block
meat and vegetable stew	4 ounce tin
peanut butter	1½ ounce tin
barley sugar rolls (4)	1 ounce
caramel bar	½ ounce
skim milk powder	¼ ounce packet
sugar	2 tablets
tea	4 tablets
salt	2 tablets

Meal 2

wholemeal biscuits	2¼ ounce packet
wheat lunch	3 ounce block
meat and vegetable hash	4 ounce tin
cheese	1¼ ounce tin
barley sugar rolls (4)	1 ounce
lime tablets	½ ounce packet
skim milk powder	¼ ounce packet
sugar	2 tablets
tea	4 tablets
salt	2 tablets

Meal 3

wholemeal biscuits	2¼ ounce packet
chocolate	3 ounce block
meat and beans, or corned beef hash	4 ounce tin
blackcurrant spread	1⅜ ounce tin
barley sugar rolls (4)	1 ounce
caramel bar	½ ounce
skim milk powder	¼ ounce packet
sugar	2 tablets
tea	4 tablets
salt	2 tablets

A magnificent buttress of azorella led us down to the cliff-edge. There were the albatrosses—dozens of proud young birds not far away from flight. Only a few still bore the incredibly soft grey down of childhood; most showed clean black wings and the lovely transition of grey to snowy white. They were about as large as geese. Each sat on a low cylindrical stool, compounded of grass and mud through a century or two, with a concave top about a foot in diameter. Their typical albatross bills, with two short breathing tubes, showed the sooty colour of the young birds; later it would turn a clean straw colour and have a handsome red tip.

While each bird in turn spat and regurgitated and made a great show of offence, we balanced along the ledges, caught each chick by the beak and lifted him to Arthur who deftly placed rings on their legs. We ringed about 40 birds. While we were in the rookery two parent birds wheeled in from the sea, wings motionless. They circled then came into land. Both wore silver rings, doubtless placed there by Max Downes [a former Heard biologist], two years or more ago. Arthur tried to catch one but they were too wary. Do they return each day from hundreds of miles out to sea, to this infinitely lonely crag, just to feed their young? Such pathfinding is beyond comprehension, almost.

Monday 13 April 1953

The day passed pleasantly for me as slushy. Lunch was a highlight— an entree of penguin steak and a main course of skua. Jim had brought down three skuas with the shot-gun yesterday. We have a poultry yard with several paddies (sheathbills) being fattened for the table. Dick catches them with a long wire hook.

A dark, wet and miserable night. The evenings, after dinner, seem to fly. By the time I have written this inadequate log, it is always not far off midnight.

Telegram

Heard Island   Apr 13 1953

MARION ISLAND

WE ACKNOWLEDGE YOUR P – QB3 STOP REPLY K – KB3 STOP

HAVE YOU TRIED ROAST SKUA REGARDS – BECHERVAISE

Tuesday 14 April 1953

All day fine rain has fallen. The sand is sodden and plastic. So far the party has maintained a high morale. Now, at about 11, Cecil has just come in with a cliff prion, an exquisite blue-grey little bird which had fallen blinded by the hut lights. Arthur feels for his birds. Occasionally, he will chloroform one and preserve it, but most of the small lost wanderers he examines gently and goes to no end of trouble to release safely. Often he keeps them until next morning and waits until there are no skuas about.

Wednesday 15 April 1953

Leon, who has been working late at night making new harnesses for the various dog teams, had his second team out today for practice. 'Too many want to squabble or play mothers and fathers!' he remarked lugubriously.

I made a small humorous notice for Fred's and Bernie's bed-sitting room.

> *Ici en parle francais* — M. Bernard Izabelle
> Aussie as she is spoke — F.W. Elliott, Esq.

Later Bernie came to me in great distress. 'John, you do not spell "aussi" like this,' he said.

Thursday 16 April 1953

Soon after breakfast, Arthur and I started for Rogers Head to obtain penguins for measurements required by the Melbourne biologists. We explored a number of arched tunnels running below the lava and opening up to the sky in a series of holes where the roof had fallen. One tunnel ran right out to an opening below the edge of the cliffs. From a sink-hole some yards back it was possible to look out to sea beyond the dangerous balanced basalt of the abrupt cliff-edge.

The azorella is haunted by the exquisite dove prion — *Prion desolata* — the little greyblue bird which flutters into our camp-lights at night. *Desolata* is most apt to describe the fragile bird of the ocean, flitting over the waves all day and returning to shore at dusk, when the terrible black skuas are less active.

Arthur made a rapid and I hope painless end for two fine macaronis and a couple of rockhoppers. The two species are alike but the fine golden plumes of the macaroni meet across the top of the bill, whilst the paler crests of the rockhopper are delicately pencilled to points just above the bright red eye.

We descended the slope, making our way between the clucking and squabbling birds, in front of the great Rogers Head cliff. Although only 477 feet high, the crag is so sheer that it is enormously impressive. The southern cliff is banded in extraordinarily even striae for its entire height. There is only one thing lacking amidst such magnificent scenery—sufficient human history to endow each yard of splendour with legends and ghosts. It needs smugglers and Vikings as much as it cries out to youth. Yet only a few old sealers a mere century or so ago may have scaled these heights, and before them, never a soul since the beginning of time.

There is a rocky traverse to the west of the Head. We followed the footsteps of Max Downes. At nightfall he watched 1500 cliff or fairy prions (*P. crassirostris*) fly to dark security. There was the old fishing rod he left to mark the place. As we lingered, even by day the prions swept in and around the cliffs as numerous as butterflies round a summer lilac, as graceful as the terns. We returned with our rockhoppers—Arthur looked like some Hebridean fowler, carrying the birds on a loop of cord over his shoulder.

After dinner I played chess with Jim and Peter. We are expecting another move from Marion and hope for a game with Kerguelen. There are only two or three minute specks in the whole wide Southern Ocean but with radio communication we do not feel lonely even locally.

Polar Lava Tunnels

There are subarctic lava tubes in Iceland, Alaska and Kamchatka, but the Heard Island tunnels are the only ones known in the subantarctic or Antarctic.

Sunday 19 April 1953

The dawn seemed like a lean, grey wolf searching and whining and snuffling while there was still no light; though no day is ever as bad as it sounds to a waker in a warm bed. My alarm rang and I dragged myself out and stumbled about dressing for the slog over to the West Bay magnetic huts. Heavy wet snow phutted against the camp, plastering the windward walls to the north-east. Only one old grey leopard was alive in a watchful dream down by the blown-back waves. The doors of the huts were completely iced over.

It is strange to enter the dark variometer hut, by torchlight peering at temperatures and chronometers, listening to the ticking of the trace-drum escapement, checking the fine twin lights, creeping about in a dim red silence. The tiny mirrors and prisms dance to invisible impulses, a great changing pattern of magnetic forces varied by a fabulous sun.

Monday 20 April 1953

Leon was cook today, a cheerful, surprisingly bashful lad and very self-deprecating when he is praised. He made a jolly good job of everything. We managed to catch Paddie with her pups outside this morning and transfer all except one to the prepared kennel. So the sleeping hut should be quieter now and gradually less odorous.

Bernie was in a low mood and refused to be cheered. He has sombre moods but they pass. Perhaps it was just the gloomy day which worsened to rain. I joined Jim in the biology hut for an hour or so. There are three clear sounds: a rising wind, the complaint of some of the dogs and the beat of the diesels, ebbing and flooding with the wind.

Tuesday 21 April 1953

The birthday of Her Majesty. The flag was flown at masthead all the grey, windy day and at night we found sufficient reason to quaff two bottles of hermitage, two bottles of burgundy, to drink her health, and to make a special issue of a packet of cigarettes or sweets per man. We rose to the toast and Len played the national anthem. So was Queen Elizabeth's birthday commemorated in her most distant—or most remote—possession.

Wednesday 22 April 1953

Ken, Cec and I started to erect the 'tank-house', enclosing the new thousand-gallon tank and making a store for galvanized iron and fire-fighting chemicals. The afternoon being relatively fine and calm—with even an occasional glimpse of the mountain—another calibration flight with a free balloon was achieved. The balloon probably was under radio observation to a height of 50,000 feet. The radiosonde flight reached the record height for the year so far—15 miles.

But perhaps the most pleasing result of the day was the strong [radio] contact with Perth. Ron's gallant work and Ken's plan are well vindicated. In the radio section we had another interest—the reception of the first comprehensive weather report from Madagascar.

We have now been on the station for two months. Enthusiasm is still at a high pitch, men are behaving courteously, and we anticipate the future with equanimity.

Thursday 23 April 1953

This is a very exciting island. Between breakfast and lunch on any day one may reach a place of lonely grandeur, a bird-haunted crag or a windswept summit commanding views of great glaciers and infinite seas. If some of the nearby island scenery were in Europe it would be visited by thousands of travellers. For me, Cave Bay and Rogers Head, Mount Andrée and Mount Aubert, the wide grey 'Nullarbor' plain of wind-polished stones, the curious lava cliffs beyond Wharf Point and a dozen other places are well-loved. The single year will go far too quickly. It seems strange that millions of people are content to live forever in streets.

Arthur, Fred and I set out for Corinth Head after breakfast this morning to photograph the macaroni penguins which have been moulting during the last few weeks. But where the macaronis had stood cackling in their thousands there was now only a vast area of broken rock white with millions of feathers. The moult was over and the birds were far out to sea—and would not return until perhaps October. Only half-a-dozen late stragglers were left. We ringed four of these, placing the metal bands round the narrow base of the wing and clamping them firmly in position. We had hoped to photograph the characteristic 'ecstatic braying' that goes on whenever a penguin returns to his mate from a drink down at the waves' edge. The birds stretch themselves and quiver, jostle each other and chortle in sheer delight.

We returned to the col and made our way to the top of the Head. Arthur went on to Corinthian and South West bays and counted 54 leopards.

Friday 24 April 1953

I always manage to pick the evil days for visiting West Bay. This morning it rained a half-frozen rain. There were not even any leopards out. On the way back, head down to the gusts and stinging sleet, I saw four Heard

Island shags—extraordinarily like penguins from a distance, with an erect way of standing and very similar coloration.

It was such a foul day that no-one had much incentive to work outside. Poor old Leon trudged round his dog-lines in a blood-stained submarine suit, but most of us found plenty of urgent enough work to do indoors. I worked from morning tea until mid-afternoon boiling and washing clothes. The great thrill of the day was the Radio Australia session which came through perfectly with a programme that included personally delivered messages from Lorna and May Dalziel. Lorna spoke and called me Johnnie and told me that everyone would be thinking of me on May 11th. From a Friday night in Melbourne, a quarter of the globe away, to a drenched afternoon on Heard Island! We have never had better reception; the blackout had cleared in perfect timing.

Saturday 25 April 1953

Assisted Leon with shooting dogs. There is a horrible contrast between the lovely leaping huskies, full of exuberance and playfulness and trust, and the suddenly immobile carcases lying out on the lava in a spreading mass, as dog after dog, up to a dozen, is laid there. Their end was swift, carefully placed bullets in the brain. Leon and I carried out the job feeling pretty low. None of the dogs, of course, saw what was happening and each victim was quite tranquil to his last instant. Still, it is hard to move amongst the dogs that remain and receive their ovation as usual.

Leopard seals are numerous now along the beaches. They are sleek and extraordinarily reptilian in appearance. Their great heads are like those of enormous pythons. Their grey, mottled bodies are immensely powerful and often reach a length of nine or ten feet. On land, fortunately, they haven't sufficient ease of movement to be dangerous but in the water they must be formidable, at least matching their sleek namesakes-on-land.

The southern end of the beach was piled high with great ice fragments from the shattered Baudissin Glacier. They stretched where the tide had left them, tens of thousands of ice boulders, many weighing a ton or more. In the shadowless dusk the blue seracs of the glaciers and the ungleaming ice on the beach made a scene of beautiful desolation. Jack decided to skin two of the dogs for their pelts but the work became so cold that in the end we returned with the carcases and dumped them on the cement floor of his engine-shed. We had an excellent meal of seal-steak before the French session at 8.30.

It being Anzac Day, the station flag was flown. We did not have any other form of commemoration. Most of the men here are far too young to attach much significance to the occasion. It is, after all, 37 years since Anzac.

Sunday 26 April 1953

At lunch Dick came in with an enormous nellie, beak secured with a leather boot-lace. He had chased it down-wind and the heavy bird had not been able to rise in time. Arthur took measurements before ringing it and releasing the creature. It waddled away completely dazed, every now and then stopping and lifting great wings, until it was far out on the Nullarbor. These giant petrels are far better adapted to the air than to the earth. On the ground they are comical and ungainly, staggering about with heavy wings loosely extended, reminiscent of old women lifting their skirts to avoid puddles.

In the afternoon, Arthur, Peter and I crossed the Nullarbor to the edge of the Baudissin which we reached by a desolate scree-filled valley. A moraine always seems utterly bleak and rather eerie. There is no vestige of organic life if the moraine is active, just rock and ice piled high as though by some enormous bull-dozer. The stone is so freshly broken, with such jagged edges that it is hard to reconcile with the imperceptible movement.

We put on our crampons and climbed steadily, no crevasses to worry about and snow-free ice glinting brightly in the sunlight or swirling with fine sago snow. We crossed the little Schmidt Glacier and splashed through the streams to Erratic Point, named after a monolith evidently deposited by some older and larger glacier. Only 14 little macaronis, hunched and lonely, were left of the 200 or more which were moulting so noisily a few weeks ago. Arthur completed his observations and we turned for home.

Wednesday 29 April 1953

Big processional clouds, bursts of sunshine alternating with quite determined snow, frost in the wind and shadows—a grand day for walking or working. Mount Olsen looked inviting, but I had promised Jim assistance at West Bay. At 12.30 Leon, Fred and I had an early lunch before setting out in the dogmobile for the magnetic huts.

The dogs become very excited at the prospect of a run. Leon selected his dogs—Butch, Mac, Smokey and the rest—and put them into their harness. I took them down—or perhaps they took me, so powerfully do they tug—to Fred who slipped them into the toggles on the main trace. It takes about 10 minutes or a quarter of an hour to harness the team. They are then bursting to be away but Leon has them pretty well trained. We loaded the 'mobile with pitch, spare cans, tools and brushes. Then with a great jerk of speed we were off careering madly down the trail seaward of the hydrogen hut. A run in the dogmobile is a splendid experience. You couldn't buy it for £50. Today, in clear sunshine by Atlas Cove, with all the snowy peaks of the Laurens Peninsula gleaming and the big mountain emerging from silver mist, it made a truly memorable experience.

At the charging hut we were all busy wielding tar-brushes and fixing the canvas. In the twilight we made a fire by pouring petrol on the debris of our day. The wind sent long streams of sparks harmlessly over the plain. We stood and watched the flames and stretched our hands to their radiant heat. The evening drew in while we stood there watching the sharp silhouette of the Olsen cliffs. The summit of the little mountain was as crystal against the sky. We strolled home. The full moon rose out of soft clouds masking Big Ben. The tide had ebbed further than I have yet seen it, the black beach being nearly 100 yards wide below the camp.

Thursday 30 April 1953

The weather was north-east with sleet; later it reversed to a colder, snow-burdened gale. I brought my auroral log up to date. Of 35 aurorally active nights—when some glow was apparent—since we arrived, on only one occasion, March 19th, was there less than 7/8 cloud.

Peter drained a 'Furphy' into the kitchen tank which was nearly empty. We worked until dark dragging the long hose between the various water units. We have, besides the two main tanks, several iron Furphy containers receiving the drainage from the smaller buildings. When water is short it is usually possible to draw on these by pumping.

May 1953

The Anniversary of Two Deaths

Friday 1 May 1953

Bernie carried through a splendid job of plumbing the bathroom drainage system. 'John, it is very bad, the manner in which thees thin iron has been put through ze concrete. It ees *corrodant*. We must take up ze bath.' Together we solve the crises, but Bernie willingly does the work, wriggling amongst the evil mud beneath the rec room where for months the effluent has been draining.

The gusts on two occasions reached 90 miles per hour. There is relative calm, then the distance across Atlas Cove is obscured by a great grey sheet. Suddenly it rushes down and the air is filled with a raging, shrieking wind charged with hard white sago snow, stinging the face and tearing across the earth. Arthur and Bernie set out in heavy snow to band the last penguins (rockhoppers) below the cliffs. They found six left.

Ron Parsons was still abed at 10.15. He has a tendency to 'sleep in' and generally has to be awakened several times. He is such a splendid fellow as far as work is concerned that I have always treated him leniently. The difficulty is that one cannot make exceptions. I awakened him and told him to get moving. In the mess, he became excited and quarrelsome. 'Just lay off me! I won't be ordered round. So long as I do my job, you can mind your own business.' The outburst was completely unexpected. He shouted away for a while in front of McNair and Fox and made the whole business public. Then he disappeared in the direction of the radio room. 'You'd better have it out with Ken!' were his parting words.

I was dumbfounded and felt miserable. Ron was morose and truculent all day, hardly speaking a word to anyone. I had the feeling that he knew he had far exceeded reason but couldn't bring himself to retract. In the late afternoon I suggested that, both of us having had our say and mine being that of the umpire in this particular game, we'd better forget the whole unfortunate business. We shook hands and I sincerely hope concluded the affair. He must have got up in a foul temper. It is odd how things add up. Some of Ron's most amusing stories start, 'I told the skipper that he could do what he damn well pleased. I just walked off the ship'—amusing, until one is more intimately concerned.

Saturday 2 May 1953

Leon killed a large seal in Atlas Cove but it proved to be ancient and sinewy and provided very little meat. Leon is temperamentally suited to his work. He comes in grinning from ear to ear and literally covered with blood; he even seems to enjoy dismembering the monster sea elephants for his dogs. His beard has grown long and wide but beneath it is a very boyish face, ruddy and set with happy eyes. His job is tough but he has grown well to it.

Sunday 3 May 1953

Peter and I set off for Mount Olsen but as we moved round the cove, Olsen itself became heavily clouded. We made for a small frozen waterfall and then worked our way to the main glacial ice-fields leading directly up to the summit. Big Ben was steadily becoming clear of cloud. The high summit of Mawson Peak became plain against a cloudless sky. The steam from the vent curled out lazily. The sea was tranquil and shaded with many colours. Westward the McDonald Isles rose sharply cut from an even blue card.

The ice gradually steepened and became broken by deep crevasses. As we looked back the whole station peninsula appeared flat. The camp itself showed very clearly, every hut being visible, but so minute as to seem merely a transitory smudge on a great ice-clad island beyond the edge of the inhabited world. As Peter remarked, we reckon distance on Heard in the Chinese fashion. Every contemplated journey is considered in terms of toil and hazard. Forbes and Hoseason lost their lives within a rifle-shot distance of the station only a year ago.

We gained our frosty summit—where else can a lovely mountain of ice be climbed after midday on a Sunday?—and descended down the south-west face. For a while we discarded our crampons but the rubble overlay ice, so we clawed ourselves again and rapidly reached the terrace. Big Ben was majestic in the evening sunlight. We moved south-west along the ridge and descended the screes to Atlas Cove in a series of giant steps, racing the darkness. The frozen sands of the Nullarbor lead us home.

Tuesday 5 May 1953

I spent the day clearing up the old laundry site, dragging out the lowest timbers and classifying everything into useful material and dross for the fire. All day I kept the incinerator stoked, finally dismissing a fragment of the past. History soon becomes ancient beneath Heard Island's shifting sands. The foundation timbers of the old laundry were buried so deeply that one might have thought 50 years had passed instead of five or less since they were laid. When we arrived, it was a wreck. The cement troughs sent down in February 1952 hadn't been unpacked but lay in weather-stained crates where they had been dumped. I changed the seismic trace at five. It was so dark when I had finished that only by the light of my distant bonfire could I stumble back to the station.

At seven, for the first time since leaving the wharf at Spencer Street, I spoke to someone outside the crew of the *Tottan* and our own party. A two-way telephonic conversation had been arranged between M. Sicaud, Chef de Missions on Kerguelen, and myself. Reception was very good. We talked of general station conditions, our forthcoming game of chess and the possibility of changing certain radio schedules. I hope we shall be able to have a weekly chat. Arthur, who has met Sicaud, describes him as far more the British colonial officer than the French administrator.

Wednesday 6 May 1953

There is very steady rain now. Every vestige of snow has left the camp. The only flash of white is from the sheathbills showing up extraordinarily clearly against the black lava and sodden sand. The dogs are howling as I write; they do not like the rain, however little notice they take of the cold and snow.

I am still perturbed about Ron. He has been very quiet and possibly sullen all day. It will require the utmost understanding and sympathy to bring him back to the right rails. He is a rather solitary individualist who makes up his mind exactly what he wants to do and then pursues that course doggedly.

Thursday 7 May 1953

Deluge for most of the day. Even the absorbent sand, dead as dripping, couldn't hold the rain and unusual rivulets streamed between the huts. The murk was so thick that it pressed visibly through the station.

After breakfast only Leon, streaming with rain while feeding his dogs, and the dogged Ron, out of sheer obstinacy, pursued outdoor work. He had hit on the idea of planting azorella and poa grass over the mounds of rock. He prowled through the dimming rain. Ken joined Ron and Kerguelen cabbage joined the azorella on the earth-covered rock anchors.

Arthur, Leon and I conveyed several tons of rock in a wheelbarrow, one man steering and balancing the vehicle, the others tugging on a rope. It was heavy blunt work in the rain, fingers scrabbling in the cold black sand, submarine suits streaming.

The power was off and we had tea by lamplight, Drygalski mutton. Finding plenty of poa grass and Kerguelen cabbage, the sheep have thrived and, at least until the big snows come, there can be no danger of further casualties, except at our instigation. The latter is no easy process for the sheep have become agile and as shy as chamois.

Friday 8 May 1953

Only Dick, silently feeling round his kitchen, was up when I set out for West Bay. For once the morning was fine with even a phantom view of the mountain, shadowless through a fine still mist. I hurried across the flooding channels from the plain, taking the stony rise above high tide, changed the trace and dawdled home, taking the microcosmic view of the curious flotsam of wood, iron and hemp. I released a young sheathbill from a couple of straying pups and set it safely, heart beating wildly, amongst its fellows down by the old wrecked plane.

We had fire-practice after tea. The idea was that the roof of the rec room should be sprayed. But the pump refused to function in spite of all Jack's work. Ron climbed onto the roof and directed a minute dribble into the gutter. It was a complete anticlimax and we all rocked with mirth. Then we let off about half-a-dozen ordinary extinguishers, foam and otherwise. Ken is gradually refilling all the station extinguishers.

A Stranded Walrus

The first ship used during the 1940s–1950s Australian occupation of Heard Island was the Royal Australian Navy's Landing Ship (Tank) LST 3501 (later renamed HMALST Labuan). On its initial voyage in December 1947 it carried a Vickers Supermarine Walrus amphibious biplane, which made only one exploratory flight before being wrecked in gale winds while tied down near the station. The remains were taken back to Australia decades later.

Saturday 9 May 1953

Arthur suggested that I might assist on a major seal-count of South West Bay. Our first encounter was with a dozen Heard Island shags, upstanding black and white birds with curious bright blue rings round their eyes. We stalked them for photographs. Like most wild-life here they are not easily disturbed.

Then we moved on to the far end of the cove and round the western end found the branded seals. I made some studies of big bulls. There is something patrician about the great bulbous nose of a sea elephant. Even the long dead carcases, relics of dog-meat expeditions, often preserve a sort of mournful and pathetic dignity. We counted exactly 300 sea elephants. This included the recording of all brands, of which we saw perhaps half-a-dozen. Curiously quite a large group inhabited the decayed shell of the old sealers' hut, perhaps built 100 years ago.

Monday 11 May 1953

It could hardly have been a finer day to have a birthday. The recent snow lay crisply in the sunlight and the beautiful mountain was clear. At breakfast there was a gramophone record. All the family wished me a happy birthday, sang songs or recited for me—Lorna, Elizabeth, Judith, Billy and Anne; then Mary, Lin and P.J. I don't know when they made the recording but not one of them could have guessed the joy their gift held. Lunchtime brought a sheaf of birthday cables arriving perfectly on time after the difficulties of reception for the last few days. There was even a cable from Johanna blending the Hertfordshire nightingales with the Heard Island penguins.

After lunch Peter went off with Arthur to slay an albatross—surely an unnecessarily provocative act on the officer in charge's birthday. Not until dark did I give any serious thought to the evening's celebrations but old Dick was going to a good deal of trouble. I rapidly fabricated candelabra from butter box ends mounted on empty earthenware jars. The uncompromising appearance was disguised with strips of cellophane and silver paper which had come in the packing of chocolate. The mess became a blaze of light. With a bottle of sherry from the store and Noel Heath's assortment of hock, claret and port, the trimmings were complete. Soon the whole company was assembled sipping sherry and sampling Dick's savouries. Ron entered in a sports coat, his moustache curled and his copious black hair smoothed down flat.

We proceeded happily through soup, entree, an omelette of cauliflower and asparagus, mutton and pork with every canned vegetable in existence, and a magnificent trifle. There was a considerable toast-list, commencing with The Queen and continuing with The Cook. Two cakes stood in the candlelight. The first, made by Lorna, had been beautifully iced and decorated by Dick; the second was Dick's own contribution, in the shape of a hut rather reminiscent of the new style paint-store, inscribed 'From the Boys to OIC'.

Tuesday 12 May 1953

Another perfect day with a hard frost and gleaming snow. I was slushy for the day. Arthur was absorbed all day in the biology hut, skinning his sooty albatross. With the usual flourish of barking huskies, Leon set off for another dogmobile run. Jack collected two or three fellows and had an attempt to drag up the old 'plane from the beach. The air was extraordinarily clear and freezing hard.

Saturday 16 May 1953

My walk to West Bay this morning was delightful, the surface fastly frozen but streaming continuously with writhing tongues of silver snow only a few inches above the ground. It seemed as though I were walking on cloud. All over the Corinth Peninsula were eddies and snow-devils; the whole land was alive.

The radio men worked on their aerial system. Blackout conditions have persisted all day and there had been no contact with Australia. We have worked Kerguelen, [Île] Amsterdam and taken down the Madagascar weather.

Sunday 17 May 1953

Such a cold, sunless and windy day, laden with blizzardly snow, that very few left the station and there were no pleasant Sunday afternoon walks at all. For the first time this year all the thermometers showed sub-zero centigrade temperatures inside the huts.

Tuesday 19 May 1953

We started the construction of a snow-melter. By lunchtime we had a coke fire burning under a full load of snow. In the dusk Bernie and

I piled some seal blubber on. The fire blazed so merrily that quite a group collected, giving advice and assistance with the shovelling of snow. By now the apparatus was rendering snow as fast as three men could keep it supplied. This yielded rather more than a gallon per minute. Provided sufficient snow-drifts are at hand, we need never be without easy water. A sort of ruddy barbecue-on-the-frozen Thames atmosphere, with Mr Pickwick peering from the shadows. The north wind brought a fall of soft snow and mantled the station, covering the ice and frozen earth very gently until the scene under the 'street' lights looked as fair as we could have imagined it.

Thursday 21 May 1953

The evening was rather clouded for me by feeling it necessary to speak sharply to Jack. He had been monopolizing certain magazines—all available copies of *Man*, for instance. I expressed the opinion that such hoarding, for several weeks on end, was not in the general interest. He murmured something about everyone else doing it and said, 'Anyway, I finished with them, now!'

Friday 22 May 1953

After tea the wind was gaining strength, hurling sand against the huts and vibrating every moveable surface. When the wind reaches 80 and 90 miles per hour every gust hurls tons of power at the station and every shift of direction is a probe for some structural weakness. I was making my bed when a violent gust culminated in the rending of iron and timber. I just glimpsed dark shadows fleeting past the small semi-transparent window of the sleeping hut. My first impression was that the latrines had become unseated. In the grit-laden dusk we inspected the damage. It was not the latrines but the entire roof of Leon's 'maternity' ward which had been lifted as one, then separated into four flying sheets of iron with beams attached and flung 70 or 80 yards. A 10 foot length of 3 x 2 had pierced the iron roof of the auxiliary diesel shed like a needle in a sock. Any one of the sheets of iron or spars of timber could have killed men or dogs.

Saturday 23 May 1953

Round the camp the snow is hard and icy but overlain by black sand. The sheathbills are visible everywhere again, like little white leghorns at a distance, moving about the lava and scratching round the station. When the snow comes they are completely lost to vision.

Sunday 24 May 1953

I decided that we should pitch the tent up on the Baudissin Glacier after lunch. Our party dipped their boots in seal-oil and departed at about 2 o'clock. Up on the ice, crampons were almost unnecessary as in most places it was overlain with good snow and névé. Many of the crevasses were completely filled and firm. We had no difficulty in reaching a suitable site 150 feet below our ice-house. We soon had the tent erected. The main job accomplished, we climbed slowly to the long bamboo marking the buried entrance of our dugout. The shelter was exactly as Bernie and I had left it, a week or 10 days ago. Everything was perfectly dry and the place snugger than ever on account of the longer tunnel entrance. We all slid down and sat on onazote squares [foam rubber] and filled the glinting confines with smoke. This form of shelter is second to none on the slopes of Big Ben.

We enclosed the entrance of the ice-house with blocks of névé and came down off the mountain. A bright moon shone through thin cloud. We gossiped back to camp in pairs. Ken had risen to the occasion with excellent pea soup, lobster entree, roast lamb and an assortment of vegetables, cherries and custard, and excellent black coffee. We consumed a good vintage hock and completed the meal with an apricot liqueur. People at home think of Antarctic expeditions as the continuous epitome of discomfort and hardship, yet here were we, sitting back in good fellowship, good food, good wine and fine, fat cigars.

Monday 25 May 1953

Nobody has left the station all day except for the sonde release, dog-feeding and snow-melting. The air is a fury of driving flakes. This morning I sent a message to Her Majesty the Queen.

Heard Island   **May 25 1953**

To Her Majesty Queen Elizabeth

May Your Majesty fulfil a joyous life and noble reign

Coronation greetings from all members of the Australian National Antarctic Research Expedition on Heard Island nearest inhabited territory to Princess Elizabeth Land Antarctica

Tuesday 26 May 1953

Being the first anniversary of the deaths of Forbes and Hoseason on the Baudissin Glacier, the flag was flown at half-mast. The morrow, a year ago, Atkinson stumbled into camp with the appalling news; grim sadness must have permeated the station then. I reminded our men of the reason for the flag but we did not hold any further ceremony.

I left soon after dawn (late now, at about seven) to change the magnetic trace at West Bay. Every inch of snow, rock and sand was glazed with treacherous ice. A strong south-westerly blew me glissading across some stretches. On one patch of black sand below the little snow-cliffs at the water's edge—which I thought would be soft—I measured my length. It was frozen hard with a film of ice. In the surf bobbed ice-fragments and lumps of snow eroded from the land. My nylon jacket became glazed with ice, cracking as I moved my arms. The absolute hut had beautiful 'rippled' windows exactly like obscuring glass.

After breakfast I assembled all available man-power—Ken, Cec, Fred, Arthur, Jack, Peter and myself—and in a keen wind but bright sunshine we slogged away with shovels removing heavy snow and then digging out the 'pit'. By dusk we were all completely tired, muscles drawn and bodies without energy. Fred and I repaired to the biology hut and opened Arthur Simson's birthday hamper. We drank to his health in Corio whiskey and nibbled his home-made biscuits. We felt very warm towards old Artie, companion on the first Central Australian expedition and friend of many years. He was 36 today.

Wednesday 27 May 1953

The first event of the day was the release of a rawin-*cum*-radiosonde balloon. It went up 'like a bomb'—a curious contradiction—before the south-west wind. The flight showed winds of about 170 miles per hour at 50,000 feet. Such flights are now likely to occur almost daily, a good deal of extra work. Today has seen the most southerly release of a rawin transmitter as far as Australian Antarctic territory is concerned.

As soon as the flight was finished we had morning tea, then commenced a heavy job of work on some of the main aerial anchorages. Dripping with rain and covered with dirt, we looked like stiff moving creations of a Frankenstein. Blunt, heavy labour, like that of convicts, stooping and lifting. I felt a sort of fierce pleasure in the drudgery.

After lunch, Arthur and Dick went out to locate our Drygalski mutton. The rest of us continued carting great chunks of lava. We filled two sleds and completed five main anchorages. Arthur and Dick found all five sheep, in spite of the snow, much too active to allow easy capture. Arthur thinks that we'll have to bring them in for winter feeding before long.

Thursday 28 May 1953

It's odd how one's values change, in some respects at least, after a few months at Heard. Today was relatively fine. The average temperature would have been about 35°F, there was fairly steady drizzle most of the morning and fairly steady rain in the afternoon and, at half past four, winds were rising to 80 miles per hour. But nearly all day I spent happily in the open air. Arthur did, too, building a yard for the sheep.

Friday 29 May 1953

Very occasionally there is an atmosphere on Heard Island that parallels that of a sunny gorse paddock with a farm or two in the background. It was so this morning, with no wind and the sun defeating the clouds for stretches of half-an-hour on end. The huskies kept up an incessant cheerful yelping. The sounds of the station blended like the rattle of a country town, engines and shouting, the thump of the bathroom pump and the clatter of the slushy's bucket, timber being stacked and wood being hammered, voices everywhere and some of them singing, a record on the gramophone, a sizzling on the fire.

The mountain was almost clear from the great rounded dome to the sea. When it is unclouded the eye may explore a dozen improbable routes to the summit. This morning I longed to be up on the glaciers.

I went down to assist with the release of the big balloon. Peter had tied on the rawin transmitter and departed to his theodolite; Bernie was left to tie the sonde transmitter below the rawin and make the release. It was so beautifully calm and away the balloon went, rising beautifully as though to the zenith. But the pity of it was that Peter's knot was insecure—and it rose majestically leaving both transmitters in Bernie's hands.

We all piled into the radio room for the Radio Australia programme and, for the first time in three weeks, heard it all pretty clearly. The session is uninspired, a random collection of scraps and repetitions. However Len Welch heard his daughters speak and was happy. It is odd to listen to a Melbourne studio—and simultaneously catch a glimpse of great frozen waterfalls plunging down from the Jacka Glacier all dulled in a grey afternoon.

Saturday 30 May 1953

Another grey, wettish day, but I was determined to visit the tent on the Baudissin. Ken, Peter and Fred were very willing to accompany me and spent the night aloft. We decided to depart in the late afternoon. The Nullarbor, recently a sheet of hard ice, had thawed to oozy mud, most unpleasant and dragging like the Slough of Despond. We treacled our way across with occasional incursions into deep soft drifts of dirty snow. The lower slopes of the mountain rose uninvitingly, misty and growing dark in the early nightfall. Our white nylons were hot and our fingers expanded and our packs were quite heavy. We soon reached the moraine.

There is no more satisfying manner of progress than crampons on gleaming ice. One is always conscious of the triumph of moving confidently on a medium that cries its insecurity and slipperiness. The crevasses were filled with heavy, slumped, wet snow and the smaller gutters were free of snow. Without any difficulty we found our way to the tent. The thaws had stripped away practically all of the many hundredweight of snow we had piled round the anchoring flap and the little lazy wind was already ballooning the outer walls. From all appearances it would only require a mild gale to cause damage at the least. We dug up sufficient snow to remedy the weakness and were soon within its shelter with two little petrol primuses roaring. We stacked our food in the centre of the tent and cooked a bully-beef stew, made a gallon of tea, served cherries and condensed milk and ate the lot cheerfully. It was immortal tent-time. Four candles; reclining bodies; much good humour; ample food and the wind baffled. Tent-time is an internal thing; outside may be ice or azorella or grassy fields.

At 7 o'clock we went out onto the ice to signal to the station, as we had arranged. There below us and across the plain were its little cluster of lights. Ken flashed his torch and it was answered by a twinkling pin-point. We asked them down below if they were alright and told them we thought we'd stay up for a week. They replied that the whole station was drunk in celebration of our absence. It was cold and dark outside and very slippery.

With boots exchanged for slippers, all the food and stoves packed carefully between the double walls of the tent, our sleeping bags laid out and onazote squares at strategic points for insulation from the ice below us, we were soon comfortable. I had brought a bottle of brandy. We smoked, yarned, read and took our tots like gentlemen. Peter lay back blissfully content with his excess of ' 'baccy, brandy and Beethoven'—as usual he was carrying round a miniature score. Warm and comfortable, it was pleasant to consider the possible hundreds of feet of cold, dark ice below us, black fossil ice of the centuries slowly making its way down to the eroding waves; and the certain thousands of feet of ice above us, up to the smoking summit of Big Ben.

I didn't sleep particularly well. At some stage of the night I was conscious of a furious gale. I knelt up and drew the tapes tighter to stop the flapping. None of us, I think, was at all cold.

Sunday 31 May 1953

By morning the gale had blown out and everything outside was held in a tight freeze. We rolled swags and cleared up the tent. Ken and I left our packs secure and climbed up the névé slope to our ice-house. The seracs held that wonderful almost unearthly shade of blue. A watery sun glinted over the hummocked ice below us.

There was a great accumulation of snow over our excavation and except for the stick and shovel we should never have known where to dig. As it was we soon struck empty space and within five minutes had slid down into the ample depths. We smoked a cigarette then decided to excavate further. We both worked, hacking into the packed crystalline snow and bringing it down in showers all over us until we lay or knelt in piles of shining granulated ice. Looking straight out along our tunnel and trench, the only sight was the grey sea out from Corinthian Bay. We glissaded down to the tent, ate fruit-cake, then descended from the ice-cap.

Since dinner I have been typing away. Arthur has gone mooching off to Corinthian Bay to count his leopards. He has just returned—26!

June 1953
'They've Climbed Everest!'

Monday 1 June 1953

All morning I was uneasy about the tent up on the Baudissin, so after lunch, I inveigled Cec into accompanying me. We made our way via the lava and Corinthian Bay, where half-a-dozen leopards lay in desperate cold—as though too frozen to raise a flipper. We plugged up steadily through mist over little glacial streams. To my surprise the tent was in good shape and reasonably well moored.

We crawled in, turned back the rubber sheet so that it was unnecessary to remove crampons and sat peacefully smoking. One of the most lovely light effects I have ever seen in ice appeared beneath our feet. The daylight, refracted through many feet of ice, penetrated below the wide flaps and gave the whole 'floor' a ghostly cold radiance of an exquisite translucent blue. We skimmed the crust from a nearby snowy depression and built up the flaps, then we crunched down the glacier and headed home through the glimmer of dusk. Tomorrow, the Coronation of Queen Elizabeth, we are having a holiday as far as possible.

Tuesday 2 June 1953

The flag-mast cord had frayed and had to be replaced before we could raise the Union Jack and Blue Ensign. Peter and I slithered about the sloping mess room roof, raised the long ladder and lashed it to the mast in the aching cold.

I had the flags in hand and was very cold, when Freddie suddenly appeared over the snow-drift near the radio shack. 'They've climbed Everest!' he shouted. I could never have put my emotion in words, no more than I could tell why mountains have always fascinated me. The greatest of all mountains has been climbed. I sometimes like to pretend that the war prohibited my only chance to be in an Everest party. Many will feel a sense of sadness, almost of desecration—what is now the greatest physical adventure lying ahead of man?

Dick turned on a splendid lunch. I made a brief speech on the Queen's Coronation, the young queen herself and the pageantry that would be enacted in London today. Afterwards all who could prepared for the picnic to the ice-house on the Baudissin Glacier. Arthur, Len, Freddie, Ken and I, in white nylons and armed with crampons, ice-axes and a bottle of brandy, set out across the white, frozen plain—the hateful sticky mud had suffered an ice-change.

We donned our claws low on the ice and plodded up, passing the well-anchored tent. My trench was well buried but easily excavated. We slipped down out of the cold wind into the calm air below, sat on onazote squares and filled the air with smoke and reminiscences. Then we solemnly drank the Queen's health, sitting in our air-bubble carved from the old snow of several seasons. There wasn't sufficient head-room to stand.

We emerged and blocked the entrance with big slabs of névé. The day was bitterly cold and darkening perceptibly. Ken tied the Blue Ensign to our marker and we photographed the scene with the strange blue seracs in the background. Then, anxious to be moving, we glissaded down to the tent and marched off the glacier.

We all dressed for dinner. I would have preferred candlelight, but Jack had gone to a lot of trouble to improve the lights so we dined in a blaze of white electricity. Jim had prepared souvenir menus. There were all the usual toasts. Her Majesty, Prince Philip, The Cook, Sweethearts and Wives, Absent Friends, Previous Parties, The New Elizabethan Age. Finally we came to the marathon film evening. We consumed 32 bottles of beer and ended at 3a.m. with savouries in the kitchen. Most of us became a little drunk but we are conscious of the sheer rarity of such experiences.

Wednesday 3 June 1953

All night the wind blew furiously from the south-west. The sea of Atlas Cove invaded the plain and washed within a few feet of the hydrogen shed. The high seas caused the dinghy and cutter to drift on their anchors, even though they were well above what we usually consider the danger level. The storm also completely demolished the remains of the old wharf from which Wharf Point gets its name.

Thursday 4 June 1953

One of the most restless and troubled nights I have passed for years. All night long I was conscious of the stormy wind thumping the roofs, vibrating the walls and howling in the wires. Twice I got up and wandered through the living quarters by torchlight. The wind scarcely dropped. For a good part of the night its mean velocity was 40 to 50 miles per hour, while gusts frequently reached 80.

Jack came down and helped me wrap the big double sheet round the balloon. We moved outside fairly easily then off went Len at a run to give the balloon a chance to rise before releasing the sonde transmitter. Poor chap, he went like a hare for about 60 yards then slipped on some ice and went slithering across the frozen rocks. The transmitter bumped along the ground before the balloon had risen sufficiently. It was a wasted effort and Len was covered with mud and abrasions. He came back blinking through his thick glasses and one could have wept for him, but he was quite philosophical.

There was a magnificent spume of snow driving up from the North Cornice into the clouds. Yesterday at 3000 feet the wind was 108 miles per hour.

Today has been only a trudging day on Heard Island—and a hundred times more worthwhile and memorable than almost any city day. There is freedom of spirit here, not the arrogant and stagnant backwater of a city. I went to bed early. It was snowing, fine diamond gleaming snow from the north-east.

Away from the City

'As the peace of the night continued undisturbed, you would say to yourself: "There's nothing like this in the cities. This is real life." You began to feel sorry for the "slaves" chained to their office jobs year after year … The world seemed big and wonderful, generous and kind … You felt as though you could stay there looking up at the heavens forever …

"Clump! Clump! Clump!" The boots of the watch climbing the ladder to the deck broke the spell. You returned to reality.'

(Arthur Scholes, *Fourteen Men*, 1949: 21–2, en route to Heard Island on the first ANARE expedition, December 1947)

Saturday 6 June 1953

The day seemed propitious for mustering sheep on Drygalski, a strong keen westerly and silver sunshine, so after morning tea all except three men set off across the plain. Blown sand, in a stinging stratum about two feet high, made a strange black blizzard, cutting off the legs of men ahead as they crunched across the ice. The sheep led us on a day-long dance. We trudged back and forward over the mountain through deep snow-drifts until we were certainly weary, and the sheep should have been if they weren't.

At one stage we had the sheep on the final moraine ridge facing the Baudissin. They stood in a group, defiant, like mountain chamois. Arthur, Bernie, Peter and I closed in to shepherd them down the ridge, but they had different ideas. They broke and scampered right onto the glacier, five immensely determined sheep, padding resolutely up towards our ice-house. Arthur dashed across, with scant care of crevasses, to head off their ascent towards the dangerous seracs. They turned and bolted across towards me and I, too, forgot the possibility of pitfalls and ran out to meet them. But they regained the moraine and turned west.

We formed a long dragnet line, moving westward in pursuit of our mutton. We were able to follow the tracks. One sheep had evidently grazed its leg and the unfortunate creature left a few blood spots. For a while we lost the trail, then we regained it heading towards the bog waterfall gully. They stood on a massive slab of rock looking at us curiously and in some alarm.

We gradually closed in but at the critical moment they leapt away. We managed to lay our fingers to the wool of only two. Then arose the problem of bringing them back to camp. We had no way of telling them that there awaited ample winter food and a postponed demise. For a while we had to carry them on our shoulders or trussed along a stick. The dogmobile had gone back, for we had been beating the bounds for five or six hours. Jim and I tried to lead them on straps while Ken made encouraging noises. For a good mile we made little progress but after rounding the Drygalski corner they fairly tugged us home along the strand separating the ice from the sea. It was almost dark when we arrived. We penned them and stacked bags of coke for their shelter and laid down ample straw for their rest. Everyone pronounced it a grand day. Even Ron, who had sworn never to climb higher on Heard than his top bunk, had reached the summit of Drygalski.

Monday 8 June 1953

Arthur counted 53 leopard seals on Corinthian Beach. Leon found one of his bitches ill and spent a lot of time with her. He is never without a dog job—exercising, driving out after seal meal, mending or making harnesses, feeding, or repairing pens for bitches, pregnant or on heat, and pups.

Tuesday 9 June 1953

I have been opening cases sent down years ago which have never been disturbed. They are mostly filled with glassware, a supply worth many pounds. Some chemicals exist in vast quantities—there are drums of insecticide, flagons of alcohol, metaldahyde and pungent unlabelled liquids. Supplies far in excess of requirements have been sent in the first years of the station. We should willingly exchange them for screws, masonite, galvanized iron, cement and other basic commodities.

Wednesday 10 June 1953

In the early darkness wild snow scurries rattled against the station and the everlasting wind carried that deep moaning which engenders vague alarm, blending utter loneliness and the cruel carelessness of the infinite Antarctic Ocean. Every wind that blows may gather the desolation of a million square miles.

There was a soiled salmon glow in the sky when Fred and I left at 8.15. Leon volunteered to run us to the foot of the Baudissin Glacier. We helped him harness up the eager huskies. Every other dog on the station is leaping and barking on such occasions. The team is gradually built up, each dog in turn being harnessed and attached to the main central trace. The most quarrelsome of dogs, huskies must be kept more or less in position until the sledge or 'dogmobile' is ready to start. A moment's lack of vigilance and they have their traces tangled or are in one glorious mêlée, snarling and struggling. Otherwise they just quiver joyously, look at you with eager eyes and panting mouths—and take every opportunity to urinate against your leg.

Leon is extraordinarily fit, as often as not running ahead of his team instead of riding. Our route this morning lay over hard smooth ice. Several times the team lost all control; so did Leon; so did the dogmobile. Eventually we slithered across to Corinthian Bay and along the beach until we suddenly crunched through the ice at a glacial stream near the Baudissin. We left Leon just as a blizzard roared down from the south-west. From up on the ice, we saw him and his team—as minute as mice—making strongly for home.

Fred and I strapped on our crampons. The air was filled with stinging snow. Visibility was practically zero, but as we could have found our way blindfolded, we plugged on. We found the tent drifted about with snow, but showing no sign of wear. The temptation to stop for a cigarette easily defeated our resolution. While we rested the weather became clearer. We were soon able to proceed onto the Schmidt Glacier. The surface was very crisp, bone dry and chiselled clean of all powder snow. Over the sea to the west a sombre snow-cloud was rushing towards us. The ice-fall of the Schmidt was sufficiently close for us to seek shelter in a small crevasse. We just got into position when the blizzard broke.

After a while we could go on again, roped on a double nylon rope. The North Cornice lay ahead. Once we left the glacier ice behind, we were struggling through dense wind-whirled snow. It was no day to be out. The wind increased in fury. After a mile or a mile and a half, it suddenly seemed to veer. Then it was everywhere, obscuring the world with clouds of fine snow, penetrating every chink of our goggles, packs and clothing. With visibility down to no more than five yards, it was obviously unwise to continue. Suspended in white, stinging space, we decided to dig-in. We soon had a fine bivouac but those below expected us back, and because we had no sleeping bags, we had no great desire to inhabit it. We smoked a cigarette each.

There was a clearing in the weather and a clear view of Rogers and Corinth heads far below against a gleaming sea, like pewter. We quickly roped, clawed and donned packs and descended with all haste. On the way down we felt the full force of the blizzard. We were several times nearly blown flat when a wind of about 50 miles per hour suddenly redoubled its efforts in mad gusts. As the force of such a wind is about 35 pounds to the square foot we had not less than 100 pounds of wind to lean on going down that slope. Most of the strength was used in hurling icy, dry snow at our bodies. Sometimes it became too much and we had to turn tail and gather breath.

With a few fortunate glimpses of the Peninsula we kept to a sound route and in good time turned down onto the Baudissin Glacier. We had had no lunch and it was now about four, so we again took shelter in the tent and ate our 02 rations by candlelight. A grand, rewarding half-hour! We were both pleased with the day and sat, white with ice and snow, contentedly eating and smoking. We were down on the plain by dusk and happily slithered across the ice, drawn by the irresistible twinkle of the station lights.

Arthur met us just outside the biology hut and shouted a welcome. Dry powder ice filled our rucksack, my camera bag and most of our pockets. I went into the sleeping hut. There we brushed out what we could and I cleaned my cameras. Probably the hut was only a degree or two above freezing, but by comparison with the day, it was filled with a gracious fug. By the time we had changed it was dinner time—a fine, slap-up four course meal in a warm, brilliantly-lit mess. Such contrasts are the best of life.

Thursday 11 June 1953

In any log I suppose there's a tendency to be egocentric. I try to know what each man is doing, more out of interest than curiosity. At meal times, I have a yarn with everyone. Routine work occupies the majority and there are always plenty of small jobs to be done. Generally, men are left to their own or their section-leader's devices.

Today Arthur and Cec took a seal-count at South West Bay. There were over 100 big fellows, and the total reached double that number. I caught a glimpse of Peter chipping away old paint from the Dines mast, and Bernie carrying boiling water for hydrogen generation. Apparently he used the water too hot and lost half his 'brew' even though Len had warned him against using boiling water. Bernie can be very pig-headed at times.

With the dogs barking outside, the world seems fresh and youthful. Perhaps unconsciously I hark back to boyhood when I was never happier than when clambering round the loft in sunbeams full of golden dust-motes, or astride the roof-ridge, or up the old pepper tree at Murrumbeena, making a noise which I thought passed well enough as singing. Up in the roof of Chippy's I am surrounded by sea-boots, skis, bamboo poles, shelves of shining glassware, lampwicks, oars, coils of rope and wire, lifejackets and sou'westers.

Friday 12 June 1953

Arthur nearly came to grief in the dogmobile this morning when the team bolted, breaking their anchor rope before Leon was ready. The vehicle careered wildly towards one of the radio anchorages, Arthur valiantly endeavouring to bring it under control instead of 'bailing out'. Only just in time he ducked his head to avoid the aerial guy which otherwise might have broken his inoffensive neck.

At dusk there was a thaw and some rain from the west. I made a round of the camp. The Met was rather peaceful, warm and studious, with Peter working and Fred checking some figures. I like the 'stationery'—blank maps of the Antarctic, beautifully ruled graphs for the various recording instruments, sheets ruled with intricate curves for plotting information from other weather stations—Kerguelen, Marion, Amsterdam, Madagascar and numerous South African centres. I turned down to the biology hut and found Jim 'scaling' and Arthur dissecting penguins.

Saturday 13 June 1953

For practically the whole day, Ken and Cec worked on the fire-extinguishers. From the vast stocks of out-dated and unserviceable chemicals in weather-stained and crumbling containers, it would seem that this has been neglected in the past.

Leon worked enthusiastically on dog-harnesses in the morning. In the afternoon he joined Jack and slushy Peter on gash disposal. 'Gash' is emptied from the large drums onto the dump near a large depression on Wharf Point. Unfortunately the boggy ground has made the dump rather diffuse, and it will be necessary to use the bull-dozer blade to gather it together. Sewerage is sledded along the beach to the mouth of a constant stream and sluiced away in a foot or so of water. It is not difficult but may be unpleasant in rough weather.

Richard spent a busy day cooking seal heart and penguin liver, all stuffed and rich with spices. The penguins had a sad little finale. Dick had asked Arthur to bring back a couple from his travels. Yesterday, as Arthur and I stood at the door of the biology hut contemplating the infinite, up from the cove strutted two purposeful penguins bound on a tour of inspection of the hydrogen shed. Their satiny breasts shone with good living and they had their top-coats thrown back proudly. Those little gentoos were walking to their doom, for Arthur strolled down to meet them and gave them their *quietus*.

I dug even deeper to the very fundament of Chippy's church and brought forth pemmican and pulleys, broken glass and biological bottles, water-glass and petrol filters, scales and spatulas. I raised crates aloft and piled up cakes of soap, stacked boards and unearthed drums of spirit, cylinders of carbon dioxide and a crate containing a hundredweight of safety matches. As dusk came I tried to sweep the bared floor but the sand lay too heavy for my broom. The boxes of glassware which I had transported from the old laundry had each disgorged 50 or 60 pounds of blown volcanic dust.

As midwinter approaches the days become divided into two distinct parts—before and after dusk—equivalent in hours but differing in occupations. After dinner Arthur made an interesting discovery among the grinding stones of a penguin's stomach—a small involute shell of a species he had never seen. He does not consider that the bird had taken it as food. It is possible that the little gastropod had been plucked from the bottom of the shallow sea somewhere. On Heard Island I have seen no shells except those of limpets.

Eating Penguins

'Penguins, it may surprise most of us to know, are very good to eat. The McNair method is to soak the meat in salt water for four to six hours, take it out and fry it, then bake it with tomatoes in the oven for about an hour and a half. It has what he called a "hard to explain, faintly fishy flavour".

'Similarly with penguin eggs. These are a good deal larger than a large hen's eggs and also a good deal stronger. You shouldn't ever try to fry them, but they make wonderful omelettes and are the finest eggs Richard George McNair ever used for making cakes. "In fact," says the man who must be one of the most experienced Antarctic cooks in the world, "you get me the penguin eggs and we'll open a cake shop and make a fortune."'

(*Australasian Post*, 31 May 1956: 8)

Grit

Heard Island is one of the grittiest and most uncomfortable places anyone could ever choose to live. The combination of strong winds and abundant loose black volcanic sand from the island's beaches means that eyes, nose, ears and other exposed parts are virtually sandblasted. And it's cold.

When ANARE worker Stu Fitch walked the beaches of Heard Island daily for four months in 2000–2001 surveying and collecting marine-borne debris, he wrote a newsletter to friends called simply 'Grit'. One day in two and a half hours at South West Bay he collected:

14 pieces of green nylon line
a spirit bottle (glass, 600 ml)
a clear plastic drink bottle
a cigarette lighter, mainly plastic
six pieces of broken glass
four pieces of apparently melted 'smalls' [plastic]
an old light globe
an old marker pen
a piece of white candle
an old plastic drinking straw
two plastic pen caps
one white plastic nasal inhaler
a piece of styrofoam (18 x 3 mm)
a square piece of white plastic with a hole in the middle (25 mm square)
three plastic line fishing floats, or parts of floats (68 x 14 mm
    diameter, 54 x 15 mm, 45 x 17 mm)
a white plastic stylus (100 mm)
a black plastic tube (90 x 7 mm)
an opaque plastic salt or pepper lid (90 x 7 mm)
an opaque plastic lid from a film container or similar
an irregular shaped piece of blue plastic (30 mm)
a small piece of blue plastic with small spheres on it (30 mm).

(Stu Fitch, Activity report and Grit, 2000–2001)

Sunday 14 June 1953

A great storm raged over us for the whole day. Repeated gusts of 90 miles per hour gave a terrible restlessness to the driving snow. The wind flung up huge continuous sprays in the cove, showered the ice-cliffs of the Baudissin to a height of more than 100 feet, ripped up sheets of ice from the Nullarbor and sent them flying like autumn leaves. Empty 44 gallon drums became detached from their dumps and madly careered towards Corinthian Bay; the air was full of seaweed. I scaled Jim's traces while the hut threatened to take off at any moment. It was quite an experience to struggle across to the main living block of the station. Suddenly there was such a blast that I struggled over to the Dines hut to find its strength—107 miles per hour.

After dinner we gathered to hear Arthur. He gave an excellent address proving that the leopard, at home on the pack ice, visited Heard Island more than any other land surface. All Antarctic expeditions regard the leopard as quite rare, yet here we may see him lying solitarily at intervals of a few yards along a mile of beach.

Monday 15 June 1953

There was thunder and lightning during the afternoon, probably the first time it has ever been recorded on Heard Island. Dick and Leon went out in extremely bad weather to get a seal for the dogs.

Wednesday 17 June 1953

A silent, sullen day, the wind spent and the world frozen; the earth tense with ice—ice blocking our pump, ice in zodiacal patterns across the bathroom floor, fine white snow lying untidily like dust in the passages, old dusty drifts hard as iron and lovely frost flowers on the windows.

I fear for the lives of our Drygalski sheep. This morning Dick rugged himself up and departed vowing to bring back mutton for Jim's birthday feast tomorrow. He returned at lunchtime with a sad tale. The trio had again taken to the glacier ice, but this time they struggled upwards to the slopes of the North Cornice where Dick could not possibly pursue them. And surely enough, through the glasses, we could make them out, a minute black group forlorn in an immensity of white, nearly 2000 feet above the camp. The short hours of the afternoon made a relief party inadvisable. Instead of retreating, the sheep moved up and over the skyline. There is no way down the great cliffs and unless they return the way they travelled they must perish.

Thursday 18 June 1953

It was Jim Brooks' birthday and the air was full of goodwill. He self-consciously accepted our greetings and was very excited about a gramophone record which Peter had received at the ship-side and kept faithfully, with everyone speaking from grandmother down to fiancée, Joy Mutton.

Arthur, Ken, Jack, Jim, Bernie and I crunched out across the Nullarbor in a perfect calm, though the upper air was streaked with malicious streamers and every horizon was piled with murk. Yet the mountain was clear. What a delight to stride across the frozen plain! An inch or two of recent snow overlay the corrugated ice. We were well warmed by the time we mounted the glacier and strapped on crampons. Each of us carried food to victual the second ice-house against future visits.

The tent has resisted the claws of many storms. The snow-flap is almost encased in solid ice. We didn't go inside nor stop to unseal the first ice-house, still marked by the long bamboo pole and shovel. After taking photographs of the tent with the rare background of a cloudless mountain, we pushed on up to the Schmidt. Our crampons left white powder on the bare ice.

The party trailed back in a line for a hundred or more yards. None of us had been so high when the mountain was clear. From the Little Matterhorn—a high, bitter tooth directly above Saddle Point— round the great ridges of ice to the crest of the North Cornice, every plunging ice-fall was crystal sharp. Thousands of feet of blue-grey ice. Amazing lenticular clouds made grey discs round Mount Dixon and Anzac Peak, the station an uncertain smudge by the edge of the smooth ungleaming water.

The climb had taken us about two hours. We had seen no trace of the sheep, although we passed directly below the place we had last seen them. While we were still warm we opened 02 rations and pecked at their concentrated virtues at the same time shovelling away the deep drifts from the buried portal of our excavation at Camp 2. It was just as we left it. The gales and blizzards which may have reached 150 miles per hour had only served to plate another layer of hard armour over the mountainside. If we can find a feasible route, I feel confident that a chain of ice-houses contains the conquest of Mawson Peak.

Arthur and Ken decided to carry on with excavations while the rest of us roped up and set away up the slope. Unfortunately dense cloud was now gathering, and the skyline of the highest cornice peak became only intermittently visible. We zig-zagged up in long rising traverses until we were on top of the ridge at about 2300 feet. There was still scarcely any wind, just tremendous white silence.

A gap in the mist made plain for a minute the tremendous overhang of ice. Below there is an almost sheer drop of 1500 feet to the Vahsel Glacier. Soon we were imprisoned in cloud that iced our beards and balaclavas. Now we were on the blue ice (2530 feet). A rather ugly open crevasse, its lips curled with frost, lay nearby. I struck my ice-axe hard into the névé and the blow was answered by a most demoralizing crack, sound not sight, that ran beneath the entire party.

We began to wonder just how thickly the crevasses were bridged. We retraced our way. The wind had already nearly obscured our footprints, without which the descent would have been infinitely slower.

At Camp 2, Ken and Arthur were still chipping and scooping industriously. We all went down out of the wind and filled the shelter with smoke. The warmth, relatively, of an ice-cave is astonishing. The heat of our six bodies and smoking breath, in the somewhat confined space, caused a slight thaw from the roof—while just a few feet along the tunnel, in the open air, there was a temperature of at least -8°C. It is uncommonly hard to leave the comfort and don packs and crampons, cut blocks of névé to seal the entrance, and face the long though easy descent. We were circumscribed by cloud all the way down to the lower Baudissin Glacier, reaching the moraine about half-an-hour before dusk.

The day was deeply satisfying and everyone was elated. It was time to dig out the wines for the evening ding. For weeks, a large snow-drift has been piled against the door of the amenities store. Tonight, I did remove some—and found the yellow legs of a dead penguin protruding at ground level. Doubtless the bird was buried by Paddie or one of the other bitches during a burst of freedom. Several litters of pups have been born during the last few weeks, the latest being Judy's eight.

Jim's birthday dinner was very bright. Dick had gone to a lot of trouble, providing savouries and a fish course, also a cake additional to the one Jim had brought down with him for the occasion. Dick's was decorated with numerous chocolate wavy lines to denote magnetic traces. The evening came to a sudden collapse at 2a.m. and everyone trudged happily off to bed. My final job was to check the extinguishing of all oil stoves.

Friday 19 June 1953

When I started out for West Bay, the snowy world reflected a grey, spectral sort of light. I heard Bernie at work in the hydrogen shed and shouted a morning greeting. He waved his torch at me through the blackness.

A few sea-leopards slept on the beach, one female apparently far gone in pregnancy. There was a faint honey-coloured flush in the sky. Every aspect of snow, sea and sky changes almost daily on Heard Island. On the way back into camp I gave a hand with the sonde release but the balloon slipped out of its sheath, struck the edge of the door and burst.

Saturday 20 June 1953

Very good radio conditions. Ken has spoken to Sydney by radio telephone, also to South Africa. I spoke to Marion [Island] this afternoon and wished them well; also to [Île] Amsterdam who came through very well. Bernie had a long conversation in French describing Heard Island.

The French Salon held in the mess at 8.15 was still going strong at 10. Bernie is completely the little dictator when it comes to *conversation*. He bounces about, snaps out his words, pretends to be very ferocious and sometimes is ferocious, and generally re-establishes himself as an important person with a mission.

Sunday 21 June 1953

Midwinter

The shortest day of the year brought fierce spasmodic winds, a slight thaw in the morning, pellets of snow most of the day, and hard frost below a silvery mist and waxing moon at night.

Midwinter greetings arrived from Pierre Sicaud, on Kerguelen. It is a great time for well-wishing in the Antarctic, at this time the nadir of many home-thoughts. It does seem incredible that anywhere in the world there can be flowery hedges and green fields. We shall have a Midwinter holiday and celebration on June 24th, the traditional Midsummer Day in England.

Arthur spent the whole day skinning a sheathbill ringed a couple of years ago. It is really a lovely bird, so white and with such exquisite satiny feathers. Jack completed the 'paper-work' I had set him to do. Poor old Jack, he is having a trying time domestically, apparently. Several cables have worried him a bit lately.

Monday 22 June 1953

I enjoyed my morning talking to Dick McNair. He is a naive, delightful character with extraordinary skill in his job. His bread is perfect, beautifully shaped 'tin' loaves. He was mixing a puff paste, and I asked him the recipe.

'Aw, it's easy. You take 12 ozs flour, nine of butter and a quarter pint of water an' then jes' roll and fold six times!' I asked him whether he used the mixer.

'Aw, Gawd no, John! But you would for a short paste. Then you'd take three parts o' flour, two of butter, one water, about six eggs an' a bit o' milk. You'd mix that in the machine.' Richard also has some very definite ideas about burnt pots. 'No, it don't matter how slight a pot burns. Once it burns, it'll always burn.'

Ten years' time became the topic of discussion at morning tea. 'So long as I'm in a good bludging job, with plenty of cash and no responsibilities, I'll be happy,' says cheerful Cec O'Brien. Arthur just murmurs, 'It's a long time!' Arthur is sparse of praise and subtle in condemnation, often silent in thought. He is well liked. Old Jack comes in, straight from his engine-room. He has a vein of petty truculence and an occasional patch of sullenness far shorter lived than Ron's. Jack is an exceptionally good fellow at heart, always on the edge of good resolutions. I couldn't help noticing this morning the entire absence of 'dirty' language. An occasional robust 'damn', 'bloody' or 'bugger', but quite occasional. Our party has cultivated decent speech, and seems no less happy for it.

Leon came in later in the morning, snow in his beard, his boyish face ruddy and surrounded by a bright green *trichot*. He had the last pair of Judy's pups in his arms, little beauties only a day or two old. He had the distasteful job of having to destroy them. He tries to make light of it, but he hates nothing more. It is virtually impossible to stop the birth of puppies, but there is a limit to the number we can feed and accommodate. For a little while he nursed the pups, loving them very much. I photographed him with them before he took them away.

Wednesday 24 June 1953

Midsummer Day in England!

Today was our Midwinter holiday. I went round the station and wished everyone a very happy wintering. The morning was unexpectedly fine and the whole of the North West Cornice was visible. Peter and I strode out across the Nullarbor, making good progress over the frozen, snow-covered plain. Light snow fell as we climbed the Baudissin. The tent was standing firmly so we continued straight on to Camp 2. We roped on a doubled nylon and commenced a slowly rising traverse to reach the col between the main peak of the North West Cornice [between the Schmidt and Vahsel glaciers] and the mountain proper. Every now and then we were able to see the huge ice-falls and towers with deep irregular bergschrunds. In the great valleys was evidence of mighty avalanches. Blue walls of ice revealed where snow had fallen away.

As we traversed below the summit of the cornice we suddenly reached a small bergschrund marked by gaping crevasses. We peered down into the dark, icy depths before finding a snow bridge. Further up we discovered two more crevasses. When I thought all danger was past I suddenly broke through a hard thin bridge. Fortunately only one leg disappeared up to the thigh before I pulled myself back. In any case Peter had the rope taut. It was too dark down in the crevasse to see the bottom.

When we had almost gained the Schmidt, we paused and looked back at the moon rising at the side of the grey, dream-like mountain. Everything was preternaturally sharp and clear. Snow, ice, cloud and moonlight—utterly desolate, completely lifeless, and beautiful. We reached the Baudissin moraine just as a fury of snow enveloped everything. Out on the plain we hurried blindly towards where we considered the camp to be. Finally faint lights showed through the mist.

Today was the birthday of Elizabeth Cynthia and William. It is pleasant to look back 15 years to that poppy-strewn Midsummer Day in Hertfordshire when Elizabeth was born. It is difficult to imagine that such scenes belong to the same planet as the ice-fields of Heard Island.

Thursday 25 June 1953

A calm moonlit night on Heard Island, with Big Ben a dome of silver scalloped by black ravines 3000 feet deep. Snowy arêtes miles away are clean-cut against the stars.

I was still considering the 'Kergie' [Kerguelen] chess move at midnight when the lights went out. Beside my bed lay small pieces of snow which had dropped from my boots in the morning. As the living rooms grew cold the long icicles stopped dripping, until the only sounds were the howling of huskies and the beat of tired surf on the beaches.

Friday 26 June 1953

This may be the centre of a 'polar anti-cyclone'. All day the mountain has stood as though sculpted from silver and alabaster. The station is an old-world Christmas card and the squeak of footsteps in the dry snow is the only reminder of the intense cold. Without wind, even the low northern sun radiates warmth.

After lunch Peter skied off to South West Bay to estimate the possibility of western routes up the mountain; I followed about half-an-hour behind him. The Nullarbor is now a frozen lake covered by a few inches of fine snow. I cannot recall ski-ing over such a perfectly flat surface before. Every detail of the mountain was clear, from the huge cliffs of the North West Cornice to the summit, more than 9000 feet above the plain known as Windy City. Far above, the crater yielded a continuous plume. When Big Ben is climbed, the weather will be the principal enemy. It looks as though an approach from the west side will be most profitable and we should begin the construction of ice-caves and igloos as soon as possible.

Two interesting cables arrived today. One from Sir Douglas Mawson wishing us happy wintering, a much appreciated greeting from the *doyen* of Australian Antarctic exploration; the other informing us that bird-ring 9532 had been recovered near the Chatham Islands. It was on a giant petrel ringed by Arthur and Dick on 20th April, about to leave the nest for the first time.

Arthur came in from a seal-count on Corinthian Beach at 10.20 in the evening; he had seen 52 leopards, some unusually far inland, apparently much at home in the bitter snow.

Windy City

'Windy City' was the name the men gave to a flat boggy area south of the isthmus that connects the mainland with the Laurens Peninsula. It was towards West Bay and South West Bay from Atlas Cove. Nearer the station it merged with the similarly boggy Nullarbor, the area south of the station between Atlas Cove, Corinthian Bay and Mount Drygalski.

Monday 29 June 1953

Possibly this has been the coldest day I have ever experienced; not on account of low temperature (which did not fall below 23°F) but the fierce, malicious wind. Hard ice clung tenaciously in dry patches to floors. Soap froze to dishes; nail and toothbrushes were stiff; the air was filled with fine gleaming crystals penetrating from undiscoverable crevices. Mats and towels stiffened like boards. Scarcely any water remained liquid. Even with the Kerotherm [a kerosene-fired hot-water system] burning, every pipe in the bathroom except the hot-water outlet froze solid.

Atlas Cove was ripped by great cold breakers, everywhere white and bleak. The sea temperature was 29°F. Spray froze on the beach and fell back to form 'brash' ice in the surf. Apart from Jim, no-one left the station; not even Arthur in quest of sea-leopards. Peter and his Met men kept the snow-melter going all day; this is vital as it is our only source of water. Flames and black smoke from burning blubber eddied in the blizzard. Most men wore at least three pullovers plus some sort of windproof garment and were heavily gloved. Two or three minutes without gloves, when I had to nail a sheet of iron that came loose on the fresh-food store, were sufficient to numb hands so that they had to be thawed painfully over a stove.

The lights beat me before my day was finished. I was due for a bath, an occasion I couldn't afford to miss. Only the hot tap was running. Thoughtlessly I ran my water—only about three gallons—and then discovered that the only way to cool it down was by making journeys outside for shovels full of snow. Unfortunately, in the dark I also brought in quite a lot of lava sand, with the result that I writhed one-quarter submerged in a black, malodorous soup. It shifted the grime of the last month or so.

Tuesday 30 June 1953

Several of us assisted with the sonde flight. I proposed that the double sheet be abandoned in favour of a very light nylon tent-lining. It not only saved the balloon but made the release possible.

Tonight there was a faint suggestion of aurora but ten-tenths cloud made any observations impossible. The few rare clear nights we have experienced have not coincided with auroral activity.

July 1953

No Water on the Rainy Island

Wednesday 1 July 1953

The wind has dropped to a whisper. Still about 25°F, but men walked about ungloved and lightly dressed. In the distance, on the pressure ice of the Vahsel or over the ridges of the Riviera, there were gleams of yellow sunlight. The station seems to avoid any sunlight unless almost the entire sky is cloud-free.

The first task after breakfast was pure water for the kitchen. The snow-melter is tainted by an oily blubber smell. Fortunately one Furphy and a rectangular iron tank (a relic from previous activities on the island) still contain rainwater. These sorts of jobs absorb hours of our time—the struggle to keep the ordinary essentials of life in a sub-Antarctic station functioning properly. Somehow the small cruciform cutter of the mincer went astray over the week-end and there is no spare. So two men have been painstakingly burning and sifting the week's gash in an effort to recover it.

Thursday 2 July 1953

For some time the mountain was clear, bathed in weak silver sunlight. At such times I am impatient to be up on the glaciers. Some of us will always be restless in fine weather until we climb Big Ben. And if we do not reach the summit, some of us will leave Heard Island reluctantly.

There was a clear aurora tonight at 10 o'clock, no colour but distinct white rays. The mountain was black as jet, the sky bright with stars. By 10.30 cloud has obscured everything. At 11.30 the mountain was again visible but the aurora had vanished. An eastern glow heralded the rising moon.

Friday 3 July 1953

There was discussion at dinner about the Antarctic Continent party next year. Heard Island will be a strange station next year, with only nine personnel. There is speculation as to whether any of the 1953 party, apart from Jim Brooks who has already been requested to go, will have the chance to help establish the station down south.

I found a bewildered Kerguelen diver lost in the slush and darkness, a beautiful trim little bird with diamond eyes, fine black plumage and strange blue legs. Arthur has a crevice between the biology hut and the little glass-store where he places storm-bound birds to rest in safety lest any dogs are loose. In the fight between Yves, a French husky, and his son Brownie yesterday, poor Yves had his ear bitten right off. Huskies are the most quarrelsome and yet the most affectionate dogs imaginable.

Saturday 4 July 1953

After burning every vestige of gash the missing mincer part was discovered this morning.

Wednesday 8 July 1953

Fred came down to the biology hut and we worked on the darkroom. We broke up cases for slats and hammered away, every now and then stopping for a smoke and a yarn. We stopped work at 10.30. I went to the galley and found the great array of cakes and pies that Dick always leaves for hungry men. It's a schoolboy's delight. I cut off some meat roll while my little aluminium saucepan boiled.

Friday 10 July 1953

After morning tea I helped harness the team, and one by one I took them down to their toggles on the main dogmobile trace. Butch and Mac, Oscar and the good bitch, Denny, Nick and Ned, brothers, very black and strong (who did their best to steer me over hard ice), Battle and Inky—and old woolly George by himself, for he pulls best that way. Oscar fondled Denny's head with his paw, licked at her ears, stood growling and quivering at Butch and generally made love to the lady in heroic manner. But his intentions were not in the least honourable, and whenever the slightest opportunity occurred he tried to break down Denny's defences. She was not interested.

We steered an erratic course out of the camp, first investigating the biology hut and then the wrecked Walrus plane down on the beach, before setting off strongly in the stabbing wind. It was an achingly cold journey across the Nullarbor. Over the icy flats of Windy City I stood 'running on the spot'; my hands were becoming numb. One of the difficulties of clothing is gloves. For a job such as sealing, heavy leather work gloves are the only covering that is not ruined, but we have no fingered 'undergloves' or linings to wear below, only fine fingerless, woollen mittens.

We ran down to the great white spuming breakers and set about carving a thousand pounds of steak from an 11 foot sea elephant. His blood-stained head rested on the sand facing into the spray. His body had sagged a little more than in life, if that were possible. Not 50 yards away a couple of listless, trusting cows lay indifferent to the fate of he who might yesterday have been their master.

I cut through the four inch blubber round the neck and in a straight line down the back to the tail flippers. Every few minutes it was necessary to sharpen the knives on the steel. We laid back the blubber in two great pale sheets, then carved the flesh in slabs to the ribs, as big as we could drag away. A short way off the dominican gulls, nellies and paddies were clustered over the remains of the other seal that Leon and Dick had dismembered a day or two ago, but their real interest was our operations. Soon the giant petrels would be dipping their strange prehistoric bills into the gory mess until their heads were red.

When we had loaded the last chunk of meat, and a side of blubber for the snow-melter, the load was too great to carry two men. I walked behind, shovelling away the snow at each halt to give the wheels a start. Finally Leon and his team were off, rapidly disappearing in the white streaming skirts of a blizzard.

Sunday 12 July 1953

During the wet black night old Harbottle with the bitch Lassie worried our two fine sheep to death. All our care had gone for nothing, and their horrible death touched our consciences. We had thought their pen secure and could only blame ourselves that their fate was not a swift bullet late in the year. By comparison the trio which died on the glacier had the happier demise. It is perfectly feasible to keep sheep on Heard Island but it is necessary to muster them in June. Dick has butchered the sheep.

Monday 13 July 1953

Bernie is excited about tomorrow, the French national day. He wanted a French tricolour so I found some white nylon in number 1 store and painted the broad bands to his great delight. He vows he is going to fly it from the dogmobile when he goes with Leon tomorrow. He is far more nationally emotional than the most ardent British patriot.

Tuesday 14 July 1953

A great clamour from the huskies announced that the team had been harnessed. There was something quite poignant in the scene. Bernie wedged firmly behind Leon, face flushed and holding his home-made nylon *tricoleur* very steady and erect, a little nervous behind the restless, milling team. Across the ice Big Ben rose frigidly remote in grey two-dimensioned precision. Bernie's flag seemed the only colour anywhere. We unfastened the team's moorings and away they shot.

I sent off messages of goodwill to Pierre Sicaud and Rouard (on Amsterdam Island). We thought a lot of Kerguelen (the French island only 300 miles away), run by Pierre with military despatch. It is a sub-Antarctic garrison isle—armed with a couple of cannon and a few machine guns, a sort of lilliputian republic all on its own in a world of ocean.

Bernie helped me with the large luncheon wash-up; we were finished scarcely before tea. After that, we could get down to the business of preparing for the ceremonial dinner. It must be by candlelight, so we trimmed 18 long candles and stuck them in beer bottles; it must have plenty of wine and beer, so we sallied out to the amenities store and collected sherry, claret, hock, port, a flagon of crème de cacao, some beer, lemonade for Dick (who has sworn off beer—he once woke up in gaol after a binge) and a few cigarettes; it must have a decorated cake, and of course old Dick was even now colouring an iced cake red, white and blue. He traced his conception of the Bastille but it became a cross between a gothic cathedral and a Western District silo.

Bernie's eyes shone brighter. When the men came in from their special sprucing, he welcomed each one with his curious blend of pomp and enthusiasm. We toasted 'The Queen!' and everyone sat down. We raised our glasses to the President and the Republic of France. The party was warming. We toasted M. Bernard Isabelle and after that there was a lot of singing. Len moved over to the piano between courses and between drinks. We had planned to broadcast the *Marseillaise* to Kerguelen but Cec came in rubbing the idea out with his hand. Too much auroral hiss, he reckoned. So we sang it just the same, and those who didn't know all the words made suitable noises. Ron shouted, '*Tout le monde!*'—which is about all the French he knows—several times in quick succession. Everyone souvenired Freddie's small French flags and soon the galley was crowded with willing helpers to clean up the mess.

Soon after midnight the party finished. Bernie stood very straight and wished each man good-night.

Wednesday 15 July 1953

Arthur came in at nine and stood by my bedside. 'Perfect day … crime to be in bed!' So I hopped out. It was a superb day. The mountain was silver and clear, the air still and the sun quite warm. An air of optimism filled the camp. In almost spring-time enthusiasm Bernie and I potted some [hyacinth] bulbs (which he had thoughtfully brought from Australia) in azorella mould and suspended them in the Met office window.

There was a magnificent light on the mountain this evening—a rose glow against a grey-blue evening. Long after dark the glow of the mountain was visible; it is still a faint paler shape in the star-lit night and a fine crescent moon rides the northern sky.

Thursday 16 July 1953

Five of us jerked stiffly in our submarine suits down to Wharf Point. We loaded the sledge several times with a ton and a half or more of black stones, weighing up to 30 pounds each. Then we'd trudge slowly behind tractor and sledge to the dog-lines. It looked for all the world like some highland funeral with terse mourners following a vast catafalque. At the dog-lines we formed chains and passed the boulders from man to man. The lines run through the tough azorella clumps and frozen lanes. Sixty 40-gallon drums have been embedded in the earth and a strong steel cable passed through holes just below their rims. A husky will be tethered to each second space so that he will have space to run and azorella to give him shelter when there is insufficient snow.

While we were busy gathering the final load before lunch, Leon came down with a rifle to shoot a small elephant seal that was slumbering on the point. Dick wanted it for the cuisine. We trailed back to lunch following a strange load—three empty drums, two mattocks, a crowbar, a ton of shining black boulders, and a grey elephant seal pup with Leon squatting on its back. We had enormous appetites, even though on such workdays the meals seem only five minutes apart.

Immediately after lunch, Dick butchered the seal. Dozens of sheathbills gathered round the blubber, quite tame, only retreating for a moment when old Harbottle lumbered up. The blood-stained snow, the pale blubber and the sheathbills, white except for their curious vizored bills, made an unexpectedly beautiful sight.

Friday 17 July 1953

The night was cold with vast ragged holes filled with stars in the clouds. I stood watching the Southern Cross very high in the sky swinging round a Pole that is only a waste of minor constellations. At this latitude the Cross never sets.

Tuesday 21 July 1953

Arthur, in his quiet yet rather fastidious way, spent a good portion of the day experimenting with his x-ray apparatus and developing the results. Leon shot two good-sized seals in South West Bay; he also saw a fur seal, a most unusual visitor for this time of year. I must say I never expected the immense volume of work. Men are still spending very little time away from station or routine activities, except in the evenings and on Sundays.

Lunch was a very good hot meal of penguin breast. The hut is now shaking violently, making one realize what sheer impertinence it is to sit comfortably warm and in a good light shielded by only a thin wall.

Wednesday 22 July 1953

A big elephant seal hauled out on the landing beach just below the camp. For Leon it was a gift from the gods as elephants are becoming rare, and his searches for dog-meat generally take him to the extremities of South West Bay. The ill-fated monster was 13 feet long—at least a ton of available meat. Great somnolent creatures, lazing away the frozen nights and days or rolling in the sub-freezing sea. For all their bulk and heavy protective blubber, they are completely mortal to an accurate bullet fired behind the eye or into the foolish, bellowing mouth. Dick and Leon went down to dispatch it; Jack was drawn away, too, fascinated. I passed him as I went into the workshop. 'Want to go down and have a look at the cutter!', he said.

After the evening meal we had unusually good telephony with Kerguelen. Both Arthur and I spoke to Pierre Sicaud, mainly concerning their biological programme. Pierre assured us that any Heard brands or rings would be reported. It is good to hear an outside voice. For the remainder of the evening I felt restless and a little irritable—and smoked one of my half-dozen cigars!

Thursday 23 July 1953

Down on Wharf Point Arthur found a whale-marker—a long bamboo pole 25 feet in length with a harpoon-like point attached. It must have drifted in from somewhere in the Southern Ocean.

Throughout the early evening the blizzard continued in patches between the racing cumulus and moonlight. We had a French session. Bernie takes all sorts of things unexpectedly seriously. There was a copy of *Man* out in the latrines with a 'Paris Letter' complete with humorous thumbnail sketches of glamorous females. Someone said, 'So that's what they're like in Paris, Bernie!' Next day every little sketch had been neatly cut out of the magazine.

Friday 24 July 1953

The night and early morning felt the full strength of a mad sou-westerly blizzard. Jim became completely lost on his way to West Bay and stumbled round blindly for quite a long time. The door of number 1 store was blown in and, to my disgust, I discovered that every inch of the shelves—every garment, every single item—was covered with at least four or five inches of snow. It would have to be brushed away before it thawed.

After dark I dug away the drifts from the amenities store and found four bottles of hock to celebrate Bernie's birthday dinner. Peter came down to the 'Yak' shack after dinner and helped me get the beer for the Friday ding. Fresh snow drifted down silently obscuring the footprints of the day. It will be good to remember in future Julys the soft, smooth curves of the snow. Perhaps in time this station will be abandoned.

Saturday 25 July 1953

I spent the day like a Victorian maid-of-all-work, washing up for a family of 13, mopping and cleaning and waiting on tables.

A thaw during the early part of the day only removed the snow from the roofs. It was accompanied by great gales, winds blowing steadily at 50 to 60 miles per hour, reaching 85 to 90 every few minutes. The disposal of gash and the latrine pans became an almost Herculean effort. Leon and I loaded them on the sled, Jack drove the tractor, and we struggled endlessly against the gusts, the highest of which reached 92 miles per hour. I would never have thought that the elements could add almost grandeur to such a job. After we'd tipped the big rubbish drums we had to hold on to them, our backs leaning against the wind along the edge of the surf. Every now and then one would break free and career away as lightly as a leaf in a March wind. Had we not pursued it, it would scarcely have stopped before it reached Corinthian Bay. Then came the emptying of the sewage in the sea, struggling knee-deep in ice-cold water; and finally the collection of blubber from the seal for the snow-melter. I used a pair of rough leather gloves dipped in black sump oil to keep them soft. You grovel in such jobs; you are filthy; the whole time is a struggle against the elements; but you become filthy with a sort of fierce delight.

I walked with Fred to the crater near Rogers Head. Right up there we found the tracks of small seals, hopelessly lost and trying in vain to reach the sea. Time and time again they turned to the cliffs but always retreated and made their way higher and higher. Some become exhausted and die in the snow or the torturous 'rope' lava, as hard and brittle as glass.

The station lights were invisible. It seemed that we were the last men left alive on a dying planet, with the eternal bitter night. We turned directly into a wind-stream for our return across the drifted azorella. Our torchlight gradually struggled across to meet the greater beams of the camp. Little more than a mile, but we arrived flayed by the effort. I just had time to lay the brightly coloured tablecloths and set out the newly issued 'silver' for the evening meal.

Sunday 26 July 1953

Rain, fog and a couple of inches of icy brash over the frozen Nullarbor, but Dick joined Leon in a distant foray on the sparse elephant seal population. All right-thinking elephants are now in their ocean wallows. Only stray misogynist bulls, lazy trollops and a few restless youngsters haul out on the beaches. Mostly they are rented by the leopards, grey, angular and shy, who on being disturbed raise their heads in anger, baring their beautiful serrated teeth, and with scarcely a sound lope into the surf where they are masters of all but the terrible killer whale.

When the rawin flight was over, Peter and I packed essentials and slogged away from camp, with no object but to stay away until dark. The station and our little balanced world soon disappeared in the murk. For a while we explored, looking for the cairns and rock left by Mawson. The black lava conglomerates stood out as edges, and the scene was curiously like a photographic negative. We were sodden. Our ventile suits are no longer even showerproof; but with layers of wool beneath, we preserved a steamy warmth. We discovered a cairn atop a large triangular rock at the base of Drygalski's main northern ridge. To an old, sandblasted wooden pole had been nailed, at some time, a tin cannister. This had completely disintegrated except for the top. The lower ring had fallen down the pole and been imprisoned beneath the rocks. Many years would have been required to cause such total oxidization, even on Heard Island. I have no doubt, from the description of the site, that this was Douglas Mawson's cairn, built over 20 years ago. The recorded position was certainly wrong—53°06′S, 73°24′30′′E—as that, according to Dovers' survey, would place it a mile or so up the Abbotsmith Glacier.

We skirted Drygalski until we found a slightly sheltered place in a wind-scoop near the old food dump found by Freddie. Now it is deeply snowed over and inaccessible. We ate our 02 rations, digging cheerfully into the embalmed meat, smoked cigarettes and decided to attempt the location of Peter's and Fred's igloo up on the Vahsel Glacier.

The obvious route lies up a valley of gigantic rocks, fallen from the high black facade of the North West Cornice cliffs. Stones so large that a human, beside them, is an ant. We are, indeed, the only ants on Heard Island. Only on the Antarctic Continent itself can insect life be more sparse. On Heard Island there is a minute wingless fly on the beaches below old rotting kelp and a small shining black dung beetle or two on the limited areas below the permanent ice-cap. Of insects found indoors there are no traces ever. Never a moth or fly or ant. Stores and clothing are forever inviolate; neither are there mice or rats, or any mammals except of the ocean.

An Exceptional Subantarctic Island

Heard Island is remarkably little changed by human activities. Other subantarctic islands have been substantially affected by introduced plant or animal pests—most notably the rabbit, currently the subject of a A$26 million eradication program on Macquarie Island. Because of its freedom from such introductions, Heard Island has special biological and historical significance.

Up the valley, immense snow-drifts hindered us until we were sinking knee-deep at every step. We followed the lateral moraine and were soon over fathomless ice but there was no sign of the igloo. It had been utterly buried; not even a faint hump showed its whereabouts. We thrust forward until the valley on our left became an abyss, corniced above bare walls of milky green ice. The snow was thin and treacherous. But the mist had closed in completely and the greyness was already in the light, so we turned back and descended.

We did not cross to the sea, whose roar carried on the moist wind, but trudged through the snow until we reached the low col over which Corinth Head is visible. The air below the cloud ceiling was quite clear when we overlooked the Nullarbor and picked up the lights of the station beyond the perfect semi-circle of the cove. The thaw had progressed considerably since morning—but every state is ephemeral here, and it may well be hard frost again tomorrow—and we slushed home wet to the skin. I peeled off three pairs of socks, a pair of pyjama trousers, a pair of jungle greens, a singlet, two pullovers, my ventile suit—all completely wet.

A sort of acquiescent silence seemed to brood over the station. I typed until 11.20. I have not mentioned a memorable aspect of today—the awesome muted whoosh of two great snow avalanches somewhere above us, just when the mist was so thick that the world seemed to end at our feet. They were a reminder of the great mountain bearing its millions of tons of ice, and of the 50 or 60 square miles of the island that have never stretched below human vision.

Monday 27 July 1953

This day seemed to run in reverse, from devitalized and pallid beginnings to a crisp finish, the morning more bitterly cold and depressing than teeming rain, far less comfortable than the sharpest frost. Men scuttled between the huts, stood dripping in the mess, crouched over their jobs away from the grey rawness. Everyone kept very busy, yet the day insinuated itself into everyone's outlook.

After dinner I commenced developing miniature films. To conserve water I used potassium permanganate wash to eliminate the hypo. Results were gratifying—well over a hundred excellent negatives recalling some great days—the Red Island expedition, the ascent of Olsen and so on. The lights winked off at 11.30 and I made Ovaltine by torchlight.

Tuesday 28 July 1953

A very low tide allowed me a firm sandy walk below the shingle to the turning point of the cove, where one may strike straight across to the magnetic huts. Leopards, four of the angular grey beasts, lay sprawled above the lap of the sea. They seldom haul out in rough weather. After a continuous spell of stormy days, more leopards come ashore—probably for the rest. I had never noticed before how red and watchful their eyes may be, quite different from the bulging, myopic eyes of the elephants.

I stayed a little while on the homeward journey to collect smooth pebbles to use as glass beads stopping oxidization in my developer bottles, then hurried back to a lazy breakfast over an old copy of The Sketch (reminiscent of hairdressers' waiting rooms), with Arthur bustling round as slushy in the galley. For the first time in months there was the contented sound of men and dogs, and none of that subconscious tension created by the raging wind.

Thursday 30 July 1953

There is a full-scale blizzard attacking the station, piling high its beautiful soft drifts. Under the electric lights the floors twinkle with diamond-like crystals. To move from hut to hut is quite difficult in the dense, icy cloud that rushes past incessantly. The blast has swept parts down to bare ice; in other places one stumbles through knee-deep drifts as fine and dry as flour.

Friday 31 July 1953

I exposed a good deal of film endeavouring to capture the mad excitement of Leon's dogs as he harnesses up a team. Before three we were away, at almost frightening speed, skidding over the ice and rocking violently over the frozen projections of rocks down by the sea. Beyond the West Bay hut lay a great sheet of ice, laminated from successive frosts and floods and in places a solid assembly of big broken sheets like table-tops carelessly welded. The team, in spite of Leon's efforts to keep them further to the starboard, made straight through the centre and crashed suddenly through the brittle surface. The dogmobile wheels sank about a foot, sufficient to bring the team up with a jerk.

We were soon underway again and reached the seal carcase on West Beach. Already the birds—paddies, nellies and gulls—had penetrated the tough hide in several places, and gouged out the eyes. Together we worked at the butchery, stripping away the pale blubber and cutting great chunks of black and red flesh. All around us strutted the snow-white paddies, clustering on the cut meat and coming as close as they dared. A loose bitch, which had followed the team from camp, every now and then made a sudden rush, but they always fluttered wildly into the air just in time.

August 1953

First Attempt on the Mountain

Saturday 1 August 1953

Ken gave a cheerful rousing to the sleeping-huts, bursting with the success of his first regular 6.30 'sked' with Perth. Dozens of telegrams— my breakfast 'mail' included messages from Lorna, my dainty Aunt Charlotte and the Queen, in that order of personal significance. Her Majesty, through her Private Secretary, graciously acknowledged our Coronation affirmations of loyalty.

Sunday 2 August 1953

Dinner was tentatively presented by Messrs Welch and O'Brien; it emerged innocent of disguise from various tins.

Monday 3 August 1953

The bathroom floor is a sheet of ice. Even our experiments with heaters overnight, reprehensible on the score of fire danger, are unsuccessful. I have decided not to allow unattended heaters even in the bathroom.

Ken, Arthur, Fred, Peter and I prepared to go up the mountain. We all wore anoraks and carried crampons, shovels and ice-axes. When we reached the tent we began to appreciate the magnitude of our task. Below heavy drifts the snow-flap was embedded in the ice of the glacier, in places to six inches. It took us five hours to free the tent in the bone-dry frost. Tens of thousands of ice-chips, powdered white like washing-soda were scooped away by hand to avoid damaging the snow-flap. A huge drift had piled up in front of the ice-fall above the tent. In places it must have been 30 feet deep, stretching for hundreds of feet.

Just before dusk we coaxed the tent, still with lumps of ice adhering firmly, into its long sledge bag, slid it down to the plain and left it for Leon to collect. So continuous is the Nullarbor ice that we remained cramponed all the way back to camp. Even so I was clumsy enough to measure my length, mooching along alone about 50 yards to starboard of the others. I landed on my left knee with considerable force and limped home full of self-pity.

Tuesday 4 August 1953

This morning there was not a drop of water outside the kitchen. Dick's tank is inside and doesn't freeze but he cannot really spare water for purposes other than cooking. Jack thawed the pipes leading from the big lower tank and cleared the pump of ice. The surroundings of the station are extremely treacherous with gleaming ice; nearly everyone has come down at some time or other.

Wednesday 5 August 1953

Arthur Gwynn received birthday greetings at breakfast. He is a self-effacing, most self-contained person, extremely sensitive, intolerant and introspective. Occasionally he shows outward irritation. He is a man of decided opinions, conservative in politics and something of an agnostic.

I made a start towards laying out equipment for an attempt on Big Ben. The first party will consist of Fred, Peter and me. I want to have our gear, including food, so organized that we could start within half-an-hour when a suitable break in the weather should occur.

Soup, savoury, a seal meat *plat de resistance* before the toast. We were all a little inebriated. After the debris was cleared away, Ron lumbered up to me, flushed and confidential. 'John, do you think that little ole store of yours might have something worthy of the end of such an aus ... aus ... pishous occasion. Don't get me wrong. It's not for me. It's for the boys.' 'Come along and let's have a look,' I suggested.

We slithered round the ice to the amenities store. 'Now, there, Ron. Fourteen bottles of sherry to last till the end of the year!' 'Well ... we'd better leave those.' 'Seventeen bottles of port! Perhaps we could take one of those in as a night-cap!' Ron glanced dubiously round the shelves. 'Do you think it will be enough?' Under the circumstances I thought so and Ron preceded me back to the mess, contentedly clasping his bottle of port.

The evening ended very happily, yet back at home it is almost inconceivable that more than two or three of us would have had sufficient in common to enter the same room.

Friday 7 August 1953

When I went to strike the small tent I was horrified to see that Leon's dogs had badly ripped a corner. Ever since the dogmobile was bogged in the ice the other day, Curley has been free. He defies recapture. Unfortunately he has been killing and worrying the young seals and harrying the paddies and penguins. I am fond of the shaggy, cunning old husky but unfortunately he will have to be shot. Arthur spent a good part of this dull day in dissecting the foetus of a leopard, taken from the mother which Leon had been forced to shoot as meat.

At lunchtime I had a signal from Lorna, full of love and affection; then we had another link with Australia in a very audible Radio Australia programme. Sue waffled even more than usual. However we did glean that Macey, 'Johnnie' Russell and someone else had been selected to accompany Dovers to the new Antarctic base next year. Other news was the statement by Mr R.G. Casey that men for Antarctic ventures should not be more than 25. That caused quite a lot of argument down here, as I gather it has at home [at the time Béchervaise was 43].

Saturday 8 August 1953

The snow has completely disappeared except where it is drifted and the ice is covered with still, dead water, never so lacklustre as from melted snow. I went to West Bay. The thaw had set all the streams running seaward from the Nullarbor and already they had cut deep channels through the névé and sand. The only signs of life were a couple of gentoo penguins, a solitary white Antarctic tern, some dominicans and the great splayed tracks of old Curley. His wild freedom and his pillaging had numbered hours. Later in the day Cec brought him down from 200 yards with the .303 rifle, and Leon swiftly provided a second fatal shot.

Ron is having one of his morose, discontented periods. He claims that he should only watch one day in three and he'll do 'no bloody more'. He is complaining bitterly about not being permitted to remain in bed as long as he likes every second day—yet the man never works after seven at night.

At about 11 our electricity supply was inadvertently cut off by Arthur who, while clearing his surgery drains, managed to cut the cable.

Sunday 9 August 1953

Ron came out from his bed at about 11 and I asked him to talk his complaints over. I found him completely intransigent and with the fixed idea that Dalziel should perform the same radio watch duties as himself. I tried to reason, and stressed the programme that Ken had. I feel desperately sorry for Ron. He insists on 'kicking against the pricks' and wishes me to refer the matter to Phil Law. As Arthur says, 'if a man wishes to approach Caesar, it is his right'. In the end I agreed.

Monday 10 August 1953

The ice is back again—hard white rock instead of riffling pools. The station was in a cheerful mood. Most men have heard about the ridiculous radio disagreement of Ron's. I sent off the cable in code. I think Ron would have liked to back down but his pride would not let him. At all events he was promptly on duty today and did not carry out his threat to Ken 'to bloody well do nothing until Wednesday'.

A crisp, still evening. Dick and Arthur have gone leopard-counting at Corinthian Bay. The only sounds are those of the diesel engine and my clock. Time seems to be passing extremely rapidly. It is about now that men start to think of home as in the future rather than in the past.

Tuesday 11 August 1953

We had a telephone 'hook-up' with Kerguelen. I spoke to Pierre Sicaud at length, discussing their works programme and gossiping generally. Arthur spoke with Mr Migot, Kerguelen's biologist. Since then I have been out here in the biology hut, working on lengthy re-order cables. Arthur, Jim and I have just celebrated—for no particular reason—with a test-tube full of brandy per man.

Wednesday 12 August 1953

There were no leopards on the beach in the early morning, only a few dominicans, a giant petrel or two and a diminished throng of Heard Island shags. High on the shingle is the head of a sea elephant.

My hyacinth in the Met office is growing apace.

Thursday 13 August 1953

Today 'From Law: The radio-man [Dalziel] is not expected to share watches equally with operators. Decision of OIC in such matters is final.' I called Ron up to the radio room and showed him the message. He didn't say anything at all. There's something impressive in the man's stolid nature.

We shook hands; now I hope the incident is closed.

Arthur had a busy evening sun-tanning his guinea pigs.

> **Good Morning, Sunshine**
>
> It was routine practice on the 1940s–1950s ANARE expeditions for the doctor to give regular sessions of 'sunshine' to the men using UV sunlamps.

Friday 14 August 1953

The radio session in the afternoon was unexpectedly good. We heard Phil outlining plans for the Continent party. In about five months the *Kista Dan* will commence her voyages, Macquarie first, and from then always on the move until we finally land in Melbourne. It was odd to sight the ice-falls across the grey afternoon sea, and think of darkness in Melbourne and shining lights.

Saturday 15 August 1953

Ron had lit the blubber-renderer and tended it, his stumpy powerful figure aureoled by the fierce furnace beams.

Sunday 16 August 1953

A day of dry dusty snow, very gloomy, cold and rattled incessantly by a keen sou'westerly. For Fred, Peter and me the day just drained away on packing. We were still wandering round with torches at 11 tonight. Arthur will be officer in charge in my absence. We worked out a system of rocket-star signals and stood outside to experiment. The cartridges shoot out brilliant red stars. Peter will film our expedition, mostly in colour.

Leon travelled with his dogmobile to South West Bay for a seal and dropped off our ski-sled. There is no man on the station for whose grit combined with ceaseless good humour I have a higher opinion.

Now it is late, a mean howling wind, sky black; air warmer than the ice which still lingers nearly everywhere.

Wednesday 19 August 1953

The weather prevented the start we desire. The Nullarbor was a morass. Leon found it too glutinous for his dogmobile and was forced to return.

Jack looks extremely fit at present. The 'ultra-violet' treatment has given him a good tan; his eye is clear. He sang as he worked and we shared the community of greasy overalls and dirty hands. I am really very fond of Jack. The histrionic Len had a quiet day, reading and mooching around after rising late; he had some slight stomach upset.

Thursday 20 August 1953

Len came in at five o'clock. 'About three-eighths cloud, Peter. Come and have a look!' Probably Fred heard the whispered conversation too but we lay snug until Peter's return over an hour later. 'I reckon we ought to take a chance,' he announced. Very soon the support party—Arthur, Ken and Jack—were also bustling round. The weather was only moderately good but the mountain was intermittently visible.

Peter, Fred and I left at 8.30, beneath packs weighing over 50 pounds. The Nullarbor was firmly frozen with a thin snow cover. On the edge of the azorella clumps we searched for the sled, discovering it just as the support party caught up with us. The six of us took on extra weight and made our way over the azorella hummocks and partly frozen streams.

Where the last black stones of the moraine give way to unbroken ice we donned crampons and loaded our packs onto the sled. As the slope grew stiffer we began to wonder whether carrying our loads would not be as easy. We were unroped. We reached the moraine of the Abbotsmith Glacier at its highest point at about 11.45. From this point there is a wonderful view of the hundreds of acres of sharp blue seracs 20 and 30 feet high, an unbroken blue barrier between the Vahsel 'saucer' and Cape Gazert. A route through them would be tortuous.

We were still in familiar territory. We had a brief lunch of sardines and biscuits. The Abbotsmith Glacier has only been crossed once. Brown, Dingle and Lied crossed at 1000 feet approx. in late November 1951. In frosty sunshine (about 25°F) we commenced the hard sledge-haul. Old Harbottle, the almost blind husky, trotted uncertainly back and forth between the leading three and ourselves. We were now roped. The summit of Big Ben, not more than three and a half miles distant, steamed furiously.

At about 1500 feet we decided to camp for the night. Not more than a hundred yards from our stopping point we crossed one small crevasse. I dropped through to waist level but soon scrambled out. We pitched our home-made tents and were soon comfortable. Arthur commenced excavating an ice-house; Jack joined him and by the time it was dark, they had made it large enough to continue working by candlelight. I made a pemmican-salami stew. The night turned very cold but our climbing party was perfectly warm in double down bags.

Friday 21 August 1953

The support party left us at 10.45 for their homeward trek. Above was a superb view of the west face of the mountain. It was still perfectly clear but a north-west wind was too strong to permit such conditions to last.

We continued up the valley, passing between the ice-fall to the north and the main broken ice of the central glacier. Without the slightest warning, I broke through into a large crevasse. Fortunately I only dropped as far as my pack. Fred had me firmly on the rope, but we realized how dangerous these innocent-looking ice-fields could be. The crevasse was 50 or 60 feet deep to the limit of vision. The exquisite blues gradually changed to fathomless black. At its widest the crack was about eight feet.

From then on I probed constantly with the axe-haft. We moved slowly and cautiously, gradually gaining height. The wind increased to gale strength and brought dirty weather. By 4 o'clock we were blizzard bound. We decided to pitch the tent. Not even the nearer pressure ice on the Abbotsmith could be seen. There was nothing to give direction nor distance; only a scrap of nylon on a bamboo pole marking hidden danger about 12 feet from the tent. The blizzard threatened to carry away the tent. We hung on to the ridge, anchored the guy-ropes and shovelled snow on to the flap.

With food, stoves and sleeping-gear in the tent, space was extremely limited. The blizzard increased in violence. We beat the fabric above our heads to keep the snow from accumulating. Our breath and the steam from our stew formed a crust of hoar-frost all over the roof; the slightest chink in the ventilator let in streams of flour-like snow. Gradually, the drift was creeping up the tent.

The blizzard came in gusts of 70 or 80 miles per hour with a steady wind of perhaps 50. Fortunately we did not have to leave the tent. We had brought meteorological pilot balloons for essential purposes [that is, urinating]. Fine snow penetrates every fold and crevice within seconds.

Though it is dry as talc outside, it must be laboriously brushed away *inside* the tent after entry, or it thaws. Then it must be disposed of through the ventilator. Every time the tent entrance is untied, snow fills the tent with a haze. We slept fitfully at nearly 3000 feet, probably the highest camp so far on the island (unless Bob Dovers camped higher in the first year).

Saturday 22 August 1953

In the pre-dawn, visibility did not extend more than three yards. We remained in our bags until seven, then made porridge and coffee. To stretch our legs we put on our nylon parkas and left the tent but could only walk a few steps in any direction. The furious driving snow held 20° of frost and without vigorous exercise it was impossible to remain outside without danger of frostbite.

I decided to dig a refuge, primarily as a latrine as we had no trapdoor in the tent. I soon had a pit some four feet deep by 20 square feet. Then I started to tunnel. Peter joined me and we got down deep enough to miss the wind. But the heat of our bodies brought the temperature to above freezing, so we became wet. Fred took my place. It took 25 minutes to rid myself of snow for every entry into the tent.

We determined to complete the ice-house and transfer everything there for the night. Excavation was back-breaking work. We had hoped to pull down the tent before nightfall, but what a dusk! To emerge to the open was to face white torment. We formed a chain gathering up all our gear and piling it down below. The tip of my bad finger was white and dead with slight frostbite.

Finally we were all down below. The enormous drift immediately created a problem of ventilation. The hole from our cave was rapidly filling with snow. It was extremely difficult to keep any opening so Fred and I thrust up ice-axes through the roof and made small vents which sent down streams of fine snow.

We lit candles and stoves for the evening meal. Though the air was warm and calm (the thermometer showed 41°F, compared with probably 10° outside) we were wet and tired. After a little while the candles gave trouble. I was stupid enough to think that it was their poor quality. The stoves burned badly. Suddenly a candle spluttered and went out. I tried to light a wax vesta; that merely sparked and wouldn't burst into flame. Then the other candle snuffed. At the same moment both Peter and I were gasping for breath. We clawed at the exit, pulling down the blocks before an avalanche of fine snow. For two or three minutes we struggled to clear a flue, holding our heads close to the icy downdraught. We lay back devitalized, very tired, with nauseating headaches. Fred, cheerful as ever, declared that he was feeling fine. Whether our trouble was just lack of oxygen or that plus carbon monoxide, I don't know. We left the entrance wide open.

The drift drove us further back into the ice-house. Our candles were rekindled and burned brightly. Fortunately our stew was almost completely cooked; we had already had coffee. We finished the meal and stretched ourselves into our damp sleeping bags, gradually feeling the sticky warmth. Peter wanted a candle left burning. We scarcely talked before settling down to sleep. At midnight I awoke and found the entrance again completely drifted over. I crawled over Peter and thrust away with the spade until I broke a hole to the blizzardly air. I enlarged the vent until it was about a foot square. Even if it did seal itself there could be no danger without a stove. I blew out the candle and we all slept.

Carbon Monoxide Poisoning

'Finally the primus went out and so did John & Pete. They began to dig feverishly for air and on reaching it gulped it down. Pete was almost weeping. I was ok as I had shoved an axe handle through the roof above & had a reasonable supply and had a grandstand view of the effects of suffocation' (Fred Elliott, diary entry, 22 August 1953).

Sunday 23 August 1953

From about five o'clock onwards we were semi-conscious of the coming day. Absolute silence. Just the grey-blue light increasing in the thinner places of the roof. One end of the ice-house was filled with drift, the blizzard still howling. We were below the cloud barrier which lies between 3000 and perhaps 6000 feet (and often much lower on at least nine days out of 10), on our fourth day with no prospect of the weather clearing. With reluctance and relief we decided to return to the station.

We packed all our ice-house gear. All we left was food on a shelf—a natural refrigerated supply for our next effort. The temperature was 13.5°F and the fierce gale was full of snow. Twenty degrees of frost is nothing to worry about if the air is still—add a blizzard, and conditions are different. Our salvation lay in moving fast.

For a little while, our snow-goggles were misted and our gropings indecisive. We were just able to see the little markers we had left at intervals, especially where there were crevasses, on the upward route. We made fast progress down, probing constantly, crawling whenever necessary. New snow had obliterated all signs of our ascent. Once or twice we broke through, harmlessly; then we were within sight of the lower (Arthur's) ice-house. Once we had regained the Abbotsmith moraine we could move freely. Before we reached the Vahsel moraine a heavy snow-storm rushed up blackly from the sea and we had to proceed blind.

With Peter lifting the nose of the sled from time to time we were able to drag it. About three times we had to carry it. We left it on the last frozen stream and trudged on with our packs to the station lights. We arrived while most of the men were still having dinner. The pure luxury of a hot wash, Ron's ample dinner, light and warmth and dryness! Fred had a frostbitten toe, white and numb.

Tuesday 25 August 1953

I spent a vigorous morning on the snow-melter, feeding it with leopard blubber until the flames rose a foot above the snow-container. The snow was striated with layers of black dust from the beaches. At tea-time, about 300 gallons had flown into the tank. It's a good job, warming on the coldest day.

After lunch there was an exodus with the tractor to South West Bay. Leon had shot a mighty big elephant seal bull and wanted to bring back the meat. The party returned at dusk with more than a ton and a half of steak, our sled, and keen appetites. Leon described the butchering of the 15 foot breeding bull as 'a fair cow'.

I am still worried by Ron, a strange, complex character. If only he had a hobby he would be happier. Today I heard him speak to Leon who had some snow on his boots, 'Get to hell out of here—bringing in all that filth!' The words were commonplace but the tone was malignant.

Thursday 27 August 1953

Late at night, there is a gusty wind and the snow is stone-hard. Earlier there was an auroral glow but it was soon completely clouded over. I found Arthur gleeful at Phil's request that he go on the *Kista Dan* for the round voyage calling at the Antarctic base. I hope I have the chance also, but I fear Phil may want me to stay here.

Sunday 30 August 1953

At about 10, a silver sun penetrated a high upper layer of cloud and the mountain began to appear. We struggled up the Baudissin in freezing clouds, then stumbled through drifted mounds to the gentoo penguin rookery below Erratic Point. The gentoo, largest of the Heard Island penguins, marches in frightened battalions, turning tail in black panic when approached. But stand still for a minute or two and the whole colony surges forward in white-fronted curiosity, surveying the intruder with myopic intensity.

Next we inspected the bull elephants. They are very different after months at sea, bellowing and distending their enormous balloon-like noses, arching their backs, magnificently sleek and virile. Very different from autumn when they lay lethargically in their ordure.

During the next two or three weeks, more and more breeding bulls will haul out from the surf until, in South West Bay, there will be a male population of two or three hundred, many weighing three or more tons. The cows will come too, probably 10 times as many, nearly all of them pregnant. They will congregate in torpid groups awaiting the relief of giving birth. Then the bulls move in and take over their chosen harems, and so provide for the propagation of the race.

Monday 31 August 1953

The history of yesterday still lies imprinted in the snow, every footstep clear. Through the station the 'trade routes' between the various buildings are gradually beaten down to hard, glassy valleys. It has been a lovely day, calm and still. Now, as I write, there are misty, uncertain stars. The innumerable sounds of the station, dominated by Jack's diesels, are distinct and clear.

After lunch there was a considerable exodus towards Corinthian Bay to watch the branding operations. Last night Arthur counted a record 108 leopards basking in the snow along the beach; some had even come far inland across the Nullarbor. About three-quarters were still there, lying asleep or cocking a wary eye. From close quarters the largest are evil-looking creatures, smooth, grey dappled and enormously powerful, anything up to 10 or 11 feet long.

The attempt to brand them proved a fiasco. They twisted and threshed their enormous sinuous bodies and easily wriggled away from the yoke, hissing and snarling almost silently, rearing to snap at the puny human intruders. If there was ever any doubt concerning both their ability and intention of biting, it was removed. The tormenters had to be brisk to avoid the threshing body-blows and terrible mouths but, perhaps fortunately, the grey animals rapidly became exhausted on land. Dick thrust one brand onto the tail of a leopard. I think probably there was little pain as the blubber is several inches thick. But by that time he was looping his way wearily into the sea.

The remembrance of the last day of August 1953 will be centred in the grey leopards, creatures perfectly organized for their cold, unsociable existence in the foamless Antarctic seas. I read for a while from Huxley's *Brief Candles* and switched my light out in our local September.

September 1953

A Memorable Aurora

Wednesday 2 September 1953

I decided that we should repair the passage bridging the two sleeping huts. Fred and I worked on the outside, flaking away several inches of hard ice and névé in wind-blown sub-freezing sunshine. We laboured steadily all day while the weather steadily deteriorated. Snow began to fall persistently and the temperature was 25°F. As the work necessitated ungloved hands, it was one of the most miserable tasks imaginable. Hands became ingrained with tar and froze until they ached. Once or twice we had to retreat to the mess stove to suffer 'hot-ache' while circulation returned.

Friday 4 September 1953

A raging gale all night with repeated gusts worrying the camp, vibrating walls, finding every loose roofing nail. I rather like the sound of wind when I am fully awake, but half asleep, I am restless and imaginative. Will our latest work on the roof be stripped away? Has some door been blown open? Has any stove been left burning? Then suddenly I am awake, filled with a vague alarm. There is no sound except the furious wind. I switch on my torch and at two or three in the morning pad round the living quarters, examining every stove.

We lit three heaters to dry out the bathroom. In removing the ventilators (sheets of masonite loosely covering holes), we saw something of the effects of last year's fire. Beams were badly charred; it was providential that the blaze was discovered in time by one of the Met men in the early morning. Some sort of fire alarm system would be worthwhile. The sleeping huts are so far removed from the living quarters that the whole place could be in flames before any one was aware of the danger.

Evidently the ventilators were the work of Dick Hoseason, for he had written his name and the date—March 1952—only a few weeks before his death on the Baudissin Glacier. It's curious how a man will enclose his signature in passing pride of his craftsmanship. I recollect a pane of glass high up in the Henry VII Chapel in Westminster Abbey, inscribed roughly with a diamond with the name of the glazier, a century or two ago, and the laconic sentence 'The wind blewed it out'.

Fire!

In March the year before, the men had woken to the call of 'fire!' in the bathroom. If it had not been 'flat calm', they would have lost their dining room and kitchen, and possibly their sleeping quarters—all of these rooms were right next to the bathroom.

Saturday 5 September 1953

Just before dawn a most memorable aurora. Bernie called me at five, and I stumbled out to find the whole sky pulsing and flashing with an unearthly greenish-white radiance. A violent sou'westerly piercing one to the bones, I rushed back for more clothing and Peter climbed down from his bunk. We stood in what lee we could find, trying to observe the whole sky at once. Overhead stretched the most vivid light. The southern edge fluttered as though in a tremendous cosmic wind, the colour a narrow range between white and faintly phosphorescent green. The magnitude and intensity of the aurora was astonishing. After only half-an-hour clouds began to screen the sky. At about the same time there was a general twilight from approaching dawn. Only for this brief time, in all the months we have been on Heard Island, has such an aurora been visible although there is no doubt that many great displays have been hidden by clouds.

Sunday 6 September 1953

Two big sea elephants were far out on the snow, making their way overland to South West Bay. By what uncanny instinct they even find Heard Island after months at sea no-one can say. It seems even more remarkable that, having landed, they should know their way about. I have frequently followed tracks right across the snow between Atlas Cove and Corinthian Bay, but these I have always put down to purposeless wandering. It may be so; this morning's pair may have had no idea of their destination—or had they heard the distant bellows of their rivals, or caught their scent, carried nearly three miles over the snow?

Arthur, Dick and James left at 9.30. I watched the trio move slowly up the Baudissin to the Schmidt, then lost sight of them in the clouds. After an hour or more they were again visible, making good progress eastwards. By about 11.30 they were high up on the Baudissin. From the door of the bio shack it was easy to see their best route, but it would be different up amongst the ice knuckles. Arthur led the party too high at first, and they found themselves approaching the scattered rock moraine above the first big black cliffs. They must have soon realized they were wrong. They stopped, conferred for a few minutes and probably rested; then I watched the tiny dots reverse direction until they were above the correct descent.

They crossed the snout of the small glacier beyond the Baudissin. By 3 o'clock they were out of sight. I looked for the agreed flare at 6.50 but there was not the slightest chance of seeing it even if it was fired. At nine I stood down by the hydrogen hut and watched for any other signals (should the party be in difficulties, a star-flare would be fired) but there was just consoling darkness.

Monday 7 September 1953

Along the shingle a magnificent bull sea elephant had come ashore. He was sleek, clear-eyed and rippling with vigour. He reminded me of magnificent sixth-formers I have known. This particular bull was never to know the promised land of adoring cows—nor the indescribable lethargy and ordure of the season's end—for Leon shortly afterwards shot him for the dogs (and men!) of the station.

The cloud lifted a little in the afternoon and the rain turned to mushy snow. Just before five Cec and I floundered up to the seismic hut to change the trace. I had hoped to catch a view of Saddle Point but it was still mist-bound. At 6.50 I should send up a flare, anyway. We returned to the bio shack and had the printer virtually finished when, to my surprise, Arthur walked in gaily and soaked. He and his companions had returned. I suppose all officers in charge tend to the maternal when they have parties in the field; it is impossible to keep one's mind away from the wanderers. It is a relief to see the dinner tables full.

The wind tonight broke all our records, reaching a crescendo of fury that persisted for nearly three hours, from eight until after 11. There were repeated blasts of up to 115 miles per hour. Roofs and walls vibrated and bowed visibly. In the rather frail bio shack I wondered whether the place would disintegrate with the next blast. Cec and I fought our way back to the galley and made a steaming brew before bed.

Wednesday 9 September 1953

The magnetic observatory at West Bay is a cold, lifeless place, *en rapport* though it be with terrestrial forces. I like breaking the frozen seals of the seldom-opened doors and replacing the icy blackness with ruby light, probing the red twilight with a narrow white torch beam, reading temperatures, chronometers, millimetres. The old trace is removed, the new trace wrapped round the slowly revolving drum. With my black cylinder containing the latent image of traces scrawled by the shivering little magnets, having triple bolted the doors, I leave the huts to darkness, the ticking of clocks.

Thursday 10 September 1953

One of the most refreshing aspects of life on a lonely island is the frequency of occupational change. Every man is from time to time impelled to take hammer and nails, a paintbrush, a cooking pot, or a needle and thread. The cook assists with the release of a sonde balloon, the radio men refurbish the bathroom. Today Arthur, our doctor and biologist, spent his day as slushy with mop and pail and piles of dirty dishes. Work and relaxation are indivisible.

Our flower bulbs in the Met office seem to be dying. They burst into green leaf and budded beautifully, but the flowers have not come and the leaves are yellowing. It may be that the azorella mould we used for potting them was unsatisfactory. We had great hopes of seeing a flower or two before we returned to Australia in seven months.

Friday 11 September 1953

Now is the turning point of the year and some of the men have begun to harp on changeover and home. Jack was gloomy this morning and Jim returned very silent from West Bay. No longer is Australia behind us but ahead.

After tea Arthur and I carried a 'Tottenham' tent to Wharf Point, and working in a fury of wind erected it near the seal carcase in order to watch the birds. We anchored it with great rocks and snow, and plan to spend tomorrow morning observing and photographing the petrels, skuas, dominicans and paddies.

Saturday 12 September 1953

Arthur and I were escorted down to the wind-shaken tent by Ron after an early breakfast. The giant petrels rose alarmed in spiral wheelings; the dominicans withdrew to the snow-mantled tussocks of poa and azorella. Well away from the scene, riding the waves as buoyantly as kapok, lay some hundred Cape pigeons.

After we'd sat smoking for a while and watching the paddies, Ron left us and the unarithmetical watchers from the skies considered the coast to be clear. In came the nellies, great wings raised to counterbalance the wind's force, pale-ringed eyes peering uneasily. In to the magnetic, bloody carcase were drawn the hook-billed, offal-loving skuas.

Our spy-holes from the tent, where we lay on down bags and foamed plastic squares for insulation from the cold, were just 17 feet from weltering commotion. Had the birds sensed our presence they would have scattered to the winds. We could see clearly the red-stained bills. The giant fulmars, less at ease on the ground than in the sky, wobbled on their legs like cripples, recovering balance by curious uncertain side-stepping. They seemed like pterodactyls, primitive terrible birds with beaded reptilian eyes. Most were almost black with grey-yellow tremendous bills.

Every now and then a panic would come over the birds—all except the paddies. By common consent the seabirds would rise in screaming commotion. Some movement far off at the station might have been responsible, or the crawling tractor skirting the Nullarbor on its weekly journey to the sea. After a time the birds would drift back, landing at some little distance from the carcase. A few possessed rings, mostly the paddies. One nelly had a band which had opened and would soon be lost. Arthur recorded all ringed birds. For two hours we lay in the tent, as though in invisible suits. Then we disturbed the feasting, and were blown back to the station realizing for the first time how bitterly cold the wind was.

Sunday 13 September 1953

A most unpleasant raw day with snow cover softening and pools of dead grey water growing in the hollows. No-one left the station except Arthur, who visited the tent on Wharf Point for an hour or two.

My quarterly turn as duty cook. Lunch was mushroom soup, followed by baked salmon cakes and potatoes and boiled vegetables. Dinner was more complicated. For the first time in my life I attempted a large steak and kidney pie. The crust was guesswork, but it turned out very well; there were vegetables—mashed potatoes, green peas, carrots and baked beans—a complicated soup and a sweet made from sponge cake, tinned cream, blackcurrant jam and canned cherries.

Tuesday 15 September 1953

The air between Atlas Cove and Corinthian Bay was charged with fine sea-spray. The big iron buoy in the cove had broken loose, its steel cables snapped. It lay rolling in the surf. Our bird-watching tent was, amazingly, still steadfast. Magnificent breakers, spray streaming hundreds of feet behind, crashed 40 and 50 feet high against the terminal seracs of the Baudissin Glacier.

Wednesday 16 September 1953

This morning the wind had almost exhausted itself. Over an ice-glazed beach I walked to West Bay, passing three very tired leopards which had dragged themselves ashore after the storm. They scarcely flickered an eyelid at me even when I moved quite close. The thaw and slight freeze had formed great milky ice-sheets rippling down from the plain level to the sea.

After dinner I had some ultra-violet ray treatment. Apparently this artificial sunshine has a tonic effect and Arthur wants to give everyone treatment eventually. It's pleasant to lie mother-naked under the warm light. The station lights were switched off before my day ended. I sat in the mess and drank hot cocoa by torchlight, then found Fred reading in bed. Into two small liqueur glasses I poured [sister] Mary's small bottle of Curacao, kept all these months for the occasion, and together we drank to her new year.

Thursday 17 September 1953

To my great delight I received a cable from Lorna.

Fred came in at 11 with enthusiasm for changes in the food arrangements for our next trip up the mountain. He believes we should cook only a main hash at night and coffee, and depend for 'sweets' on dates, biscuits and the like. I was a bit terse but think he is probably right. At the age of 40 it is essential to retain a plasticity of mind. God, how I loathed the 40-year-old omniscients of my youth! On a remote island station, where every existing emotion tends to be accentuated, any older man must be always on his guard to *appear* sympathetic with the youngest men and never suggest that age per se is valuable.

Geelong, Sept 17 1953
Béchervaise, Heard Island

Darling John glorious weather massed polyanthus golden willows ... we miss you so—fondest love—Lorna.

Saturday 19 September 1953

A slight thaw, only serving to set the silver icicles dripping, backed to very heavy snow in the afternoon. Falling continuously and very quietly it seemed a white, descending hush. It was so soundless, working indoors, that one might suddenly have heard a thrush.

A current topic of boisterous if not bawdy comment is provided by Denny and Paddie—and probably a couple more bitches—being in season. The utmost of Leon's ingenuity has not prevented innumerable matings, old Harbottle being the ablest and most willing sire. If it's not the ladies breaking loose, it's Harbottle, for all his blindness, leaping and clawing his way over seven foot fences, 'Come an 'ave a look,' yells old Dick excitedly, 'He's on her agen! Wot a dawg!'

Sunday 20 September 1953

This month has beaten all our previous records for wind and snow. Much has remained frozen where it fell. Drifts are three or four feet deep. The even cover over the Nullarbor and in the station is perhaps six or eight inches deep, overlying inches of ice and feet of iron-hard earth.

Monday 21 September 1953

Owing to the huskies' lawless love life, Leon was anxious to top one of the pens with cyclone wire. He spent the whole inclement day struggling to free a coil which lay firmly frozen in about six inches of ice. For an hour or so he hacked away with a pick, sending ice-chips flying far and near, but that was useless. Then Jack made a couple of attempts to free it with gelignite. The second effort, using a whole plug, removed about a hundredweight of ice, shattered a large rock used in tamping the charge, and blew the feathers off an indiscreet paddy. The coil, dented and fractured in one or two places, remained as firmly embedded as ever. So poor old Leon lit a vast fire. For two or three hours he poured on oil and piled on wood. At dinner time he had to admit defeat.

A long chat with Jim just before afternoon tea. Things appear to have been getting him down. This isolated life is far harder on young men than on chaps Arthur's or my age. The trouble is probably sexual but most often is entirely unrecognized as such by the bearer, who blames hard work or the weather or just the boredom of routine.

Tuesday 22 September 1953

The mountain was clear to at least 4000 feet. A heavily pregnant elephant seal cow was making her way determinedly over the snow from Atlas Cove to West Bay. Her route was quite straight, yet it lay slightly uphill. By taking the 'overland' the cow was saving herself at least 20 miles of swimming. She found it hard work, puffing along then resting, much out of breath. The directness of these apparently unintentional shortcuts is uncanny. Having spent months at sea this expectant mother hauls out on a fine sunny morning and immediately sets off over featureless snow!

Shags were parading in full force; two pairs of gentoo penguins strolled along the foreshore to inspect three prone grey leopards, one very emaciated, perhaps sick. In the water the leopards are probably the penguins' most terrible enemy.

Thursday 24 September 1953

The great excitement of the day was the discovery of a Ross seal (*Ommatophoca Rossi*), probably the rarest seal in the world. Arthur considers it a new record for all sub-Antarctic latitudes, the creature being normally a denizen of the pack ice, leading a solitary existence and very seldom seen.

In 16 weeks we should see the relief boat in the Atlas Roads. So much must still be done. Time is beginning to seem like water passing over Niagara.

Friday 25 September 1953

We slithered and crunched across to South West Bay. It was an utterly desolate beach, strewn with thousands of ice-fragments ranging from boulders to chunks of 100 to 200 cubic feet. Shapeless by sheer bulk and gravity the huge old bull elephant seals, many every bit of four or five tons in weight, lay sprawled amidst the ice. They are almost incredible creatures, their enormous distended noses drooping down a foot or more from their red lecherous eyes. Like immense shapeless bags of flesh they mostly lie as though exhausted. Every now and then they will rear up inflating their proboscis and roaring ineffectually. A bull that has taken over a harem will defend it vigorously against all comers, his sheer towering mass his principal weapon. When the pups are being born, the cows are still being left more or less in peace but the libidinous old breeders, although mostly prone on the outskirts, appear quite aware of events.

These vast mountains of flesh have a habit of scratching themselves with one of their flippers, extraordinarily out of keeping with their flaccid bodies. It is raised, arched, extended, an amazingly articulated organ rising and moving with the graceful gestures of a ballet dancer. Often it is the only sign of life, appearing unexpectedly, hopelessly inadequate, one would think, for preening the huge area of flesh. At times it appears ludicrously like a human hand.

The cows are equally shapeless but smaller. Many are now accompanied by their pups—wide-awake shivering little elephants covered with long, moist black hair. They are mostly about three feet long at birth: quite beautiful by comparison with their parents, possessing definite form and bright bulbous little eyes. They nuzzle their tired immobile mothers. They appear to feel the cold but are quite energetic, raising their heads almost as soon as they are born in plaintive little yapping barks, just like canine puppies.

When we arrived at the forlorn beach it was blowing a gale of rain. James was on ahead. Just as we came level, I saw something arching its way into the surf. It was too small for any elephant likely to be entering the water. It was the Ross seal. James dashed down into the water and managed to turn it back up the beach. The little beast, no more than five feet long, puffed his throat and bared his sharp beautifully pointed teeth. In the scurrying, icy rain we set about photographing him. After a while it seemed apparent that he had no real intention of leaving.

It is now 11 o'clock. These 16 or 17-hour days all seem too short.

Saturday 26 September 1953

Leon, whose need for meat was urgent, swept out over the Nullarbor in his unloaded Nansen sled. But on his return, with 600 pounds of meat, the continuing thaw made the load impossible. Time and time again the sled broke through into icy mush and in the end Leon had to heave off practically all the steak in order to get the sledge back home.

Just before dinner Ken attempted to boil up a rather derelict leopard skull. The stench became overpowering, from the bathroom through the rec room, even as far away as the sleeping huts. Just at this time everyone came in to wash and dress, and Ken was the centre of good-humoured complaint. Then, to everyone's amusement, Ken carried away the offending cauldron and became violently ill.

Sunday 27 September 1953

There was little sign of life about the station when I left for West Bay shortly after seven. There were no leopards but the shags had returned in force and seemed tamer. It was easy to approach closely enough to see their beautiful blue-ringed eyes.

One of the most striking sights was the continuous flow of sparkling water from beneath the ice-sheet of the Nullarbor. The night's frost had not been sufficient to re-freeze the plain to any depth. The pleasant, mild day really gave me the feeling of approaching Spring. Then, of course, there were the inevitable thoughts of Big Ben. It is a pity we are not quite ready—perhaps the next good stretch of weather.

Wednesday 30 September 1953

At breakfast time, Jim, flushed from his wet walk to West Bay, reported on the state of the elephant seal harems in that quadrant, 'Fifty-seven cows, sixteen pups, two bulls … the first bull seems to be willing to divide his mob but the second doesn't seem to want to come in … at the far end of the cove there are ten cows and no pups—the "40" brand is still there. The beach harem has twenty cows, five pups and the one bull.' Arthur notes down the information on his cigarette box. 'No leopards, I suppose?' 'No leopards.' Arthur is endeavouring to keep a census of the elephant seals. Last year Les Gibbney was able to be very thorough as his main responsibility was biology and his chief interest was seals.

Len busied himself with boarding-up our sleeping hut passage—by the end of the day the walls advertised Foster's Export Lager, Heinz Baked Beans and somebody's Tropical Fruit Salad.

October 1953
Half a Nelly's Egg for Breakfast

Thursday 1 October 1953

News of our Ross seal has reached the press radio and even Macquarie Island. Sturrock, the doctor there, sent Arthur the following telegram: 'Seen pink seal with purple spots near surgery Sunday morning. Query identification.' Arthur replied: 'Obviously *Phosterphoca lageri*'.

Saturday 3 October 1953

During the night useful rain fell—we always think of rain in terms of snow-melting saved. Most of the day it snowed steadily, becoming at the same time colder. When it was dark the familiar hurricane whine began. Throughout the night the whole station crouched down, shuddering and vibrating at each fresh onslaught of the wind. It is easy to imagine that the wind encircles the station, frustrated by the first human habitation in a million square miles of dark wilderness.

Wednesday 7 October 1953

Leon, at lunch: 'Jim, when I was over at West Bay the other day, I tested my personal magnetism.'

'Oh,' said Jim, always a bit anxious whenever anyone goes near his sacred variometer house, 'How did you do that?'

'I just stood in front of the place and beamed all over.'

Thursday 8 October 1953

There was no vacillation about today; the wind remained uncompromisingly sou'west and solidified the mushy snow to hard treacherous glass; a morose, mean sort of day. Well ventilated, Arthur patrolled Corinthian Bay inspecting the harems there. He has located several branded cows—all bearing the 1949 marks.

Friday 9 October 1953

For the first time in weeks, I opened a window of the mess and let the air waft through to the galley. The sounds of the station at work can be extraordinarily audible on a calm day—Leon with his dogs, men talking as they paint hungry walls, someone hammering in the paint shop. Jack I happened upon at the moment he was considering using some of the surgery oxygen apparatus for paint-spraying.

The Radio Australia session, for a change, was extremely clear. Sue announced the marriage of Tim Ealey and Mary Binet, which was received with considerable comment. Tim is about five feet four inches and small; Mary is vast.

Saturday 10 October 1953

It was one of our rare fine, still nights with pale auroral glow. Sirius was magnificent, quivering with colours beyond the northern glacier. It had been an uninspiring sort of day but two things are memorable. One is a sound, the long whispered note that ran through each snow terrace as we strolled up to the seismic hut. Evidently there had been some thawing and our weight caused the large sheets of snow to fracture, invisibly but audibly. The other is the black dome of Big Ben outlined against the aurora.

Sunday 11 October 1953

Bernie asked me if anyone was going out in the afternoon and looked so lost for a companion that I said there was nothing I should like better. We straggled along the beach to the first big elephant seal harem just in time to watch the big-chief bull rear up and pursue an escaping cow. At least she appeared to be a fugitive, slyly looping down to the icy sunlit surf. She probably weighed a ton but he caught her by the nape in the water and struggled to bring her back by force. Whenever he relaxed his grip his vast bulk blocked her from the open sea. From the distance we watched the cow returning up the black sand pursued by her triumphant master. The magnificent breeding bulls who mate the vast majority of cows ensure that the most virile strain is perpetuated.

As we climbed higher there were superb views of the North West Cornice and the northern glaciers. We dropped down a steep snow gully just too soft for glissading and discovered the shelter of a rock for a quiet cigarette. 'John, we shall remember this when we are away far, isn't it?'

We walked home tranquilly to a really excellent dinner by Arthur, a complex soup with a tomato base, a lambs-tongue toad-in-the-hole and a fruit salad. Fresh snow lay sparkling like naphthalene.

Monday 12 October 1953

Ron installed special little shelves in the latrines for bottles of 'Airwick'.

Wednesday 14 October 1953

Arthur made a couple of seal-observation journeys searching for brands, the only method of tracing the growth and movements of the sea herds. He said the other night, 'The longer I study leopards, the more I find that is unknown'. One of the puzzling features about the small leopard population at present is the number of small beasts. If they must be yearlings at least, their rate of growth is slower that some authorities have stated.

Today I cleared a space for our mountain equipment. I have moments of depression concerning our mountain-climbing, probably the fundamental reason that brought me to Heard. No-one who has not spent three or four nights high on the lower slopes can realize quite how formidable the weather can be. How quickly it all comes upon us! The year is almost gone. Suddenly, one day the *Kista Dan* will be in the Atlas Roads. The thought fills me with as much sadness as joy. Heard Island is a beautiful and memorable place.

Thursday 15 October 1953

Not so long ago men were talking about their future on Heard Island as though it were broad enough to contain their planning; now there is a sense of the brief weeks that remain, weeks that will teem with activity.

Vicious winds and snow-showers parried the thaw for a few hours in the morning and it remained an unpleasant morose day throughout. In the afternoon the dull pools amidst the drifts grew deeper and overflowed. In parts of the station the drifts, now aggregates of old snow, ice and blown sand, form curved dams round the walls of the huts and contain lakes from their melting. With picks and mattocks, Arthur, Jack, Dick and I chipped out gutters and built levees to save the kitchen store from flooding. It was an islanded hour of heavy physical work straight after lunch, when we set the lifeless waters moving, carried coke to the big hopper and tried in vain to move a drum of kerosene. The last one was punctured in the effort to free it from the ice; we gave up the attempt today and moved the pump down to the drum dump.

I spent most of the morning experimenting with constructing waterproof outer-gloves, having found a nice 'bit of material' in Chippy's. Fitting the thumb is the very devil. I tried handsewing, and didn't like the effect. I tried machining the thing inside out—and it reversed a poor forlorn puckered thing. In the end I discovered that it could be stuck down with the heroic PC 49. As I worked in the rec room men made rude noises and likened my masterpiece to a phallic symbol in the least aesthetic terms.

Arthur meanwhile was skinning a Cape pigeon; Jack toiling on number 1 engine—he fixed the mended radiator in place today; Jim was calculating 'absolutes' at West Bay and Leon out killing and carrying a couple of seals—for both men and dogs. In the afternoon Len and Cec made a happy combination lining the sleeping hut passage with hessian. You wouldn't know the place now; no longer damp, dreary and smelling of mouldy wood. Peter, for a while, cursed over the multitude of minor repairs to our mountain tent. He hates little time-consuming things; he'll probably be a very impatient father if or when he becomes so circumscribed. 'Oh, curse the bloody thing,' he keeps muttering, but in spite of his irritation, he does a good job.

Friday 16 October 1953

A high wind during the night reached 90 knots. I spent a really satisfying day, finishing my gloves (using for their lining the blanket conveniently shredded by the dogs), making another pair of outer canvas boots (to which I affixed a pair of heavy rubber soles, for use out of crampons) and fussing round our growing pile of mountaineering equipment. It will only be days before we are ready for the attempt to climb Big Ben.

Overnight old Harbottle escaped from the leopard seal pen. During his captivity, affairs in the canine world had altered and poor old Harbottle gained his freedom only to be bitterly disappointed in his advances to Fran, Judy and the other bitches.

Monday 19 October 1953

The trip to West Cape originally planned for yesterday was expanded. The party had a wonderful day in the nelly rookery at West Cape, bringing back three or four dozen big white eggs for the kitchen; Arthur ringed a number of birds. The most exciting discovery was a number of fossils in a volcanic conglomerate boulder on the beach. As far as I know fossils have not previously been reported from Heard Island, except for 'abundant foraminifera', but the molluscan fossils of Pliocene age in the ash-beds of Kerguelen are well known. These pecterns [sic] discovered by Arthur and Ron may be of the same period—when warmer, or even tropical, seas existed here a couple of million years ago.

Tuesday 20 October 1953

At seven my alarm went for West Bay and I cursed the very thought of it, let alone its sound. However I was soon on the way through misty rain and thaw. On the outward journey I was hurrying and on the homeward way lingering, as usual picking up stones. Each man will doubtless take home something to remind him of this place. On bedside ledges there are little hordes of bones and teeth; Bernie has a great fierce leopard skull; Arthur has his bundles of 'dicky-bones'; Jack has his dog skins.

> **Picking up Stones**
>
> Béchervaise's father used to bring home stones from his travels for John and his brother Herbert. 'I have a special love of smooth worn stones,' he said once, 'traced doubtless in those distant rattlings from the bottom of my father's Gladstone bag' (Helen Phillips, oral history interview with John Béchervaise, 10 June 1976: 5).
>
> Today, no materials of any sort can be removed from Heard Island without a permit.

For breakfast half a nelly's egg, served by the day's slushy, Leon. Shortly afterwards an unpleasant incident, again concerning Ron Parsons. We have a rule that each man may sleep as long as he likes one day a week, preferably Sunday, and on other mornings appear for breakfast (cooked) by 8.30 or coffee and toast by nine, or at all events be out of bed by nine. Ron stayed in bed till lunchtime on Sunday and was still dead to the world at 9.30 this morning when I told him the time.

He turned on his side, looked at me very angrily and said, 'Well, what of it?' I told him I expected him out of bed at once, to which he replied, 'Go to hell!' or something to that effect. Thoroughly annoyed, I yanked off his blankets. That really set things going. He bounded out with fists clenched and eyes blazing, threatening to attack me forthwith. I walked off but realized that I should clear up the matter. After morning tea I warned him that I would tolerate no more of his ill-temper. He glowered away, talking quite irrationally but in the end, declared that he would in future be out of bed by nine each morning. The only man who has given any trouble so far this year is Parsons. He is a difficult, limited sort of fellow. He has erected barriers between himself and everyone else on the station. I should give a great deal to see him as happy as the rest of the fellows and have not yet given up hope. It is very difficult to record this without seeming horribly priggish and self-righteous.

Wednesday 21 October 1953

Arthur set out mid-morning bearing a long bamboo with a paintbrush attached and some red enamel to mark the calf belonging to cow number '41' in the small end-of-the-cove harem. He wants to be sure of this particular animal when the time comes for branding. The pups will then have withdrawn from the harem and be otherwise indistinguishable. This is probably the first time on Heard Island when a second generation branding may be fully documented. The cow was branded in 1949, so she has reached maturity in four years.

Friday 23 October 1953

Arthur gave most of the day to preparing penguin flipper-bands for the macaronis, arriving daily in greater numbers. He was experimenting with pigments to make the numbers clearer from a distance through binoculars. I helped him, but chiefly my day went to final mountain preparations. If we don't succeed this time it will not be the fault of equipment.

Saturday 24 October 1953

At breakfast time I received a bewildering cable in code from Phil telling me about a meeting with Charles Holmes [editor of *Walkabout*], when the latter spoke of next year's retrenchments. At this distance it is impossible to fathom but it has an ominous note.

Ken was intrigued with the acts of mating amongst the elephant harems. He vowed that one bull had a penis nearly three feet long. Arthur timed the act which took four minutes.

Tuesday 27 October 1953

In the morning the weather seemed so fine that I fretted that we were not away. Peter and Fred had consulted early and decided against our chances. But in the afternoon the weather was bitterly cold with frequent drift snow showers.

Wednesday 28 October 1953

Just before five Peter called me. He anticipated a good day. The temperature had fallen to 27°F overnight; the mountain was clear to some distance above the North West Cornice. We had a good breakfast and were on our way just before seven. Within minutes of rounding Drygalski an almost imperceptible change of temperature occurred, just sufficient to change the texture of the snow in the hollows, not a thaw but a variation in crispness. At the same time the wind veered a few points. Out at sea, a long way off, a grey mist grew higher. That was the time we should have read the signs and turned back. Later on I discovered that at 5 o'clock, almost to the minute, the barometer had started to tumble.

But we pushed on and were soon on the final rocks of the moraine. Leon harnessed George and Binder. They dashed off downhill towards the sea and for a few minutes I envisaged the whole outfit coming to grief. However Leon lurched off yelling at them, and fortunately the sled over-ran its hauling ropes and was thereby slowed up.

A heavy blizzard suddenly enveloped us. One minute we were all visible to each other; the next we were struggling. We found ourselves completely uncertain as to where we were, blinded by the whirling snow of the blizzard. When a knuckle of ice showed on the left I realized that we were not far off our route. Even then I should have had the load dumped with markers and turned the party about.

We kept going, Arthur and I in front, Peter, Fred and Leon with the dogs and sled, and Ken struggling along nearby. In our determination to avoid the crevassed areas low down we rose too high. In a break in the streaming white snow we saw the faint grey wash that was the upper rocks of the Abbotsmith moraine. We arrived on the icy ridge where a couple of furiously vibrating markers told of our other visit more than two months ago.

We were in a furious Antarctic blizzard as strong and thick as any we had experienced. Behind us visibility was completely removed. It was essential that we either make shelter or keep moving. On account of the uncertainty of a return into the face of the white hurricane, the tent had to be erected.

Down in the hollow, where Arthur made an igloo about three months ago, Fred, Peter and I fought the possessed fabric of the tent. It would have been better if the temperature had been lower; as it was—28°F—any shelter would provide thaw conditions owing to the heat of our bodies, and there were six to fit into one small tent.

The air was dense with spindrift. Ken, Leon and Arthur crawled into the tent before we finished staking it; their weight helped to hold it down. Even the nearest rocks 20 yards away were invisible. The whole operation seemed clumsy: for long minutes poles refused to fit into sockets. I was annoyed with myself that I had not turned back at the first indications of the blizzard.

Such icy malignant fury on the lower slopes of Big Ben makes one realize that willpower, careful preparations, and thoughtfully designed equipment, are not sufficient. Immediately upon the onset of bad weather, it is necessary to pitch camp until the storm abates. To move on, as we had done, spells quite unjustifiable danger.

Eventually we joined the others in the tent. For two hours we smoked, ate chocolate and rations and played an alphabet game. Then, fortunately, the wind dropped somewhat. We made an orderly evacuation. Fred and I struck the tent while Ken struggled up for a pack-frame; Peter, Arthur and Leon were making the dump secure on the ridge.

Now it is all over, it is easy to discount the misery of staggering round with frozen limbs, prising up stones from the moraine to anchor the yellow tarpaulin. At 2 o'clock, we started down. As we descended the visibility improved and we covered the five miles to the station in under three hours. Our specially made boots had kept our feet perfectly warm. Our fully laden sled was half-way, horizontally, to Big Ben and one-ninth of its height. As things turned out the day had been successful.

Thursday 29 October 1953

Snow-showers and high winds continued all day. The barometer was at its second lowest point for the year. Bernie walked over to West Bay to fish but arrived back drenched by an unexpected big sea. The tides sprawled right over the flats, almost meeting between Atlas Cove and Corinthian Bay.

Friday 30 October 1953

A frozen windswept day with a little weak sunshine filtering through magnificent clouds in the afternoon. In 24 hours the Nullarbor was transformed from a quagmire several inches deep to a steely plain of frozen sand, set with immovable boulders and abraded by racing clouds of frozen grit and dry snow rising only a few feet from the surface. To be out on the plain under these conditions, seeing only the heads and shoulders of companions rising from turbulent brown or white fog and feeling the full force of particles hurled with hurricane force, is to realize how stones are worn down to fine, curling edges and fantastic pyramids.

Old Dick gave a splendid day's work to painting the rec room. He is a stalwart character and once he becomes interested in anything, time and energy mean very little. Most men were absorbed by end-of-month work. I completed my boots, grinding down the heels in Jack's workshop and typed a few signals, completed the drying of our mountain gear, and ordered some stores. Radio Australia was clear in the afternoon. Sue gave a description of the boots being used on the forthcoming Antarctic venture and we thought of our own home-made efforts.

It would have been a bad day on the mountain, yet I am restless. While all our gear reposes on a snow-swept ridge of the Abbotsmith moraine there is a sense of urgency. So far our meteorological forecasting has been completely astray. On the two occasions we've started out the weather has worsened from the very beginning of our attempts.

Saturday 31 October 1953

A boisterous morning with neither rain nor snow made me restless to be up on the Abbotsmith. The quality and quantity of weather information available over this sector of the world make accurate forecasting completely impossible. A cyclone over Marion Island, 1400 miles west and north of us and apparently headed in our direction, may easily be diverted; even Kerguelen may be inundated by its fringe while we escape. On the other hand, weather fair or foul may be generated over millions of square miles of ocean and reach us by paths devoid of any convenient islands. As far as I can see, even when clear air and sunshine have blessed Heard Island, it has been impossible to know whether the day will end in starlight or blizzard. It is reasonable to believe that our weather reports are of value in Australia but a weather station in the Antarctic could provide information of inestimable value.

Several times today I watched the rising barometer and probably showed my impatience at our inaction. Peter doggedly continued to expect adverse conditions before the day was out. Oddly enough, when the wind turned easterly at night and heavy snow whitened the station and all the sea-level plains between the four bays, whirling quietly down from an ebony sky, Peter was as surprised as any of us.

November 1953

Second Attempt on the Mountain

Sunday 1 November 1953

This morning I felt depressed, mainly because of the passing of time and the necessity of making an attempt on the mountain soon, if we are to try climbing it at all. So I decided that if Peter and Freddie agreed, we should just start out tomorrow if it should be reasonably fine.

Late in the afternoon James returned from a second visit to West Bay, bringing a handsome king penguin, a large and unusual visitor to Heard (which, however, is common on Macquarie Island). The poor creature was very puzzled but was much admired. Arthur finally put him in the pink store for the night.

> Only three pairs of king penguins were seen on Heard Island in 1947, but by the summer of 2000–2001 observers saw some 25 000 pairs there (Eric Woehler, quoted in *Aurora*, vol.20, no.4, 2001: 32).

Monday 2 November 1953

Camp 1, 2700 feet

Before breakfast we decided that today was as good as any. By the cove the fat little 'porkies'—small only in relation to their mountainous parents—sprawled, their skins fairly bursting with nourishment. The divers are excavating their burrows in the sand. For Heard Island it seemed high summer.

The Vahsel was unclouded, though there were a few flecks of snow in the air. We crossed two miles of uncrevassed ice without any difficulty and climbed to the thousand foot level. The yellow tarpaulin covering the sled had been ripped to shreds but the sled and our gear were in good order. We attached our hauling ropes and made excellent progress up the great snow valley beside the Abbotsmith Glacier.

The depth of snow that had fallen since August was apparent by the mere four inches of bamboo marker, which we had left projecting about five feet above the surface. At about 6.30 we camped on the far side of the large crevasse, not far above the ice-house which was our terminal in August. Blessedly calm, fairly cold at 18°F but very comfortable.

Tuesday 3 November 1953

Camp 1, 2700 feet

It is about half-past nine, snowing furiously, the tent completely rimed over on the inside. It would be hard to conceive a wilder night. We're in the same place as last night, with a furious blizzard blowing. If this snow keeps up we shall be entirely drifted over by morning.

It has been a world compacted by cloud all day. Space is white with faint grey and blue shadows. Gusts must be reaching in the vicinity of 100 miles per hour. The little tent seemed poised for flight a few minutes ago. Only one seam needs to go and the whole will disintegrate like tissue.

Wednesday 4 November 1953

Camp 2, 3400 feet

For hours last night I lay half asleep, miles up a glacier with no retreat possible. Before dawn, the storm blew itself out. By seven, we caught glimpses of the dark ocean, so we commenced the terribly slow job of striking camp. From awakening to loading the sledge takes the better part of three hours in such weather. The temperature in the flying white dust is 17°F. Our boots, virtually home-made, of felt and canvas enclosing ordinary military boots, have not allowed our feet to become cold. We hauled the sled nearly a thousand feet up the route we had poled yesterday.

Thursday 5 November 1953

Camp 2, 3400 feet

We are in the midst of our second severe blizzard and completely immobilized, fully dressed and in our sleeping bags. At five this morning there was no visibility. Then at eight, there was a sudden lifting of cloud with incomparable views of the Laurens Peninsula and the Vahsel Glacier about 3000 feet below. We were on the point of leaving after lunch. Fortunately we didn't go. To be caught in this present blizzard in the seracs and crevasses would be serious. When we are able to move again progress will be very slow, through feet of dry powder snow. We have ample fuel and food to last about a fortnight. No-one has ever camped higher on Big Ben than we are. It is a vast, lifeless place of perpetual whiteness with the almost eternal sound of wind and the rush of avalanches down the immense ice-cliffs.

At Atlas Cove

Today the men on station took 'Kingie'—held captive in the pink store since 1 November—back to West Bay. He was 'last seen preening himself on shore, having fallen in with a party of gentoo' (Atlas Cove station log).

Friday 6 November 1953

Camp 3, 3700 feet

The morning turned marvellously fine and through big silver clouds we could see the Anare Isthmus white with snow. At eight we left on a reconnaissance, leaving bamboo markers until we struck an *impasse* and dense fog. We returned to the tent below and packed everything onto the sled. The haul was very difficult—a total lift of perhaps 500 feet and a distance of half-a-mile constantly probing for crevasses. We reached this campsite pretty tired. It is in the centre of a sort of ice-knuckle, dissected by crevasses in all directions. We probed for a good space round the tent and put in four markers as a sort of safety boundary.

After some coffee we made a further reconnaissance, up about 600 feet and almost right across the glacier. Extraordinary visibility revealed the coast as far south as Cape Arcona. We reached a series of vast parallel crevasses choked with snow, about 20 feet wide and 40 or 50 deep. A most encouraging day. Given such progress we should make the summit.

Saturday 7 November 1953

Camp 4, 4200 feet

Heavy snow. About eight inches fell during the night, dry powder that has made sledge-hauling very difficult, purgatory where the snow overlies hard ice. At dusk the temperature was 15°F but it has dropped. The tent is a sheet of hoar-frost sparkling like stars. We are now camped between two vast crevasses at the margin of the Arrowsmith. Tomorrow, if the weather holds, we should have the final slope of the plateau ahead. It appears that our greatest difficulties are already behind.

Sunday 8 November 1953

Camp 4, 4200 feet

Snow falling most of the night. It was impossible to do more than leave the tent. In the dim grey cloud, crevasses dropped away to unimaginable depths. Many drop down from blue to black depths, often denoted by a slight depression in the snow, or by nothing at all. We never move unroped.

Monday 9 November 1953

Camp 4, 4200 feet

We have been completely immobilized since last night. It was snowing then fairly steadily—and with no more than half-an-hour's pause it has been snowing heavily ever since.

The blast and blizzard gave us the idea that preparing for another day's march would be wasted effort so we lay tightly jammed in our sleeping bags and just dozed. Snow drifting from the north started to rise up the sides of the tent, sometimes half an inch in a minute. For two hours we kept pressing and compacting it, to consolidate the snow as a sloping wall outside the tent. Eventually the tent, up to about a foot from the ridge, was encased in a cast of snow. The two ends were likewise completely snowed up. On Peter's side the snow only came up about 18 inches.

The trapdoor from which we carve snow for melting is under Peter's head, while the hole itself is stuffed with stoves, billies, plates and things. As it grows deeper, its beautiful translucent depths become more and more useful as a receptacle for food bags, stoves and the like. At about three Peter and I donned anoraks and went outside. We stamped about in a phantom white world with the great crevasses showing as dim blue shadows. The drifts are now protecting the tent to a great extent. The glass is rising a bit. In height we are only half-way to our summit after a week, but in distance we are five-sixths of the way.

Tuesday 10 November 1953

Camp 4, 4200 feet

A wretched day immured by dense cloud and intermittent blizzards. About 20° of frost. We have been in this camp too long.

The tent only showed a rime-covered ridge. We dug our way out, just to be able to stand erect. The tent sides were now so compressed by drifts five feet above the floor that we were squeezed like sardines. The fabric in many places was frozen to the drift. Scraping off the frost with a spoon onto a plate was a hopeless task with two other men in the tent.

I dressed and went outside and cleared the snow from one side. I had completed a side when Peter came out, as impetuous as his biblical namesake. He set to work with great gusto. Then suddenly he put the spade through the tent! I was annoyed; I am afraid I showed it. Such accidents simply mustn't happen on trips like this. Soon we were all back in the tent. Peter cobbled the rent skilfully. Gradually the atmosphere cleared.

> **At Atlas Cove**
>
> Found the first macaroni penguin egg of the season (Atlas Cove station log).

Wednesday 11 November 1953

Camp 5, 4800 feet

We had nearly 12 hours' rest and struck the tent, leaving a great hole in the snow. Our tent site had slipped about six feet towards the lower of the two crevasses.

A terrific sledge-haul at the start, in dense silver mist. We were only the second party ever to cross the Abbotsmith, the other having passed some thousands of feet lower.

Visibility improved for a while and we saw the frosted summit of Mawson Peak, but the clearing was short-lived. We strained at the ropes until we could scarcely move. Ordinary man-hauling, on such an incline, was too difficult. We roped independently on the 120 foot rope and hauled the sledge at intervals, hand over hand.

All afternoon we struggled. Just as the sun was lost we reached this little flat behind an ice knoll. The slopes of Big Ben reddened. By the time we were all inside the tent it was after nine. We are at about 5000 feet. With another day's good weather we could be on the plateau.

At Atlas Cove

Flag flown at half-mast till 11a.m., when hooter was blown for two minutes silence; then at full-mast till sunset.

Arthur went to Corinth Head in afternoon, bringing back two penguins for dissection, also providing penguin steaks for the kitchen.

Skuas killed two days ago made a disappointing meal, being tough and tasteless [the three skuas included one ringed there a year and a day earlier] (Atlas Cove station log).

Thursday 12 November 1953

Camp 5, 4800 feet

We are utterly bored. It is snowing lightly and there is no view. Last night brought us within such close distance that we could see every detail of the final peak. We had tugged our sled for many miles; the rest of the climb can be done with rucksacks, probably in two days—from this camp and back again—with good weather. All we can do is to have patience. Ten days since we left the station, and we have only 12 days' food.

If only the right weather comes soon. This mountain was my real reason for wanting to come to Heard Island. Now that it seems to be within our reach, surely we'll be allowed to get there!

Friday 13 November 1953

Camp 5, 4800 feet

The tent is completely buried under snow! At nine last night I awoke to see the tent bowed under tremendous snow, drifting fast, powder-dry and not easy to consolidate. I hated doing it but it seemed necessary to go outside and dig the snow away. This meant fully dressing from a warm triple sleeping bag and facing the blizzard. In a fury of energy I removed a mass of snow, working in blinding white dust.

The night wore on. At 1a.m., I asked Peter to get up and remove snow. At five, I asked Fred to 'do his stuff'. The drift was increasing every hour. At 9.30 this morning it was my turn again, but no longer could my spade even keep pace with the snow. Before I had finished one side, it was almost up to the ridge again. I had to give it up. There was only one thing to do. All of us exerted pressure on the tent against the high piling drift. We held it from crushing the tent. Soon it topped the ridge-pole and we were in a strange sub-nevean gloom. The effect of the cyclonic wind was lost—it became a recurrent booming sound—but the sides of the tent bulged inwards alarmingly.

We lit a stove in the timeless morning. This melted the hoar-frost lining the tent, but another serious problem was air. We had to struggle to keep one remaining ventilator free of snow. When we had warmed our water, we were forced to extinguish the stove. Now the entrance and both ventilators were completely snowed over.

At about midday I decided we'd have to build an igloo over the entrance to the buried tent. It was blinding, evil work. In the height of a blizzard we cut blocks, carried them and gradually constructed our dome. I have never worked more uncomfortably. Our faces and beards were entirely iced. I couldn't work with snow-glasses and the light was dazzling. We finished the igloo in about two hours—a big one, almost high enough for us to stand—but found the tent sagging more heavily than ever. We made the igloo drift proof and I was able to sit out there and relieve the crowding. We may be able to move tomorrow. We are rationing food fairly tightly.

Saturday 14 November 1953

Camp 5, 4800 feet

At 5.30 we pierced our igloo, but there was nothing to see except cloud and endless drift. The tent was bowing heavily everywhere. The space was slowly becoming more and more constricted so that we were more or less lying on top of each other. The barometer started to fall again, and continued all day.

At 7.30 I struggled out and got dressed and sat in the igloo which at least had light. The drift poured in through several air-holes. Some I re-blocked with snow. At the apex I left a hole over which the snow blew without much entering. Lighting a couple of stoves, we made cocoa and scrambled egg. Gradually we got dressed and just sat about under the snow. We didn't eat lunch (apart from a little barley sugar) as it was now urgent to conserve food for working days. The decision to descend is being forced upon us. Weather and lack of food (or lack of time to sit things out) may remove our chances of success.

No-one has ever been right under the peak as we are. With a single day's good weather and visibility we could probably reach the top, though there is always the chance of a three-day blizzard and we must allow perhaps a week for our return. Perhaps the most galling thought is that it will be extremely difficult to make another attempt.

In the afternoon, Freddie gallantly dug his way out of the igloo and tried unsuccessfully to locate the sled. However, he found some cigarettes which was a comfort. He returned white-glazed and spent an hour in the igloo getting rid of the snow. Then Peter went out, and he found the sledge under four feet of snow. He was able to send down much-needed fuel, a candle and some food. Evening meal half-ration pemmican stew, coffee and dried fruit. Freddie and I slowly prepared the tent for sleeping—we take turns in position—and we wriggled into our bags on either side, pressing hard against the snow-bulged walls. It takes an eternity to manoeuvre in such constricted space.

At Atlas Cove
Jack Hughes' birthday menu, 14 November 1953

SOUP :	Creme of Dieselene
ENTREE :	D4 Caterpillar Pie
JOINT :	Roast Crankshaft of Bull Seal
VEGETABLES :	Boiled Radiators, Centre Bearings with Powdered Graphite, Steamed Injectors
	Gravy X100
SWEETS :	Concrete Custard Electric Currants Petroleum Jelly
SAVOURIES :	Broken Drills served with Hard Words
DRINKS :	Range Fuel and Kerosene Punch Sump Oil—on tap in 44 gallon drums

(Atlas Cove station log)

Sunday 15 November 1953

Camp 5, 4800 feet

The barometer was still dropping. While I cooked breakfast in the dripping igloo, it steadied and for the first time in 26 hours showed an upward trend.

After breakfast I put my boots' outer-covers on and broke through the igloo. Visibility was nil. No sign of the tent below. I returned and sealed the igloo. It is no good just sitting here while the snow piles deeper. I went out again. From inside the tent they shoved an ice-axe up through the rear ventilator to show me the position of the tent. I commenced digging. My hole was finally about six foot deep. Gradually the rear end of the tent was uncovered.

The guys disappeared into the walls of snow and the snow-flap at the bottom was regelated in solid névé. Inch by inch we got everything free. We were able to lift the tent bodily out of its pit and re-erect it on the other side of the igloo. We made a ground-sheet connection with the tent and another entrance to the igloo from above. By about 11 we had finished our meal and were preparing for bed, here on top of the new snow. We have had a very busy day but are really happy to be on the surface once again.

At Atlas Cove

The men collected 15 dozen penguin eggs from Aubert de la Rue rockhopper rookery for the kitchen.

Worried about the mountain party, which had now been out for 14 nights, they sent up flares without getting any in response.

Nearly all the macaroni penguins at Corinth Head had laid their first eggs (the first egg of macaronis is smaller and rarely hatches a chick), and a few second eggs were appearing (Atlas Cove station log).

Monday 16 November 1953

Retreat

This morning the snow fell steadily and the wind howled. I got up and dressed and rolled my gear at about nine and urged the others till they did the same. The food situation was bad. We would have to take the risk of a descent through dense cloud, even over the crevassed ice ridges. We pulled down the tent.

After a small lunch—a couple of biscuits and some cheese—we pushed down the steep traverse of a great snow slope. It was extremely difficult to believe the compass. For a couple of hours we descended; slow, gruelling work, especially for Fred and Peter who had the side-slip of the sledge to control. When the altimeter showed that we should be up against the first great ridge of crevasses, there was a sudden clearing in the mist and there, right ahead of us, was the solitary marker we had left days before.

Through the crevasses it was infinitely slow, deadly careful work, probing the white emptiness. We found a route through to the site of our great crevasse camp, returned along our line of markers and retrieved sled and packs. Proceeding downward in dense cloud and driving blizzard, the great effort kept us warm. We pressed on towards our final marker—and a camp for the night next to the broken pediment crossing of the other crevassed margin of the Abbotsmith. The marker was only 50 yards ahead. Next thing I knew I was dangling on the rope, 20 feet down a crevasse! The suddenness of my fall was such that I hadn't even felt the jerk of the rope.

The crevasse narrowed to a foot or two 30 feet below; then there was just blackness. My ice-axe was caught in a coil of hauling rope and I was able to pull it up, but in so doing I lost one of my prized home-made gloves. In the same instant I became aware that a few yards behind me but some six or eight feet above, Peter was also down. That meant that Freddie was supporting both of us. Very rapidly I made a few niches with the axe and wedged myself, feet to shoulders, so that the strain was off the rope.

I wedged my way up about eight feet onto a ledge where I could stand. Peter had nearly reached the surface. After a while, I made myself secure and the others moved my climbing rope to a position vertically above me. I was then able to cut further niches and climb out while the main rope was kept taut.

Just as I got out there was a clearing in the cloud and we saw West Bay immeasurably far away and below us. In the same moment, 4000 feet and several miles distant, I glimpsed a flare. It was impossible to answer it before clouds filled the breach again.

It was about nine by the time we had the tent up. The intense cold—about 5°F—made it essential for us to get inside at the first possible moment. It took about two hours to scrape and brush away most of the snow and ice. Then we could light the stoves and prepare an extremely frugal meal. Food is now down to about 24 hours' supply of half-rations.

At Atlas Cove

Counted 239 nests in West Bay gentoo rookery. Collected 350 eggs from Rogers Head (Atlas Cove station log).

Tuesday 17 November 1953

In Retreat

Our 16th day, conditions much worse than yesterday. We made breakfast of biscuits fried in a little butter and drank our second-last brew of coffee. Then we went outside, but the weather was impossible. It is now mid-afternoon. We have sat in the tent, fully clothed, waiting for any sort of break and trying hard to keep warm. Fred has his feet in his gloves, inside his damp sleeping bag. I feel sure we will get through soon.

Later

At about 5.30 we made a pretty desperate effort to break through the cloud and blizzard. We had been sitting very cold for seven or eight hours, cramped in the tent, listening to the wild movement of the fabric. The end of our food, rationed now for more than a week, loomed.

There was nothing to indicate that the same conditions might not continue indefinitely, so we went out into the flowing ice. On a 120 foot rope it was just possible to see the shadow of the man at the far end. I probed incessantly with my ice-axe for crevasses. In three-quarters of an hour we moved something over 100 yards, leaving three bamboo markers for our return direction. But when I saw some big ice-hummocks looming up and found we were moving parallel with a great crevasse, we plodded back into the ice-laden wind. Our footprints were drifted over.

It was good to get back to the poor little tent. We made a little stew of pemmican and butter, much watered for we couldn't afford any other drink. It was one of the coldest and most restless nights imaginable.

Wednesday 18 November 1953

In Retreat

It was a grey, comfortless dawn. At about 7.30, a shadow of a frosted rope appeared on the brown japara! The sun! It seemed utterly impossible. Peter, in the middle the only man who could move, sat up to look through the ventilator. It was true. The mountain top was clear and we were above a vast bowl of cloud.

We dressed and ate our remaining biscuits and butter. The sun removed some of the frost so that the tent could be folded. We adjusted our goggles, and took some photographs. Queer hogs' backs and zeppelins of black cloud drifted about the high horizon.

We commenced the descent. Hard work urging the sled over crevasses, preventing side-slip and trying to keep our climbing rope taut. Probing frequently, we reached the broken pediment crevasses. We saw our marker beyond, and at last reached it. The Abbotsmith ice-falls were behind!

Then followed the long descent over sastrugi with immense lateral crevasses, deep blue and black. Sometimes we broke through with a leg but scrambled out without more trouble. Once the sled half dropped into a lower lip and caused us much difficulty. We spent hours belaying ropes on ice-axes driven into hard névé. Sometimes the surface was hard and blue, at others feet deep in drift. A furrow looking dangerously like a bridge would be secure; a smooth drift would conceal a pit.

At long last we reached the hollow where, perhaps 50 feet below the drift, was number 3 ice-house. Only one more crevasse. We ate some barley sugar. While we were sitting I heard voices distinctly and shouted. No reply. Then voices again.

We got up and tugged at the towing ropes. My foot found the final crevasse, the last dark, destructive hole. Then Arthur Gwynn, Ken Dalziel and Jim Brooks appeared over the skyline, roped and rucksacked. We made a joke in greeting. We ate chocolate and biscuits, and sucked from cans of fruit juice. Arthur led the way down over the smoother, un-crevassed slopes to the safe, flat Vahsel Glacier, and we plodded gladly behind. Their company was better than the benzedrine we had planned to take for the final miles.

The crossing of the Vahsel moraine used up almost all the energy we had. We fell forward on our towing ropes down 'Blizzard Alley' and reached the edge of the azorella. A new world of green and black, after 18 days of whiteness.

We left the sled at the edge of the snow. What from high above and miles away had seemed a tiny dark sea-level patch, became the weary miles of Windy City and the Nullarbor—snow-free and soft with dry sand, or hobbled with boulders. The harems had gone, leaving hundreds of irresponsible seal pups.

We reached the station at 6.30. It seemed as gay and bright as a Walt Disney cartoon. Familiar faces; very, very old friends. I stripped naked and bathed. We were all somewhat emaciated. There followed a meal and a ding. For the first time in my life, I couldn't finish a beer!

Now there is endless station work to keep me busy until the *Kista Dan* arrives. There is a curious peace of mind now that we have made a really firm attempt to climb our mountain. We had bad luck. Perhaps, by some miracle, there will be another chance, but the mind quails at the thought of the time needed for preparations. Perhaps the job will be left to someone else.

Thursday 19 November 1953

Our period away separated two very different landscapes down on the Anare Isthmus. Everywhere over the black lava the azorella gleamed as though transmitting light through green glass; the Olsen cliffs showed streams of black rock, Drygalski was colourful on all its ridges to the summit. Scarcely any snow remained at sea level. All round the station buildings lay the winter debris—splinters of wood, pieces of rope, a few old tins in soft black sand.

I composed a brief signal outlining our attempt. Arthur had not reported it until the fourteenth day. There was one signal from Phil 'anxiously awaiting details'. In the evening I was too restless to settle down to any one of the innumerable jobs I must do.

Friday 20 November 1953

Jack, Jim and I were up on the lava by the seismic hut, mixing concrete and building for a thousand years. Long after the last station building has disappeared, our concrete piers will remain four-square to the weather. Little short of another eruption will destroy them.

Arthur returned from Corinth Head and his penguins. Ken, holding the fort in the galley and also slushy, provided a fine dinner. The mess now has an excellent radio receiver. When reception is good programmes flow in from London, Melbourne, Moscow, Amsterdam. The station seems less isolated with the world entering the mess.

Sunday 22 November 1953

After dinner I gave an account of our mountain journey. We sat in deck-chairs in the rec, by warm stoves and with a couple of bottles of port for further comfort. Later some of us listened to the radio in the mess. We heard the BBC news extremely clearly—the young queen about to start on her Empire Tour. Men turn on the radio generally during or after meals. The other morning, suddenly, over a Radio Australia news session, there was quite a lengthy announcement concerning our efforts on Big Ben.

Penguin Cottage Pie for Dinner

'Stewed up minced adelie and gentoo penguins and made cottage pie. Found a recipe for Pineapple Betty so made it for sweets. Everyone seemed to enjoy it' (Fred Elliott, diary entry, 22 November 1953).

Monday 23 November 1953

All day it wept heavy, unceasing rain, soaking the already lifeless black sand and flattening the waves. Down on the beach a dozen black nellies performed a clumsy gavotte over some unpleasant remains of a once-living creature.

I cooked the lunch. There are endless tins—potatoes, carrots, soups, pineapple, cherries, goose-berries, milk, cream—and ample butter, eggs, flour, everything. All that is necessary is heating and disguise. I sliced ham and enclosed it in batter, browned by some essence, and fried the result, baked some potatoes, carrots and peas, and made a complicated soup and two large pots of coffee.

In the afternoon Arthur became absorbed in separating the yolks and whites of penguin eggs and weighing the first and second eggs of the clutches.

Tuesday 24 November 1953

Exceptionally high tides and big seas threatened to inundate the desolate grey Nullarbor. The hydrogen shack was almost isolated by the flowing tide and thick glutinous mud. Every man huddled at his work, except Dick and Bernie, who were away.

Cecil was slushy—nothing ever dampens his spirits. For people like Peter, Len, Dick, Jack and the radio staff, there are never-ending 'skeds and obs', 'weathers' to receive and concoct and send and interpret, meals to prepare, engines to maintain and service, morse-keys to tap and signals to listen to. For James there is the daily West Bay trudge, and scaling and computation. Yet this sort of work, faithfully carried out and not chronicled, is the whole reason for the existence of the station on Heard Island.

Wednesday 25 November 1953

A hundred years ago today, Heard Island was first sighted by the old American sealer whose name it now bears. Subsequent history appears almost as misted as the grey glaciers. Sealing operations were conducted on an extensive scale by rugged Americans who spent long years in stone huts, the broken walls of which remain alongside the rusted iron rendering pots. Apart from such unobtrusive relics nothing remains except almost certainly a good many burial mounds humping the azorella. The desolation that followed exploitation of the great elephant seals may have exceeded the natural state of the island, but it had largely recovered its seal population by the time it became an Antarctic base.

On various maps where it appears—frequently it is overlooked—it is marked as French, American or British. I had the jack raised and, following ANARE's suggestion, a celebration in the evening.

Towards lunchtime Dick and Bernie trailed into the station, weather-beaten but fit and well and full of enthusiasm. They had observed sooties, nellies and penguins of various kinds including two chin-strap penguins. With the adelie penguin which wandered fatally into the dog-lines last Saturday, and the king which Jim brought back from West Bay, we have now seen all the Antarctic penguins except the mighty emperor. Dick also noticed a number of kings at Red Island, apparently at home in the gentoo rookery.

We all had dinner at a big square table in honour of Len's birthday and the centenary of Heard. It was well supplied with sherry, chablis, burgundy and port. The day seemed overlong by 11.30 and I folded myself away, pretty tired.

Thursday 26 November 1953

Ken and Cec had their heads together on a 'homer' for the *Kista Dan*. 'That'll bring 'em down like a dog to a bone,' reckoned Ken at morning tea. The apparatus apparently will give the ship a constant signal during the voyage from Australia.

Leon went out and got a young bull seal—some of the meat was carried in to the galley for human consumption. He is a persistent, utterly reliable chap and often his work in bitter weather carries with it the need for a sense of humour and a streak of gallantry.

Friday 27 November 1953

Exact knowledge is at such a premium on Heard that men will frequently invent what seems reasonable and pronounce it with authority, rather than be silent—this morning at breakfast, sheep, breeds and habits and suitable locations on Antarctic and sub-Antarctic islands. Then it passed to goats on Campbell Island and livestock generally on South Georgia. The personnel, almost to a man, is engaged in scientific or technological work; all senses are tuned to accurate weighings and measuring, listening, seeing and thinking. The 'humanities' are not rated so high.

After dinner I continued printing until the film was finished. Washing is the big problem here, even using permanganate of potash as a hypo-eliminator and indicator. I swished the prints round in bowls of icy water until my hands ached with the cold. Then I laid them out on glass in the biology hut, using the glazing solution Cec and I made from the gall-bladder of a sea elephant.

Saturday 28 November 1953

I am longing to see the family and know again the soft, familiar places of home, but the thought of leaving Heard Island fills me with sadness. There is something splendid about rolling out of bed in the morning and donning windproof clothing and striding along the scalloped seashore that lies outside the door. To meet, instead of suburban cats and sleepy dogs, a score of great elephant seals and innumerable magnificent birds, the exquisite dominicans, the dark skuas; to feel the wind in a treeless world. To lift eyes to silver shrouded Olsen and the glowing azorella of Drygalski—all this cannot be taken for granted.

We wandered over the springy azorella, looking for skuas' nests. Everywhere were the burrows of divers, thousands of them which had returned for the summer. These South Georgian diving petrels excavate long tubular tunnels in the sandy parts of the plain, where there is sufficient stone to prevent collapse. Whether these dainty little black-and-white petrels return to the same burrows is uncertain but there seems to be some evidence that they do. After the plains have lain for months under thick ice and snow, the nesting-sites must require almost complete renewal. They are not seen in hours of daylight when they would be helpless victims of the fierce skuas. They only leave their nests at night or in the grey dusk and dawn. The Kerguelen diving petrels are similar in colour; they nest in the azorella tussocks.

Fred made off for the food dump he and Bernie had found at the base of the Schmidt Glacier. Jim and I soon joined him, and sat on what I think is Dovers' old station-made tent and ate sardines. There is a great stock of food there and we removed the tomato soup before replacing the rubber sheets covering the store.

Len's birthday ding—Jim and Fred's special menus, with Len's photograph, were much admired. Savouries, tomato soup (from the dump we had rifled), braised seal heart and a great variety of sweets. Hock, burgundy and sherry. The Queen's health was drunk; then Len's.

Sunday 29 November 1953

Dick and Ken ambled round Rogers Head collecting skuas' eggs, rather like thrushes' in colouring but the size of large hens' eggs, and those of Cape pigeons and rockhopper penguins. Several men are making collections—great white nellies' eggs, the rounder, dumpier ones of the gentoos, the delicate bluish-greens of the rockhoppers, the mottled skuas' and the Cape pigeons', unbelievably large for the bird—almost exactly like those of the domestic hens.

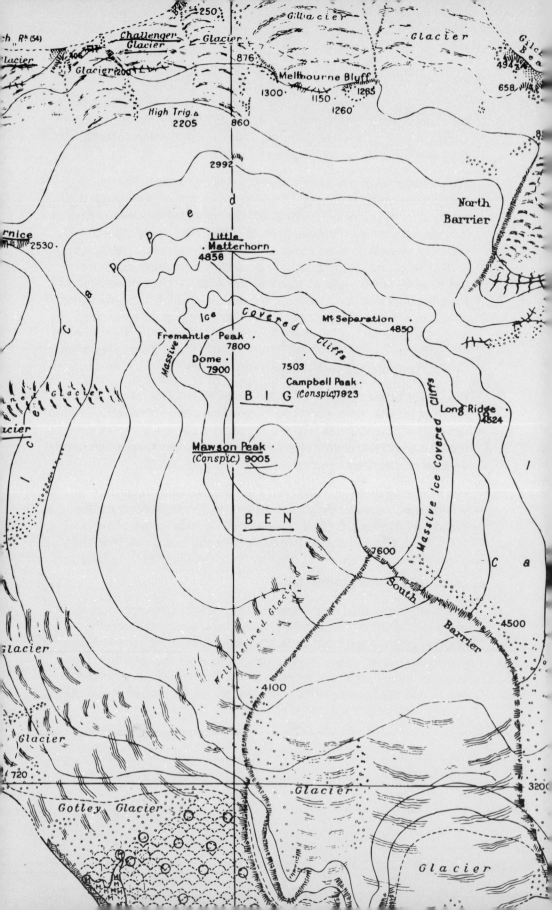

December 1953

Branding the Elephant Pups

Wednesday 2 December 1953

Richard McNair's birthday good wishes at breakfast. As cook he has made a magnificent contribution to our stay on Heard. We have never sat down to a meal without bright, clean table-linen; no slushy has ever lacked spotless tea-towels. Outside the galley he has been Arthur's most constant and enthusiastic assistant, tramping miles to report on birds and seals. He's a cheerful, level-headed fellow respected and liked by everyone. Not the least admirable aspect of Dick is his self-control. For the year he swore off grog (from his own accounts he was a confirmed drunkard up to the time he left Melbourne); he has stuck to his resolution unfailingly.

Leon removed the boards from the passage floor near the bathroom and collected Carrie's pups. He destroyed them shortly afterwards— an unpleasant but necessary task.

Jack, after a morning's rest, continued on number 1 engine. Last night at 11 o'clock I found him still working in a cloud of smoke and fumes. He had disconnected an exhaust to hear the sound of the engine, with the result that he had made himself ill.

Thursday 3 December 1953

Bernie was slushy—he has exchanged with Arthur to be free on Christmas Eve, when he has a great desire to camp on a glacier. Bernie is a true romantic. In his mind he wants to link up Christmas here with Christmas in Greenland.

Jack continued on number 1 engine (and by the evening had it to his satisfaction: 'No more bloody graphite!'). At lunch I had a tiff with Peter who had spent the morning painting the Dines mast, and had then washed his brushes in the troughs and left them lined with sticky red lead. He flares up when attacked on such trifles but cools down and is apologetic after. James is very pleased at the possibility suggested yesterday that he may be called upon to do some astro work along the coast of Antarctica after Dovers has been landed.

After lunch, I went with Arthur and Dick to brand seal pups at the far end of the cove. We had a couple of petrol blow-lamps burning in a sonde case, their flames directed into a heat-insulated kero tin where the irons were heated. Arthur bestrode a pup while Dick branded him, and I kept up the supply of the second irons and logged the letters used and the size and sex of the unfortunate animals. This year each pup is marked 'HC' — 'H' signifying Heard and 'C' the year 1953 — with letters AA, AB, AC, etc.

The branding is done on the tail, a short distance from the hind flippers. It does not penetrate the blubber and does not appear to cause more than momentary distress. It turned out a miserable afternoon, cold, with showers of rain and snow from the south-west. We branded 15 pups and were back at the station by six. The little 'porkies' will grow and roam the Antarctic seas, and most of them will come back to Heard Island. Some will attain vast bulk and be huge harem bulls, and some placid, shapeless cows. Future biologists will patrol the beaches looking for our brands.

Friday 4 December 1953

On the mountain, the crest has not been visible once since we came down on November 18th.

An unexpected leopard dozed above the tide-wash, a lean scrawny male tapering away to a concave belly; it is weeks since any came ashore along the cove. There were plenty of porkies; they are utterly carefree yet they wear the most worried expressions, funny wrinkled faces with an individuality that is lost when they become older. I saw one exactly like Dr Samuel Johnson. Yesterday, on our way back from branding, Arthur broke away a diver's burrow and found the two birds — beautiful little Kerguelens with the black leg stripe easily seen. He had to go down about a foot below the surface and more than a full arm's length from the entrance. I walked home into the wind. It's a pleasant time to ponder, walking back along the beach to a good breakfast — an omelette of penguin eggs.

In the afternoon I mounted photographs and filed negatives. Some of my prints seemed good. I became depressed, thinking of the mountain and the wonderful pictures that might have illustrated a successful climb, if only the weather had let up. A brief message came from Lorna; she was 'frantically busy with end-of-term' but somewhere within me I was irked and disappointed. The rain thudded softly yet heavily into the sand.

Saturday 5 December 1953

We really got down to it this morning. Arthur jumped the seals, waiting for the favourable moment to leap on their backs and hold them. The clusters of pups at the end of Atlas Cove now have a high percentage of branded members. We moved to a small azorella gully out of the wind and a few feet higher than the stench of a squalid huddle of elephant seals of various ages, and ate our sardines. Then Ken wandered off in search of skuas' eggs, and Arthur and I talked of the evolution of seals and their place in the *carnivora*. Ken was annoyed because Ron, who had promised to come out, hadn't materialized. Still, lately, Ron has apparently been much happier.

After some coffee Ken and I continued the day by painting the mess. The branders arrived back early; the blow-lamps had given trouble. Arthur took a brush and helped paint. For the first time in weeks the mountain cleared. Some day, someone will stand on the summit.

The BBC in London played request numbers for Dick, Ron and Leon, giving the Australian National Antarctic Research Expedition on Heard Island quite a build-up. They expressed great enthusiasm at including music for such an outpost. It seemed, suddenly, that for a few minutes the whole world was focused on minute Heard. Every word and note was almost fantastically clear. The Gounod 'Ave Maria' was sung; I shall never hear it again without watching hundreds of birds, black against the sea, and the beauty of the changing light on the mountain.

Sunday 6 December 1953

My day as duty cook. For about an hour I was busy frying ham and penguin eggs. Then Arthur, Dick, Jim and Jack set off in good weather for the albatross colony on the cliffs facing the Jacka valley and glacier. The mountain was still clear, but hard and white, waiting for cover which the north-east wind promised soon enough.

Dinner: two large mutton and bean pies, baking in the oven. The basis of everything today has been tins—four of potatoes, three cauliflower, four Scotch broth, two cherries, three tropical fruit salad, two herrings in tomato sauce, two kippers, two more potatoes, one cabbage, two asparagus, three onion soup. And I forgot the four tins of corned mutton! The food supplied to the station, supplemented with a good deal of seal, penguin and occasionally skua, leaves nothing to be desired. A man feels like nuts—walnuts, almonds, cashew nuts or any other kind—and they are instantly available. There are pure fruit juices, cordials, every kind of jam, cheeses, biscuits of several types, a great range of breakfast foods, crystallized fruits, wines. Dick makes perfect bread. There is ample good butter, marmalade, spices, essences. Every kind of fish and meat is available in tins.

My piecrust looked marvellous but the boys hurled the usual insults, asking whether I had used plaster of paris instead of flour, talking about pneumatic drills. They did justice to the meal, all the same. The excursionists had a good day: about a hundred black-browed albatross in the rookery, all sitting on eggs.

Monday 7 December 1953

This is the time of year, and of our term on Heard, when there is evidence of the strain some men feel. The nearer the relief boat comes, the harder it is to preserve normal tranquillity. *Minutiae* cause turbulence--the way a man talks, some imagined slight, some action that is thought inconsiderate. We are all affected.

Feeling the Strain

'Had row with Bech ... It has been brewing for a long while as I as well as most other chaps on the station are getting fed up with his pompous attitude. I told him finaliy that I had no wish to make any more attempts on Big Ben with him if he continued his attitude' (Fred Elliott, diary entry, 7 December 1953).

Tuesday 8 December 1953

The excitement of the day was Ken's operation. He had a small mole-like lump on his leg which Arthur had promised to remove. Arthur and Jim seemed to spend all the morning preparing the operating table, theatre and in sterilizing instruments and scrubbing. The job was carried out using a local anaesthetic.

Pierre Sicaud called me tonight over the radio. Although I heard most of what he said, he couldn't receive me very clearly. The French relief ship will be arriving at Kerguelen in about a week and Sicaud will return to France. There will be no chance of meeting him and his colleagues in person. Perhaps they will always remain just welcome voices, neighbours who helped relieve that loneliness of the ocean.

Wednesday 9 December 1953

Blizzardly conditions in a sou'west wind. A somewhat uninviting prospect for the West Bay walk; still, it snows here at least 300 days a year.

On the way back, head down and dreaming, with my eyes on the fine snow, I walked up to a fine, large bull elephant seal and might have stumbled on him, but he gave just one brief frog-like croak, on full volume, and looked at me with careless scorn. I find it very hard to analyze or describe the snorts, snuffles and croaks of elephant seals. They bellow on so low a note that you can easily appreciate the individual vibrations; there is often, in the briefer sounds, a bell-like quality but completely without sustaining reverberation; they belch foully and noisily.

Breakfast: Ron slushy, with Ambrose Heath's *Good Puddings and Pies* ('Not so good,' says Dick, 'It's mostly taken straight out of Mother Beattie's book'). Perhaps my 'concrete' piecrust of last Sunday was responsible. 'There was nothing wrong with it,' said Dick, encouragingly, 'Except that you left out the baking powder!'

At morning tea Leon announced that he had a job for someone—helping him 'worm' the dogs. The unpredictable Peter instantly volunteered to assist in the cold, miserable job of trudging round the dog-lines.

Friday 11 December 1953

A walk to West Bay in mild weather. Four gentoos strolled up for a chat, surveying me with great interest. Sea elephants frollicked on the plains. They lift their weight onto their flippers and hurl their bulk forward in a sort of rippling movement, the brunt of which is taken by their bellies, every organ of which is bounced up and down and back and forth with considerable violence.

We emptied the depleted Furphies until they were dry, and even then only half-filled the tank. Unless we have soaking rains, we shall be forced to cart water from the glacier. Everyone was very cheerful in the rare sunshine.

We gathered in the radio room to hear 'Calling Antarctica', an unusually good session. The *Kista Dan* is leaving for Macquarie tomorrow, earlier than expected. It may be she will reach Heard earlier and possibly have more time south.

Saturday 12 December 1953

Today spent branding elephant seal pups. We sat on the sledge looking out over the sparkling cove and along the impressive wall of Olsen's cliffs. The days may sometimes pall and often we may feel glad at the thought of relief, but this place would take a lot to equal it for grandeur.

At the northern end of South West Bay were sprawled at least 200 porkies and a number of older beasts, including some fine clusters of large bulls. We took the sledge right in amongst them. The process was much swifter than the portable blow-lamp forge. The most tiring job is waiting for the correct moment, rapidly bestriding the seal, sitting down on its back and holding him firmly on each side of the neck while the branding, measuring and sexing is performed. A porky up to five feet three inches long and weighing 300 to 400 pounds takes a lot of holding. All the time he is endeavouring to snap but fortunately his teeth are not very large. After holding down about six or eight pups I was extremely tired. Arthur must have 'ridden' several dozen. By 1 o'clock we had branded about 70.

We moved up to the slopes of Mount Andrée for lunch. A tiny Wilson's storm petrel, home to nest after spending the southern winter in the northern hemisphere, flew out into the driving snow from the azorella, seeming so swift and fragile as the snow-flakes themselves.

Sunday 13 December 1953

After lunch Arthur asked for my company on a walk to Corinth Head to see his macaroni penguin family. I can never tramp over the soft azorella hummocks, past quiet pools, over broken lava mossed by small olive-green hemispheres, without wild, vicarious joy for the 13-year-old boys who should be here. The lava uplands would give them sheerest delight, wonderful places to hide in and to explore. What grand natural historians some of them would become, knowing the ledges where nest the gentle sooty albatross, finding the crevices of the fairy prions and the green tunnels of the doves.

Skuas dive-bombed us whenever we walked close to a nest. It is hard to understand, as they possess no natural enemies. They swoop down to within a few inches of our heads at tremendous speed. It is intimidating. The average skua wing-span is fully three foot six inches. All over the lava and azorella are the wings of prions and divers caught emerging from their tunnels and torn to pieces. Prions are seldom caught on the wing for they can twist and turn and evade the fury of a skua's attack.

Everywhere one looks, Heard Island cries out to be visited. Sometimes one imagines that here, someday, there will be men and women and children living in strong stone houses. If human life could be established here long enough—but there is no sufficient reason—it might give Heard Island what, in reality, it will always lack, a literature and legend.

Soon we reached a hole in the lava where a tunnel of buckled lava had collapsed. Extending far into the shadows were dozens of rockhopper penguins complaining of our presence. Arthur soon spied a ringed bird but it retreated down the black tunnel. Some distance away there was another opening to the light, so I walked over the top to this hole and waited while Arthur shepherded the flock underground. Then I caught the little fellow and Arthur was able to take his measurements and observe how the ringing had stood the test of several months in the Antarctic seas.

He also made the exciting discovery of many nests of the fairy or cliff prion, formerly only known to nest in almost inaccessible narrow cracks and crevices in the cliffs. By torchlight, one could see them sitting on their eggs, exquisite, fragile blue-grey little petrels with characteristic black-tubed bills and bright eyes shining. I went down and brought one up to photograph. So fine and delicate are these prions that when they are flitting like swallows below the cliffs they seem almost transparent.

Monday 14 December 1953

Arthur asked me whether I could photograph the penguins for him. Following my inclination rather than my conscience, I agreed willingly. There is now so much to be done on the station.

The rookery, about 2000 pairs, climbs the steep rock and scree slope rising from Corinthian Bay to the brink of the largest crater. Macaronis are possibly unique. Soon after the second egg is laid, the hen sits for half the incubation period while her husband is away feeding at sea. Then the watch is reversed; the husbands are welcomed ecstatically and given charge of the stony little nest. About five days elapse between the laying of the first and second egg. Although both eggs are fertile, only the second, larger, egg is hatched. If the second egg is stolen or broken, the first may be brought to fulfilment.

Towards the end of October the males arrive, racing in from the sea, leaping out of the water as though pursued. And of course they often are, by hungry grey leopards! They advance on the rookery and peg out their claims. Ten days later arrive the females. They soon get together. Some unfortunates miss out, for the hens are in a minority. The courting and stone-gathering and pilfering are very active for about a week, at the end of which the first eggs are laid. Amongst the penguins strut the snow-white sheathbills, industriously thieving the eggs of their hosts. We returned in worsening weather in time for a late lunch.

In the long twilight after dinner, Ron, Leon and Dick sat yarning round their fire, rendering down seal blubber in a small bay of the azorella.

Bernie at the piano, introspectively: 'John! For you it is different. You have your lady and your children who are thinking of you. You live in them but me, I am alone. Down here on Heard Island I am a ghost!'

Tuesday 15 December 1953

In the darkroom I exposed some mountain enlargements, which make one dream of a second chance. Blizzard snow raced across the Nullarbor, whitening the windward slopes of every minute depression. At the same time an immense many-layered lenticular cloud towered above the black sea-bound gloom, each vast circle resting on the one below, fabulous architecture of the sky, faintly tinged with rose when the rest of the world was cold as the ocean.

I re-read odd chapters of Gilbert White. How good it would be to write such a natural history of Heard Island! But the days are too short. Midnight found me restless in my bed, in sheets that should have been changed this week, surrounded by spectres of things that must be done.

Friday 18 December 1953

A very soft, grey morning. Both water-tanks were empty down to the black sand sediment, so I decided to take a team to South West Bay with the empty Furphies. We scraped and jarred over the stony places until we reached the waterfall gully, but the waterfall was dry when we arrived. It is erratic in its flow. Sometimes it is immense, yielding thousands of gallons per minute; at other times it provides not even the merest trickle. I wonder whether its intermittent action could be caused by thermal action. About half-an-hour after our arrival it suddenly commenced and what had been a dry rock-face was inundated. We loaded about 750 gallons, too much for the tractor. The sledge sank deep and in the end it was necessary to 'winch' the load 20 or 30 yards at a time. Slow, heavy and cold work.

Skuas gathered in case we should disturb any divers. One poor little bird panicked and flew out into the wide, cruel daylight. Instantly the skuas were in pursuit, overtaking the bird in its straight, swift flight and seizing its small body. Four or five joined in the chase of the successful hunter, and when it tried to alight it relaxed its grip. The diver flew away as though unharmed, but the skuas had it again within a second and tore it to pieces.

Steady soaking rain continued all night; the tank of course overflowed.

Arthur Gwynn, Leon Fox and Cec O'Brien crossing the sharp volcanic rubble,
probably on the Laurens Peninsula, 1953.

Photograph: Fred Elliott

The remains of a sealers' stone hut, Corinthian Bay, 2002.

Photograph: Bernadette Hince

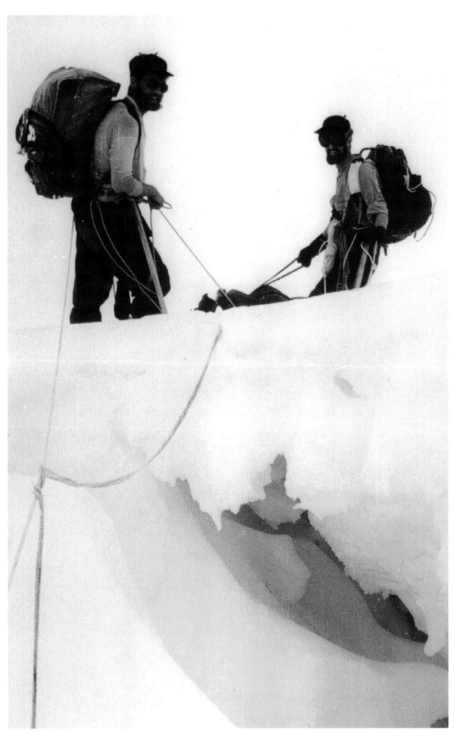

Fred Elliott and Peter Shaw on the Abbotsmith Glacier during the attempt on Big Ben, 1953.

Photograph: John Béchervaise

Branding a 'porky' (young elephant seal), Heard Island, 1953. 'Future biologists will patrol
the beaches looking for our brands,' wrote Béchervaise on 3 December 1953.

(L to R) Dick McNair, Cec O'Brien and Arthur Gwynn
Béchervaise Papers, National Library of Australia, MS7972

The Ross seal, a rare visitor to Heard Island, 25 September 1953.

Photograph: John Béchervaise
Béchervaise Papers, National Library of Australia, MS7972

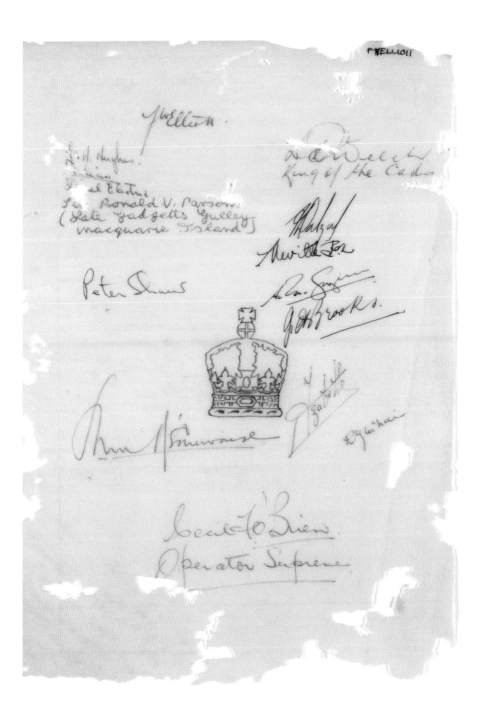

Cover of the menu of the celebratory meal held on Heard Island for the
Coronation of Queen Elizabeth II, 2 June 1953.

THE CORONATION OF HER MAJESTY QUEEN ELIZABETH THE SECOND

CELEBRATION DINNER

HEARD ISLAND

BILL OF FARE

RELISH : Glaciated Egg
        Atlas Cove Anchovies
SOUP : Cream of Mother Carey Chicken
FISH : Balmoral Salmon
       Cave Bay Cod
ENTREE : Antarctic Penguin Breast
         Station Skua
         Seal Steak ANARE
JOINT : Roast Drygalski Mutton
VEGETABLES : Potatoes, Peas, Carrots, Parsnips,
             Snow Cured Kerguelen Cabbage
             Royal Mint Sauce
SWEETS : Edinburgh Pudding with Philip Sauce
         Peach Elizabeth
SAVOURIES : Stuffed Heard Penguin Pie
            Patty of Fatted Sheathbill Liver

Azorella Olives   Crevassed Cheeses

    Brandy   Wines

              Liqueurs
              Iced Beer

_____

The menu of the celebratory meal held on Heard Island for the
Coronation of Queen Elizabeth II, 2 June 1953.

Reproduced by permission of Fred Elliott

Surplus to requirements: sardine cans rusting in their box, Atlas Cove, 2002.
Béchervaise wrote on 4 December 1953, 'We moved over the wind-sculptured stones
to a small azorella gulley out of the wind and a few feet higher than the stench of
a squalid huddle of elephant-seals of various ages, fat, dirty, away from the sea and
content to remain amidst their ordure. We ate our sardines.'

Photograph: Bernadette Hince

Elephant seal pups among nineteenth-century try pots used for
rendering-down elephant seal blubber, Corinthian Bay, 2002.

Photograph: Bernadette Hince

The *Kista Dan*, on which the men of 1953 returned from
Heard Island to Australia in early 1954.

Monday 21 December 1953

A flood of Christmas cables came in, personal ones for nearly every man, many from other islands and groups wishing us well. Sir Douglas Mawson congratulated the mountain party on 'a record climb'.

Tuesday 22 December 1953

One of the most settled spells we have had for the entire year. Think of the different story that would have been told had our mountain climbing coincided with a week's weather even half as fine. It would take a week of pretty hard work to prepare for another attempt, and it is impossible to take that week, let alone the time of the ascent itself. Owing to the earlier departure by the *Kista Dan* for Macquarie Island, we can count no more than a month to the time the vessel will be lying in the Roads. If we all work every hour of that time, we may just be ready.

In the morning a velvet-grey mist slid in along Atlas Cove. Gradually the mountain cleared until it stood out in all its fantastic beauty. All day, wherever men worked, they had beauty and majesty that perhaps we shall never know again. The meteorologists watched a sonde balloon reach a lonely height of 65,000 feet, more than twice as high as Everest!

I 'emu-paraded', burning all the rubbish I could find. Fred balanced dangerously round the conical sections of the rawin hut, dabbing with red-lead. James, Arthur and Dick painted at West Bay, completing the absolute house and making a sound start on the variometer house. Peter wandered round making the theodolite screen, snow-gauge and other odd items a brilliant buttercup (the yellow enamel was prised, not without some gloom, from old Jack. I discovered, tucked below his benches, a great stock of other paint lifted quietly from the paint store). The station is acquiring the look of a newly dressed shop window—quite a place to inherit. How pleasant to be about to land and start the year all over again.

Wednesday 23 December 1953

Towards lunchtime Dick arrived in the biology hut with a large, grey-headed nelly which had struck an aerial stay. It had been dazed but otherwise uninjured. Arthur found its weight to be 15 pounds and its wing spread six feet ten inches. While Arthur measured the beak, culmen and mandible and overall length, it was gently bound with transparent Scotch tape, extremely baffling and thwarting for the big prehistoric-looking giant petrel. When we released him he ran madly downwind without becoming airborne. We watched him calm down, smooth his ruffled feathers, assume his uncouth dignity, turn into the wind and wheel away.

Thursday 24 December 1953

The Christmas lanterns which I bought years ago in England and have been hung each year at home, are now brightening the mess. Christmas without children, without bright stores and the rush of traffic.

For Bernie Izabelle, Christmas Eve has the utmost significance. For weeks he has been talking about the day. I invited him to accompany me to West Bay and visit the sooty albatrosses on Mount Andrée. We conversed in unequal French most of the way round the cove. James was painting when we arrived but soon set up his instruments—the dip circle, the magnetometer (Lloyd Creek pattern), the 'QHM' (quartz horizontal magnetometer) and the 'BZM' (magnetometric zero balance)— and went to great pains to explain them.

We had lunch then sallied out to see the skuas and their chicks. It would be hard to imagine fiercer and more devoted parents. They scream and wheel round, making great threatening swoops, landing back within a few protective inches of their fluffy little khaki chicks. An adult skua standing with black beak wide open and magnificent wings raised like the heraldic German eagle is glorious to behold, the predator of the Antarctic lands, a carrion bird and tireless scavenger. There must have been a dozen nests in an acre or two of azorella. With no apparent enemies it is difficult to understand why the skuas have perfected such ferocity of defence. Compared with the magpie, he is as an eagle to a sparrow.

We scrambled up the cliffs to the beautiful sooty albatrosses. They are the most gentle birds imaginable and probably the most beautiful large birds on the island. They sit patiently on their airy nests, tranquilly watching their fellows off duty wheeling magnificently below. I was easily able to climb to a nest and sit right beside the dusky bird. She moved to let me stroke her plumage. After I had been sitting completely fascinated next to the albatross for some five or 10 minutes, another bird landed right beside me and proceeded to talk to his mate. Then a third came. It was an experience to remember forever.

Bernie decided that he wanted to take a rockhopper from the far end of the bay. He would kill it and mount the bird, and take it back to France with his leopard seal skull. Such trophies have little appeal for me—I can imagine them covered with dust, moth-eaten travesties of the living spray-washed birds. I looked for stones while Bernie committed his little murder. After a time he joined me looking very solemn and unhappy, the bird in his bag.

I folded my Christmas cards before dinner and laid out an ample table of wines. After the meal Peter provided cigars. In the final hour of the day, I addressed all the cards and cancelled the stamps with the Heard Island postmark. At midnight I found Jack about to turn off the lights. He gladly agreed to keep the power on while I played my Christmas record. So in the first minutes of Christmas Day on Heard Island, I listened to Lorna, Mary, Lin, P.J., Elizabeth, Judith, William and Anne singing 'The Twelve Days of Christmas'.

Friday 25 December 1953

Christmas Day

A dull day, grey and nondescript, the weather completely neutral. On the whole, men's thoughts were far away from Heard Island. By six everyone had gathered in the decorated mess. Big 'pilot' balloons had been painted with topical caricatures by Fred, and the scraps of Christmas decorations I had brought from Australia gave the place a festive air. Someone had hung a Kerguelen cabbage over the door as mistletoe.

The meal started rather self-consciously. Fred's Christmas menus, Dick's wonderfully dressed table with every kind of savoury and cake and sweet, the decorations, all just brooded for a while. Then gradually reserve broke down. I proposed only two toasts, 'To those we love!' and 'To ourselves'. Bernie presented everyone with little view-books of Paris. The Met men presented everyone with 'certificates of merit' for the releasing of sonde and rawin balloons. Everyone was very happy in the end, wearing caps from the Christmas crackers (which my sister Mary had thoughtfully provided) and shouting loudly across the table. Once again I played my Christmas record and those who hadn't heard it in the morning gathered round. Then we all washed up and repaired to the rec room to see the only film that had not been previously screened, *Edison, the Man*, with Spencer Tracey.

Monday 28 December 1953

The prions are spinning through the air in great numbers. It seems quite unknown, why they swarm in this way. How like swifts they are, swifts pursuing numberless insects, but here there are no flying insects.

The small and fragile prions could weave circles round the skuas, whose only chance lies in stealth by a burrow in the azorella, the merciless swoop while the little bird is adjusting its vision from total darkness to sky-wide light.

It is no longer the fashion to attribute sheer joy of living and delight in performing dangerously to the actions of birds. In the absence of any other explanation it is possible that the birds are making familiarization flights. Often by the light from the station windows, especially when the air is confused with mist, one glimpses the swift flitting of wings. Many of the smaller birds are nocturnal feeders. Some, both prions and divers, fall prey to the confusion of the station, a vast malicious geometry in the gloom, offset by unimaginable blisses of light. Doubtless the air-weaving is an annual, rhythmical festival. Year after year, 'all this juice and all this joy' [from Gerard Manley Hopkins' poem *Spring*].

In Chippy's I find things saved magpie-fashion, bound to be useful in the long year. They remain unmoved. We arrived on an Antarctic island back in February. What numberless things we shall do! There is plenty of time, endless time. Then, for a while the weeks race but the months pass slowly in a queer stroboscopy. Now we are all busy putting our estate in order. No-one will ever know all we have done.

Tuesday 29 December 1953

I wished Fred happiness on his twenty-fifth birthday. He is certainly a very popular member of this party.

Thursday 31 December 1953

I spoke over the phone to Gerrit Prinsloo, on Marion Island, over 1400 miles distant. We could hear each other pretty clearly. After that I wandered up to the grave of Dick Hoseason and Forbes. At the base of the cross, Fred had been attaching the memorial plates. The Hoseason one had been altered by Fred to read correctly. 'John' had been altered to 'James' by brazing in the letters and then etching with nitric acid.

So the working year ended in a crowd of small labours. Towards evening the mountain cleared. It's only weeks now before we'll see the mountain for the last time. We had a fine Old Year dinner, charging glasses from a bottle of Corio (all the whisky we possess) and drinking to 1954. We joined hands and sang 'Auld Lang Syne' at our local midnight, half-way between Melbourne and London. The end of a wonderful year.

January 1954

The *Kista Dan* Arrives

Friday 1 January 1954

I went to the bathroom and was appalled to see that the kerosene heater had been on fire during the night. The heater was black with burnt paint mixed with little dobs of solder, blistered paint stretched up the side of the main storage tank to the ceiling. Had the fuel tank been full, a serious fire could not have been avoided. Fire, the greatest dread of an Antarctic station. The dread of fire had several times rolled me out of bed in the middle of the night to make a tour of all stoves and heaters. I feel sure that water in the fuel caused the flue to catch fire.

Down by the cutter a large leopard seal had hauled out. All day long he made strange and sometimes melodious noises, once a sort of chromatic scale of high-pitched notes.

Sunday 3 January 1954

Nineteen years ago today I was married. It is as good a memory as the years that lie since, and Lorna and I exchanged anniversary cables in almost precisely the same words. It was grand after breakfast this morning, sitting in brilliant, warm sunshine watching the skuas blowing against the sky and hearing all the dogs barking.

Sometime tomorrow the *Kista Dan* is due to leave Melbourne for Heard Island. Within three weeks we should see new faces, receive mail and feel the world again with us. It is not a prospect of unalloyed pleasure.

Monday 4 January 1954

A drizzly day with occasional unenthusiastic snow. Everyone is extremely busy; it is a testing time for men's tempers. Ken spent a good part of the day repainting the bathroom, partly because of the soot left by the heater fire and partly because the continuous fire over months has grimed our previous work. Arthur concentrated on his logs, and Len and Jack continued painting and re-conditioning the cutter. Len never fails to come up from his task complaining of the cold and the general difficulties of his labours. He's really tremendously proud of his painting and everyone must be kept informed of its progress.

Tuesday 5 January 1954

All day long there have been thunderous ice-falls from the faces of the glaciers overlooking the sea. We sometimes sighted the falls themselves, thousands of tons of ice seeming to fall slowly, silently, raising clouds of spray to a height of a hundred or more feet, and all over before the sound reached us. All along the coast the grey seracs are slowly toppling as the ice-face is undercut by the waves. Long after the position of the ice seems to be fantastically defying all the laws of gravity, the pinnacles and leaning towers remain firm—until suddenly, without the least warning or indication, the vast masses topple. There must have been about 20 major ice-avalanches during the day.

A great gathering of terns appeared along the cove today, both Arctic and Antarctic species flying together and 'fishing' at the mouth of the broad tidal stream flowing down from the Nullarbor. Arthur and I went down to look at the exquisite birds more closely. The Antarctic terns are mainly blue-grey, with sooty black heads and bright red bills. Their Arctic cousins, who have flown the length of the world, are generally smaller and have white heads, black beaks and feet, and a less definite colouring, often brownish. The terns hovered with swiftly beating wings over the small waves, beautifully clear-cut against the grey screes beyond Atlas Cove, their sleek heads thrust downward towards the water, their bodies often a motionless core to the flurry of their wings.

The *Kista Dan* left Melbourne yesterday and should be here in 12 days or so.

Wednesday 6 January 1954

It seems strange that, although right throughout the year men have kept plugging along, there should now be still so much to do. The painting, of course, has depended largely on the weather and normally the entire month of January can be given to it. The early relief has deprived us, in a sense, of nearly a month. We could use 30 men.

All through the night the heavy ice-falls continued. I worked out in number 1 store, experiencing for the thousandth time surprise that in the quiet night there should never be the rustle or squeak of a mouse, nor the flight of a moth round the lamp.

Thursday 7 January 1954

Peter tells me that December was the calmest month so far recorded on Heard; a mean wind of 14 knots I think he said.

Bernie helped Leon to hunt seals into the station. There are now so many wandering up in the azorella that with patience it is possible to drive them. The three that Leon brought down were all shot to fill the meat boxes for the dogs going south.

Friday 8 January 1954

A wild, wet day, the glaciers looking very grey, old and eroded. Peter, Fred and I still toy with the idea of another attempt while the *Kista Dan* is away.

Ken made a great mess in the bathroom with his washing. He is easily encouraged and easily disheartened but his moods don't last very long. At times he possesses a grand enthusiasm but he frequently wilts. Arthur made inventories all day, striding determinedly between the surgery, Chippy's and number 1 store. He has an amazing single-mindedness when he is on a job. He is full of nervous energy, lean of body and buttocks, sharp of tongue and yet retiring, unexpectedly bawdy at times, never suffering fools gladly and doing nothing unless he is certain it's worthwhile.

It is midnight. The wind has been steadily rising and the rain lessening. It will seem strange to return to a comparatively windless world.

Saturday 9 January 1954

A vile day—very windy and wet. From now on until after the boat arrives it will be just one long day interrupted by guilty sleep. Every man is very busy; it is increasingly difficult to take men away for general station assistance. So I worked alone and felt miserable. The day just rushed. When the evening came I cancelled all my plans and attended the film—*Weekend at the Waldorf*—and went to bed before midnight.

Wednesday 13 January 1954

Another non-stop day for everyone. At midday a message from Phil Law stated that he would require some helpers for the Continent and suggested, apart from Gwynn and Brooks, Dalziel, Elliott and Welch. He also stated 'require you remain OIC Heard until our return, as new OIC not yet chosen'.

That was that. In one sentence were lost the alternatives of going south or having another crack at the mountain. I cannot recall ever a keener shock of disappointment. Poor old Len's hopes were dashed later in the day when a cable requested him to remain in charge of Met while Peter went south. The only man who was outspoken in his disappointment is Jack. Still it is grand news for old Fred, Peter is quietly elated and Ken runs round like 'a dog with two tails'.

Friday 15 January 1954

A gusty, unpleasant day, cold and filled with grit. I worked with Jim, Fred and Arthur at clearing up dumps round the camp. The worst eyesore, an entire old aeroplane engine, we winched away from near the hospital. The timber and iron dump has grown but is reasonably useful now. We unloaded and loaded until our arms were stretched.

Then we finished and at 7.30 sat down to a final 1953 party dinner-ding. I had put out all the wines necessary plus a bottle of brandy. I was conscious of a sort of finality about the evening. We drank mulled claret, laughed at old jokes, anticipated the speech of the films (which most of us can now quote from memory) and were as merry as ever. The evening ended at 12.30; the last real relaxation before the arrival of the *Kista Dan*.

Saturday 16 January 1954

A furiously busy day in weather calm and grey with a moistness turning to light rain. Arthur packed in the biology hut, surrounded by broken cases and sawdust—skulls, jars, bones and all the collections of a long, busy year. Midnight saw bright lights still. Ken, Cec and Jack had been painting the engines all evening until they looked like bright red and green toys.

Sunday 17 January 1954

The quiet day was accompanied by innumerable little explosions as cans of condemned fish-paste flew apart in the incinerator drums.

Monday 18 January 1954

Every man on the station has been brought up to concert pitch. I am proud of their efforts. Looking back over nearly a year I recall little but happiness. Now, there is a ship only a few miles out beyond the grey sea mists. Before another day has passed, it will lie swinging at anchor in the Atlas Roads. New faces, mail. The heavy disappointment at not going south with the *Kista Dan* will fade, for it cannot be sustained while new enthusiastic men are taking up life on the station.

From lunchtime onwards we had telephone skeds with the ship. We heard that the *Kista Dan* would arrive in the Roads at about 2.30a.m. tomorrow. Tomorrow!

Tuesday 19 January 1954

Cec was on radio watch throughout the night. He awakened me at 2.30. The *Kista Dan* was below Rogers Head, fairly rough sea, probably coming in. Nothing to be done and I turned over and went to sleep, requesting another report after the 4a.m. sked.

Four a.m. is the deadest time of a night's sleep. Again Cec beside me. 'She's in the Roads, John. No, nothing further. Another sked at eight.' I slept for another three hours, had breakfast, saw the *Kista Dan*, a fine small steamer rolling in the fiord-like narrows under a low, sombre sky.

Soon after nine came the order to take the cutter out. A great big circle was closing. I felt no particular elation and wondered why. We chugged out against the slop, bouncing through keen spray, bungled things a bit and came in on the second run. There weren't many familiar faces. We tossed up a rope rather unprofessionally and tied up. I went up the ladder and found myself shaking hands with Phil. He looked tired and drawn; they'd had a rough voyage. There was a good deal of activity. Mail-bags, the personal gear of those going ashore, Phil's cameras— there seemed dozens of them—and two or three men other than Phil Sweetensen came. Gore, who had been on Heard, the new radio chief, came. He has oriental blood. An incredibly young-looking medical officer, Budd, was there. After about 10 minutes of lowering bags and rather chaotic conversation we were on our way back. And that's all I saw of the *Kista Dan* except from a distance.

Phil was anxious to commence unloading. One pontoon was unloaded. Twelve sheep were brought ashore and before I could intervene were turned loose on the beach. There was no time to retrieve the situation. After a brief attempt to drive them towards the dog-yard we had prepared, they had to be forgotten and were allowed to stray away towards Corinthian Bay to find what sustenance they could.

Load after load came ashore, men in waders grabbing pontoon ropes, the tractor hauling sledges. We stopped briefly for lunch—seal meat which Phil enjoyed greatly. We were too busy to count time. The stacks grew higher and longer. Dusk brought rain and early darkness. We dragged tarpaulins out and covered the stacks. Finally we worked by searchlight.

Phil asked to be called at four. I saw that all men ashore were bedded, mostly in the Nissen hut. Thompson, swearing vigorously, reclaimed his wet rucksack from the sloppy cutter drawn up on the beach. The day had brought 15 or 20 new acquaintances. Some I took to instantly, some I wondered about. Only one fellow, very assertive and with vulgar tongue, I disliked.

I glanced through mail before a very short night's rest. I found myself choking a little as I read dozens of letters full of affection breaking in through the long months and the broad sea. One letter from Charles Holmes telling me that my work in Melbourne with *Walkabout* had ceased to exist. Disenchantment and disillusionment coming into my little Heard Island bedroom in envelopes, piled up with the beauty and tranquillity of friends and loved ones.

Wednesday 20 January 1954

The whole camp was moving soon after four, floating the great elephantine rubber pontoon, loading the RTA crates onto sledges.

The greatest effort was that of Dovers in driving the heavy caterpillar tractor up a crazy ramp overlying one of our sleds onto a pile of criss-crossed sleepers almost awash in the rising tide, a job I should have hesitated to ask anyone to do. Bob confidently drove the dangerously tilting tractor, and remained unperturbed as parts of the ramp broke away under its weight. Momentarily there appeared the danger that the machine might fall over backwards, but with a great roar it surmounted the angle and came to rest squarely on top. Arthur had been murmuring, 'Someone will be killed if this is kept up!' and even Phil was too preoccupied to think of using his camera. Bob came down out of the tractor seat smiling quietly. 'There was plenty to spare,' he reckoned.

Phil made a tour of the station and seemed very satisfied. We walked along the beach to West Bay, investigating Jim's magnetic station. The weather was constantly worsening, a nor'easterly with cold rain, backing north. The brief occasion was the only time during the changeover when Phil and I talked together. The ship sounded its hooter over the grey rainy sea and we hurried back. The Atlas Roads are no comfortable anchorage and it seemed likely that the *Kista Dan* would put to sea.

There were quite a few extra men ashore, left stranded. I scuttled round finding dry clothes—overalls and singlets and flying-boots—and arranging places for them to sleep. There was a sort of confused relaxation in the mess. The place was hopelessly overcrowded; men stood eating their meal from the surrounding shelves, drinking their beer the best they could. Phil played the piano. Most people drifted off to bed pretty quickly, the long days beginning to tell.

Thursday 21 January 1954

Another early start, but the weather foiling everyone's efforts. The cove was white-capped and gusts came out of the sou'west bringing snow and sleet. Phil decided to abandon the effort of launching the cutters and pontoon. It was grim work, wading up to the armpits in the ice-cold sea. Dovers was of an entirely different opinion. 'It's nothing,' he muttered, 'I go fishing in weather like this!' And he probably does.

Eventually the weather abated and gradually we got all the gear on the pontoon. The mean weather drove most of the chaps back to the shelter of the station as soon as they had nothing further to do. Just before Phil left he thanked me for my part in things. I said that I hoped he'd give me a trip down south some day and he said, 'How'd you like to take over the station for a year?'

Leon and I waited until the cutters were under way, drenched with spray. Fred, James, Arthur, Ken and Peter were aboard. 'Heard Island 1953' was really over.

I put out a few wines and a bottle of brandy to celebrate the first meal of the new 'mixed' party. The new men are Vic Cleland (weather observer), Keith Lodwick (geophysicist), John Gore (radio), George Delahoy (radio operator), Jack Walsh (Met observer), Grahame Budd (doctor), and Lin Gardner (engineer).

So we are now 15, with about six weeks to go before the 1953 party is reunited for the homeward voyage.

There is one member of the 1954 party whom I don't know even slightly; Henderson, who spent most of the changeover on the *Kista Dan*. I can see Phil's difficulty in appointing an officer in charge, the uncertainty (according to Phil) being the reason he requested me to remain on the island. Sweetensen, who has gone south for the trip, is an assertive, critical, not very intelligent fellow with a foul tongue.

I would hate to pass the station over to the man. It would lose its graceful nuances, its deep comradeship and the finer sensibilities which have united practically every member of the 1953 party.

Bound for Mawson

The voyage south John Béchervaise had hoped to make with some of his fellow Heard Islanders successfully established Australia's first station (called Mawson) on mainland Antarctica. Less than 10 months after returning home from Heard Island, he was aboard ship once more, this time bound for the new station. There, he was officer in charge in 1955 and again in 1959.

Friday 22 January 1954

After lunch a few of us wandered round the lava uplands towards Corinth Head looking for the 12 sheep. I wondered whether any of the newcomers experienced the sharp, thrilling stimulus of jagged black lava, brilliant azorella.

We traversed the sharp lava, climbing up to the top crater overlooking the macaronis. Once we found sheep tracks but I felt sure they were no longer on the peninsula. However, some of the men went down to the Shag Rocks and found the whole 12 in good condition with plenty of grass and water. It might be possible for them to remain in this place, and it would be easier to muster them when winter comes.

Saturday 23 January 1954

'Johnny' Walsh made a cheerful slushy. He's a gentle, ineffectual sort of person with unexpected saving graces. He'll potter along with his Met observation work and his dogs, and probably be very happy within himself and good-humoured to his companions. Though one might not suspect it on casual acquaintance, I think he is deeply sensitive.

The new radio operator George Delahoy seems a useful type. He is quiet and self-contained. I think he and Gore will have a good year together. Tonight I felt rather out of touch. The mess seemed full of schoolboys.

Sunday 24 January 1954

Soft, depressing rain for a good part of the day; a low cloud ceiling and the glaciers looking very dull and lifeless. At breakfast I still felt a sense of loneliness; there seemed no intelligent conversation.

It is unfortunate that parties of two different vintages should have to work common ground for the next five or six weeks. My fellows are tired from the great efforts of the last few months; their eyes are turned towards home; some still feel a deep disappointment that they should have been left here whilst others are experiencing Kerguelen and adventures further south.

Monday 25 January 1954

Len Welch was slushy. I've never seen old Len looking so tired and dispirited. I tried to cheer him up but he doesn't find much fun in losing Fred and Peter and in inducting the new Met team. 'All I want, John, is to be on that boat heading for Australia!'

Tuesday 26 January 1954

A bitterly cold, windy day with grit blasting the station, and in the afternoon snow-showers. Budd and I made an early sortie to West Bay to relieve Keith Lodwick and allow him a morning's rest. It was a miserable head-down walk out, but Grahame was very interested in all he saw—and in my beloved stones. The man is becoming more assertive and in spite of his youth might be able to lead the 1954 party.

Wednesday 27 January 1954

A day of slushy duty with endless washings-up. I enjoyed Dick's company. I asked him whether he'd ever thought of going south as cook. 'Not enough dough in it for me, John. I'm goin' to be in the money from now on! Reckon I'll go to Canada!'

These next few weeks are going to be trying. Jack Walsh, today: 'Nobody in the Met seems to have shown any initiative since 1950!' The natural reaction of the newcomer—especially the returning old timer. The new party naturally wants to make the station its own.

Thursday 28 January 1954

News that at last the *Kista Dan* had left Kerguelen on her southward journey. The main problem had been shipping sufficient water through very rough seas. Pontoons had been overturned and drums lost. The French helped magnificently.

Another sombre day of drifting sand and marching showers. It was Ron's birthday and I just let him find his own peace all day. He rose late and occasionally appeared in his submarine suit. Otherwise everyone was energetic.

I am interested in Keith Lodwick, the new geophysicist. His outlook and philosophy are very different from Jim's. He is nothing like so neat in his work and far less particular; he seems to be quite oblivious of worry. Today he actually lost a magnetogram on his way to wash his traces in the lagoon. James would have been almost beside himself with anxiety; Keith searched high and low then ceased to be upset. He works very hard but takes off time for occasional walks and dings. I think he will be much happier than Jim, in fact temperamentally he is more mature, but already I miss Jim greatly. Keith will never drive himself as hard as James did but I don't doubt that he will be very efficient in all his final results, even if he brings his traces back to Melbourne in a dog-eared bundle.

There is a new atmosphere in the radio room. George Delahoy has installed a tangle of amateur transmitting equipment which trails all over the main apparatus. At the changeover the radio room was as sedate as a newly polished dentist's waiting-room; now it is an operating theatre. Gore is quiet, enthusiastic, even-tempered and knows his stuff. He is too withdrawn to run a station, but I think the radio room will prosper.

Bernie commented on a photograph showing Peter Brown, the great gangling storeman and field-tripper of last year's party. 'There is a man I do dislike,' he said. 'He used to make me very sad. He said during the changeover "If I had my way I'd get rid of all these bloody little Frenchmen!" He was a big bully, John!' In my three days sight of Brown, I had only considered him as a very kindly, immensely strong fellow.

I brought in as much grog as I thought suitable for Ron's birthday dinner. Since the departure of the films and projector, dings take a different pattern. There are several musicians in the new party and the evening soon became merry with instruments and tunes. Len Welch was in his element with piano and mouth organ; Jack Walsh blew his trumpet and the pleasant George Delahoy swayed about with his piano accordion. Grahame brought out his recorder, 'genuine Elizabethan plastic' he called it.

Friday 29 January 1954

The mess presented a sordid sight, littered with bottles and spilt ash-trays. The later stages of last night had brought out a couple of privately owned bottles of rum. I was thankful not to be slushy and went out into a wild, wet morning with relief.

Everything was forgotten in the sight of a most amazing congregation of birds feeding off-shore practically for the entire length of the cove. Evidently the sea was full of krill or plankton; I have never noticed such vast numbers of Cape pigeons smugly riding the surf nor so many Antarctic terns, suddenly diving in pursuit of some invisible morsel. Further out the blue-grey prions were also feeding in long straggling rafts and the rainy air was filled with all three birds. The funereal skuas seemed disconsolate compared with the joyous floating birds. They pecked disdainfully at ancient sand-drifted carcases on the shore.

The *Kista Dan* was expected to reach the pack ice today.

Saturday 30 January 1954

A mean wind steadily increasing to nearly 50 miles per hour, with gusts to 75, filled the air with sharp black grit, and laid bare stones and debris long buried. Men staggered along, heads down and eyes closed. Through the finest chinks of buildings it poured in a glistening black stream and fell in a gritty rain on food and tables. In less well-constructed huts, such as the biology, many pounds of sand gathered. This weather is the most uncomfortable we have ever experienced. Worse than any north-wind in the Mallee and yet only a degree or two above freezing. The supply of sand from the beaches is inexhaustible.

Dick set out soon after breakfast with Grahame Budd for the Jacka Valley. They reached the high point turning towards the final scree, but were so bombarded with grit and thrown off balance by the wind that they wisely returned and were back at the station soon after four with report of several king penguins, one very young. It seems that the kings are returning in some force to Heard Island; they may well form new colonies at this end of the island if they are undisturbed.

Sunday 31 January 1954

After lunch Budd, Bernie and I garbed ourselves for a walk on the ice, carrying crampons and ice-axes. Along Corinthian Beach we encountered a magnificent king penguin with brilliant orange side-patches and throat. He drew himself up very high, bill pointed almost vertically, and declined to be interested in us.

The Baudissin was more eroded than I have ever seen it. Travel was labyrinthine but perfectly safe. We passed onto the Schmidt, also deeply pitted but I decided to turn on to Drygalski when our unroped progress was no longer safe. So we left the ice and followed the small stream to the waterfall gully. A strong wind blew the spray back in drenching rain. The cascade seemed to be composed of huge falling feathers.

We soon reached the food dump, now bare of snow. Here we ate biscuits and sardines before turning home. As we crossed the azorella mounds the skuas swooped down, curtailing their attack a few feet from our heads. Idly I swung up my ice-axe to scare them off, I suppose, but the action was almost involuntary. To my great regret I killed a bird, an entirely unnecessary slaughter which flooded me with self-reproach. It was quickly dead, leaving its mate flying round alone.

February 1954

Sheep in the Azorella

Monday 1 February 1954

All men are children but in the cities they pretend to be men, hedging themselves with conventions, dressing to fashion. Down here their feelings are less screened, their thoughts more transparent; they show swift happiness and sullenness like children, in a manner that often calls for sympathy and affection. Men are far away from home and suddenly some feel a sense of insecurity and a great longing for the herd.

Explorers are boys, every one. Tonight as I read Phillip Law's despatches from the pack ice, I felt the same envy I once possessed of schoolfellows who were able to take vacations in distant parts, far beyond the ends of the roads I watched disappearing towards the Dandenong Ranges. But now I have measles or mumps—I wish I knew how the bug came my way—and I must stay on a very restless bed while Fred and Jimmie and the others are down south. What have I done to deserve this? Oddly enough I am also a little glad I am here, for there is a real job to do in blending the larger parts of two diverse groups. I should not have envied a new officer in charge's task; at least I can understand how my 1953 men feel at the end of a grand, hard year; and I believe I can live sufficiently in the enthusiasm of the new arrivals.

George Delahoy is engrossed in the construction of a minute transmitter, built in a chocolate tin, to be used on field trips. When Johnny Gore had finished a long and cheerful day's slushy duty, he induced cicada-like buzzes from the new apparatus. Ron, having a day off, settled at rendering down blubber.

Wednesday 3 February 1954

Rain threatened but did not fall for my early walk to West Bay. A skua walked up to me and tested my rubber boot with his beak. I have never met such a fearless, curious skua. For several minutes I examined him at my feet, his lovely mushroom plumage, bright eyes and capable talons—the latter seeming odd on webbed feet. I rather wonder whether any other bird possesses such formidable claws on swimming paddles.

I mustered 10 men to catch a sheep out on the lava uplands. The little flock has become completely at home amidst the azorella and tussock grass, and very man-shy. We stalked them for miles in pleasant bursts of sunshine, at times all on hands and knees crawling in towards the puzzled knot of sheep. Time and again they eluded us. Finally, Cec managed to grab a healthy, fat ram and it was coaxed back to the station and execution.

In the evening the splendid mountain almost cleared and was no less magnificent than on the first sight, nearly a year ago. The avalanche scars had been healed by recent high snow. Each towered ridge cast long, late shadows; each great ice corrie seemed so close—and yet is so infinitely remote.

Thursday 4 February 1954

Tonight a signal from Phil. 'Separated from objective by belt fast ice 16 miles wide through which ship attempting smash at about 2 miles daily.'

Friday 5 February 1954

The anniversary of our departure from Melbourne. Soon after breakfast six men left for day field trips. Dick and Grahame started off for the Jacka Valley and I followed a quarter of an hour behind. I lingered fascinated by the immense wind-sculpted stones at the south end of the cove. Clean-cut edges separate the sandblasted southerly face from the lichen-warmed northerly face. An orange lichen growth gives an appearance of perpetual sunshine; clumps of Kerguelen cabbage, now at its lush best, spring from the crevices.

I caught up with Dick and Grahame and we reached the foot of the last scree before the Jacka Glacier. From below, the cliffs at the top appear quite unnegotiable. The ascent is easier to the northern end where masses of azorella have taken hold. The route rounds the main buttress and gives onto a sharply tilted scree disgorging loose stones abruptly over a considerable cliff. Far below the sea lay very calm and deep blue.

Treading circumspectly we crossed the scree to the cushioned safety of the azorella. A few yards of pleasant, springy descent and we were on the ledge where the albatrosses nest. From this high, secret nursery birds fly all over the hemisphere and almost certainly circumnavigate the globe in the middle latitudes. It would be interesting to know how many black-brow colonies exist in faraway places (Alexander says it breeds at South Georgia, the Falkland Islands, Kerguelen, Auckland Island, Campbell Island and Ildefonse Island, Chile).

Immediately upon reaching the ledge one is greeted by dozens of downy, oyster-grey fledglings, standing and bleating with alarm on their high inherited stools. Like many such birds they have not only raucous sound for their defence, and a fairly powerful if but slightly developed bill, but the unpleasant ammunition of a crop filled with oily and malodorous chyme. Whilst Grahame and I photographed the chicks they rose in indignation and regurgitated violently. Fortunately their supplies of ammunition are apparently limited to recently taken food. Two chicks disgorged little fish about six inches long.

The stools on which they sit so securely are cylindrical, almost 13 inches in diameter and concave on top. Each year the parent birds provide a thin lining of new material which soon becomes matted down to a layer only a fraction of an inch thick. There are both fairly new and very old columns in the group. I can't really see why some of the very old nesting sites, judging by their mossy, time-smoothed sides, should not be the heirlooms of a century of more. Perhaps very occasionally a snow avalanche might destroy a few stools, though they are as firm as pize [*pise,* rammed earth] and there is no sign of such interruptions.

The air is a great clear ocean all round us with magnificent birds swimming below, banking and gliding effortlessly into the hidden caverns. Every detail of their plumage is visible as they sweep past. Their snow-white heads with never a satiny feather ruffled support deep yellow bills, flushed rose-pink. Over the eye is the dark brow-line exquisitely pencilled and fading imperceptibly at the edges. It gives the bird a rather studious and sleepy aspect. The great birds have an air of absolute innocence. They are clean-cut and wholesome almost beyond belief, embodying the pure sea air and the incorruption of the waves. Dick and Grahame ringed over 30 juvenile birds. There must be a last time for everything; perhaps I shall never revisit a lonely island where the black-brows nest. The day was good enough to last a life time.

Down on the moraine Grahame and I found ourselves surrounded by about a dozen Antarctic terns. The little birds 'dive-bombed' us with a ferocity and persistence outdoing that of the skua. They made their queer twittering cry incessantly except when it changed to an angry rattle at the moment of attack. They dived again and again, actually striking our heads after they had become sufficiently enraged. I wonder whether in spite of the thoroughness of our search there were not eggs or chicks? Black-capped, crimson-billed, body a delicate blue-grey paling to almost white, the Antarctic tern is one of the most beautiful birds. We joined Dick and moved slowly homewards over the wearisome beach boulders. No shoreline in the world could be more desolate and majestic and beautiful in a way that is unknown to most people on earth.

I received a signal from Lorna tonight. It's odd that this last month should seem so lonely. Probably because one's thoughts are turned so constantly homeward.

Saturday 6 February 1954

Vic Cleland expressed the opinion that I was an absolute fool, more or less, for 'giving' all my pictures to the Antarctic Division. He reckons that he will hand over no negatives except those taken with the rather poor camera supplied and on films sent down by the Division. The whole matter of expedition photography poses difficulties but I am sure that all worthwhile negatives should be deposited with the central authority. Like any enthusiastic photographer I have used my own equipment through the year and much of my personal film.

Sunday 7 February 1954

A sullen, wet morning. In the afternoon Grahame and I dressed for a brisk walk. We followed the beach, splashing through streams, then climbed up on the windswept spur leading down from Drygalski to Windy City. The place is a chaos of frost-shattered rock. Then we crossed the big plain to West Bay and climbed up to look at the sooty albatrosses and their chicks. The latter gulp and click their bills in the same way and prepare to disgorge oil if one approaches too closely. The lovely grey parents swept round and below us. On the summit of Andrée, an icy blast swept the hilltop.

We examined the cliffs north of Cave Bay. Appalling declivities drop into the turbulent sea. Between stretches of quite vertical cliff nearly 400 feet high are steep ridges. Most are covered with pumice and scoria in a highly unstable condition.

Tuesday 9 February 1954

News today from the *Kista Dan*, ice-bound. Dovers and some men are camped on a small island about a mile from their intended station site. Apparently the ice is moving quite a lot.

Wednesday 10 February 1954

A day spent with Cec doggedly finishing the last of nearly a thousand prints for the ANARE album. At night, after 12 hours or so, the atmosphere of dim light palls and we cheerfully 'gave it away'.

The great news was that things are moving again with the *Kista Dan*. The ice has moved, the blizzard has ceased. Explosives and pick and shovel work failed to clear a path for the ship, but natural ice movement apparently did the trick.

Thursday 11 February 1954

Grahame and Keith came into lunch with a report of a large penguin parading the beach below the hydrogen hut. He sported none of the king's magnificent colouring although the breast had a very faint all-over tinge of yellow. The marked side-patches of the king were absent; the throat was white to the base of the bill, the eyes surrounded by a grey circle. We escorted him to the biology hut and wished that Arthur could have been present to identify him, but believe he was a young emperor. If our photographs can be identified as such, it will be a new record for Heard. Apart from a single record from Kerguelen, probably a new record for sub-Antarctic latitudes.

Dinner brought further news of Phil and the *Kista Dan*. What would I not give to be down there!

An unusually clear night coincided with a brilliant aurora, shaped by the silhouette of Big Ben. A huge lenticular cloud streamed northward, black and pear-shaped. Every quarter-hour I recorded the form, altitude and intensity. I hope someday I shall see a splendid green aurora shivering the polar skies, and have nothing to do but watch it. There must be auroral activity on Heard on the majority of nights throughout the year. Nothing could illustrate better the almost perpetual cloud than the fact of only seven or eight observable aurorae in more than 11 months. I remained on watch. Towards 1 o'clock nothing was visible except a very faint glow like a sheet of almost invisible white gauze softening the glitter of rare southern stars.

Friday 12 February 1954

I heard the Met man's alarm clock and, after a long irresolute pause, the stumbling toward the 2 o'clock obs, and the wide-awake, less noisy return.

Cec spent most of his day with me, trimming several hundred small file photographic prints. Photography is a young man's hobby; old men do not take photographs. I have reached the stage where I contemplate vast collections of negatives with abhorrence, negatives that will never all be printed. I am only too glad to classify them all while I am still on the island, file them so that every single one is accessible should it ever be required, and hand them over to the Australian National Antarctic Research Expedition's photographic archives. *Sic transit Gloria*. To think of film exposed high on Big Ben, when Peter, Fred and I were the highest men in more than a quarter of the world (the coldest, darkest, windiest quarter!) being stowed away in dusty Collins Street.

During the year Béchervaise took more than 1100 photographs.

Today was Leon Fox's birthday. Very much by chance we heard of it — the Radio Australia session announced his mother's birthday greetings. Leon stumbled out with a grin, blushed beneath his beard and returned hurriedly to his dogs from our greetings.

Heard Island has clothed Leon more suitably; in Melbourne his garb was deceptively lamb-like. Here he looks almost as tough as he is, almost as happy as his spirit, and oddly gentle. At dinner we drank his health. The ding that followed developed into a brilliant occasion, doubtless assisted by the wines of our country. George swayed about with his piano accordion, Grahame piped away on his recorder and Jack Walsh blew his trumpet lustily. The piano, several mouth organs and tin whistles contributed, but Jack Hughes' one-man percussion band using buckets, frying pans and egg-beaters gave the concert its most memorable note. He sat in gloomy concentration, enjoying himself immensely.

Sunday 14 February 1954

Slept long and late then strode over the rough azorella mounds in a big circle, taking in the ropey lava along the sprayed cliffs, leaping from mound to mound, delighting in the uneven stresses and sudden shocks to my legs, returning in time for lunch. Lin Gardner and Jack Walsh shared the galley. Jack redeemed the day with a fine tasting if somewhat sodden Bakewell tart.

At 6 o'clock I walked to West Bay. Along the grey, morose beach I found a dying macaroni penguin struggling to keep three skuas at bay. They were in no mood to wait and were strutting in mercilessly to an unequal, cruel struggle. I killed the mac with a piece of elephant seal bone with one blow. Further on there was a king penguin amongst the ocean-worn stones. He stretched up his beautiful throat and displayed his fine, sharp beak then relapsed into uncontemplative stillness as I moved on. For hours on end penguins will stand huddled and immobile, almost in a state of suspended animation.

More than 30 dark skuas, a dozen dominicans and even a giant fulmar or two, wheeling nervously over the surf, were now assembled at the carcase of the macaroni. The skuas were trying to tug it from the water (they much prefer dry-land feeding), the dominicans stood daintily apart but alive to the possibilities of crumbs from the feasting of their fiercer cousins. It is astonishing how swiftly food news is communicated along the cold, hungry shores.

Tuesday 16 February 1954

Just before dinner I took a brief, brisk walk over the lava to Corinthian Bay—that is if one may use the word 'walk' for progressing over the torturous, buckled sheets of rock. The clouds pressed heavily on the world and allowed no shadows. The ice beyond the Nullarbor, and the rocks and azorella rising to the heads, possessed an unusual illumination. Black rock and grey sea, dusky blue ice, and mosses and azorella glowing brilliantly green and yellow as though transmitting light, like the glass of cathedral windows.

Sprawled along the Corinthian Beach the sombre leopard seals (only large, immensely powerful adults now) lay stretched to reveal sinews at rest and their extraordinary economy of flesh tapering from the thorax, like bodies in shrouds. Twelve to 14 feet long, they lay like corpses. Their pallid speckled underbodies were both cadaverous and plague-ridden. But, when you walk close enough to vibrate the sand, they start up alive, vital polar monsters with reptilean heads gaping teeth like cross-cut saws.

The dominican gulls wheel round in screaming flocks to warn you away from their fledglings. The cry of some birds cannot be described; the dominicans utter a series of short, high-pitched yet infinitely lonely and mournful notes, typical gulls' cries but transmuted by loneliness and the landscape of a dream. Sometimes, as they leave their speckled young to threaten the intruder, a sly, black skua sees his chance of a meal. Like the skuas, the dominicans also dive-bomb intruders but they terminate the downward swoop much earlier.

I ran back over the rough moon-mountains, the last living creature on earth except for birds—and gained a great hunger for dinner! Tonight the first home-brewed beer was sampled. It was very good, and more than justified the order we put through for hops.

Wednesday 17 February 1954

I was foolish enough to argue with Vic Cleland about the great mass of silvery, cloud-like mist that billowed out from the Black Cliffs, near Red Island. Cleland was really annoyed, apparently, that I would not agree with him. 'Call it a cloud, if you like,' I said, 'but I am sure it has been caused by wind blowing away falling spray and not by vaporization of water.' Here Vic with supreme contempt said, 'Clouds are condensation; not vapour!' and proceeded to lecture me on the properties of steam. Shortly afterwards the waterfall was visible trailing off into a 'downward smoke'. 'Oh, that,' commented the haughty Vic, 'I was talking about another cloud altogether, down below the Jacka Glacier'—which was a not very successful lie. I felt that Vic was a silly little 'twerp', but I was more annoyed with myself for treating him seriously.

Thursday 18 February 1954

Cooking breakfast today—plenty of bacon and eggs, coffee. About nine I handed over to Jack, cook, and Vic, slushy. Vic, who regards all domestic chores as below his dignity, who seems most happy drawling away to a group of lesser mortals, interspersing his sentences with many 'bloodies', will have a pretty unhappy year. Of all the 1954 party, I consider him least suitable. 'Oh, Christ Almighty,' he'll say in a slow, affected voice, 'do I have to do the bloody cooking again? I can't even cook bloodeh watar! Oh, God! I'll do my best but I'm no bloodeh cook.'

Dick, Grahame and Leon arrived back in the late afternoon. The tent had given excellent shelter, hundreds of birds had been ringed and 50 fur seals sighted at Red Island.

Friday 19 February 1954

Keith and I made a brief brisk circuit of the azorella to inspect the fur seals. They leapt towards us very aggressively, moving with great agility over the rough azorella and pools between the mounds. The sleek fur seals are completely different from the torpid elephants. They romp along on their flippers, using these very much as feet. Sharp little ears, pale, almost white, lie back on the neck in a line from the nose, the eye occupying a place roughly central between the two. Most observers have remarked on the aggressive nature of the species which Gwynn states as probably *Arctocephalus gazella*—the same as that found on Kerguelen. It is still doubtful whether the fur seal breeds on this island. Gwynn considers the considerable population of Kerguelen overflows to here during the breeding season.

Sunday 21 February 1954

Throughout a very warm night (maximum temperature 52°F between 7 and 8p.m. yesterday), it must have rained lightly. After lunch Dick, George Delahoy and Jack stumbled away over the wet azorella to find and shoot a sheep. They returned successful; a good shot of Dick's slew a sheep outright. Ever since the mighty hunters returned, the placing of the shot has grown more precise, the wind more furious and the distance progressively greater.

The wild, sombre day held intervals beneath low drifting clouds when the glowing greens of the azorella on Mount Aubert were preternaturally clear. Every needle of the Baudissin ice-foot seemed distinct although the light was utterly shadowless. When the showers were briefer than the pauses I set out gumbooted across the shallow flood of the Nullarbor for Corinthian Bay. Attracted by an unusually white leopard I made my way to the tumbling surfy beach.

The huge volume of water from the ice-caves in the Baudissin had ripped millions of cubic yards of sand from deep channels in the beach and the plain sweeping back to the ice. It made high, dangerous ripples as it rushed to the surf and in some places was far too deep to cross without risk of being swept away into the icy waves. So I scrambled up the sliding rubble of the moraine. Much of the stone, sand and gravel overlay black ice; in the hollows were sloughs of quick-slime and sand leading down to ice and little pits. I didn't test their depth. I was alone and found the atmosphere quite horrible. Even out on the open beach the sand was a little quick. Rain beat in my face all the way home.

I let my dripping clothes fall on the floor whilst Jack told me about the day's hunting and cleaned the rifle.

Monday 22 February 1954

A year and a day since we arrived on Heard Island! I have missed so little of civilization; chiefly my family, a very few friends and a garden of fruit and flowers.

When I read Phil's press message about the foundation of Mawson I experienced a fleeting surge of bitterness and envy. Bitterness that a year's unceasing labour and enthusiasm, and a desire never ceasing from boyhood, were insufficient to take me south; envy of my companions. My mind was taken off the matter by seeing a reference to the destruction of the great fig tree in the main street of Cairns. I thought of the old elms in the main street of Harpenden, Elizabethan trees to which for centuries men have gladly paid the small tribute of repairing pavements and even, once in a century, a house or shop-front.

The great triumph of the day was the removal of the old Walrus. For years it has lain more or less close to the site of its destruction; for years men have souvenired odds and ends. No party has landed on the black beach of Atlas Cove without the wreck of the old 'plane providing an initial impact and an enduring memory. Finally today Jack and Lin hitched up the tractor-winch and in a very short time it was dragged away to disintegrate further in a more suitable grave.

Tuesday 23 February 1954

Keith was very excited because he 'had' an earthquake. Leon came looking for bullets. He had to shoot six bitches this morning and he hated the job like hell. I helped him and Jack throw the carcases into the sea off Wharf Point.

In worsening weather a large muster of us gathered on Wharf Point after lunch and toiled bluntly through the afternoon building a rough little jetty to enable the 'D4' tractor to be loaded on the *Kista Dan* when she returns. Keith Lodwick and I donned waders and splashed round beyond our waists in the cold water endeavouring to build a 'pig sty' of heavy railway sleepers.

Thursday 25 February 1954

Jack Walsh received a telegram giving the completely unexpected news of his father's death. He was very depressed about it. There is practically nothing one may do to help. Apparently his mother is left by herself with a house to pay for. A younger brother cleared out some time last year.

Friday 26 February 1954

The *Kista Dan* has left Mawson and is surveying the coast of Antarctica eastward from the new station. I commenced cancelling some hundreds of letters for the return mail to Australia. The majority by far is philatelic mail, chiefly from dealers. They have printed and stamped strange slogans and devices on envelopes—'Australia's sub-Antarctic Outpost' etc. Storrer, at Mawson, must have had a tremendous job cancelling stamps on 23,000 letters.

Sunday 28 February 1954

In the evening there was a great congregation in the 'Bilge', holding animated conversation. I was terse about the sudden invasion of station headquarters and suggested I might change homes for the night with Budd—since when there has been a measure of peace. Should I become officer in charge of another remote station I shall appropriate some small space as an unalloyed retreat.

A signal from Phil has just come in. It gives his ETA Heard as either next Saturday or Sunday.

March 1954

The Expedition Evaporates

Monday 1 March 1954

An extraordinarily calm day with pearly mists gradually disappearing from the headlands. The cove grew steadily bluer.

Six of us went up on the Baudissin to the seracs, the ultimate contrast with the flat, soft plain that stretches from the camp. For two or three square miles the ice is in fantastic peaks and valleys, with ravines up to 50 feet deep. The weird ice-scape is terminated by cliffs; some rise more than 100 feet above the breakers of Corinthian Bay. We scrambled cautiously about in the sunlight. When the mist commenced drifting across Corinth Head I decided to return. By the time we had extricated ourselves the light had lost its magic. As we finally left the pressure ice the Nullarbor was rubbed out by mist.

For a while I was busy issuing a tobacco ration and laying out wines to celebrate the birthday of Vic Cleland. Len Welch, as temporary Met chief proposed his health and Grahame Budd seconded. When Vic is natural, I like him very much; he has a sensitive outlook and a well-developed aesthetic taste.

Soon after 11, to bed with a new book on Amundsen [Bellamy Partridge (1929) *Amundsen: The Splendid Norseman*].

Tuesday 2 March 1954

There are few days left before the ship returns. I have ceased to be particular about how my 1953 men employ their time. Most have a lot of personal packing to do. The 1954 men are absorbed with skeds and obs. The day started like yesterday, with pearly visions of the mountain, but there was less time before the cloud intensified to a dull day with mist just blackening the sand.

Wednesday 3 March 1954

Another splendid morning of low mist and calm sunshine breaking through to irradiate the sea and azorella uplands. Big Ben showed in all perfection, a heart-shaking sight.

At dinner we had another sample of Heard Island home-brew beer. It forms a terrific head and opening the bottles provides some hazard, but the taste is not bad. Cec and I have almost finished the photographic programme—for every man of the 1953 party, about 30 large prints of the island.

Thursday 4 March 1954

Keith Lodwick went to bed soon after breakfast. He had worked through the night. He is only 22. He came in from West Bay grinning, hitching his trousers over fairly prominent buttocks, sweeping back his straight, black hair. He has begun to grow a villainous beard. He is a thoughtful lad with very wide interests; he moves in bounds physically and intellectually.

John Gore is anxious to increase the scope of the Sydney radio skeds which are for contact and emergency. He is not appreciative of Ken's work in achieving day-to-day contact with Perth. There is a natural antipathy between incoming and outgoing parties. Ken is a showman and possibly he hasn't half the interest in technical matters that Johnny Gore shares with George, but he made the radio room a place fit to be entered, and he cleared traffic both inwards and outwards with an unfailing regularity.

The mountain cleared in the late afternoon, and steel-grey clouds gave a strange intense light to the high snows. I thought worse weather would follow but darkness brought a night of stars. Perfectly calm and cloudless; not a faint glow of the aurora even to mask the brilliance of the Scorpion over the dark mountain; nothing to mask the Cross right overhead. In the night air there was that faintly astringent smell of a still, frosty night.

Friday 5 March 1954

We started burning some of the debris that's been there for years. We continued the work until the smoke of many fires was drifting tranquilly across the Nullarbor. The mountain showed through a thin veil of cloud but later cleared at the summit, and glowed pink long after sunlight had vanished from the rest of the island. I was quite happy about the condition of the station. I am ready to hand it over to the 1954 party and the *Kista Dan* cannot return too soon. A signal has come from Phil: 'Delayed by severe storm in Mackenzie Sea. Shall advise you when we get moving again.'

Saturday 6 March 1954

Late last night the radio operator on the *Kista Dan* had given Cec details of the storm in the Mackenzie Sea. 'The most dangerous we have had ever. Nearly wrecked this morning. Wind about 90 to 100 knots. The ship went about 78° over to starboard side. The aircraft is away in the sea, strong winds pushed it overboard this morning. Some are more afraid than others.'

In this morning's clear sunshine, a film of green I have never noticed so high before is visible to the brinks of waterfalls tumbling from the Olsen ice. A number of small prions and divers lay dead in the black sand. I picked up two, almost indistinguishable except for the black line down the backs of the legs of one.

Sunday 7 March 1954

A quiet day. After breakfast I spent some time examining the two little divers. When I had finished I threw them to the skuas. Within seconds, there were 20 birds involved.

At six I set out for Corinth Head. It was good to be out. To my satisfaction, not having smoked for some weeks, I felt extraordinarily fit. The skuas do not swoop down so forcibly now their chicks are mobile. They struggled up against the wind and swept down it in graceful glissades, inaudible in the gale. I suddenly caught a glimpse of the high snows of the mountain glowing in the late sun, rising completely aloof from the murk and teeming rain that enveloped me.

Monday 8 March 1954

I walked across to West Bay, interested in the number of small seals (scarcely larger than some of the porkies we branded) hauled out. None of them was branded, that I saw, out of 15 or 20.

I did a little washing of clothes and ironed all my shorts and handkerchiefs for the voyage home. Then I packed practically everything including clothes.

At about six I suggested to Leon that he might like a quick walk to the top of Drygalski. He was glad enough to splash across the Nullarbor. The wettest parts are firmest, oddly enough. Several acres of stony ground is a quagmire. Even when one treads on the stones they sink uncertainly into the slime. These last 'beatings of bounds' fill me with a vague sadness that I may never tread the paths again.

We stayed on top for a few minutes while Leon smoked a cigarette. A grand horizon is broken by the northern glaciers, Saddle Point, the North West Cornice, the Vahsel and the Abbotsmith moraine, the bays and the cloud-pressed Laurens Peninsula. For a year and more none of us has moved more than 10 miles from camp, and almost all our destinations lay before us. On the way back Leon said, 'You know, I often think of that camp at Red Island, so desolate. Sometimes I think if only the eyes of the soul could remain here forever, they would see the station moulder away, and the rocks and the mountains would say how brief and meaningless was the whole life of man!'

Wednesday 10 March 1954

Most of the time went to completing my sketch of the camp, in an odd gloomy mood of grief that I had not been on the *Kista Dan* and sadness at leaving Heard.

Thursday 11 March 1954

The 1953 and the 1954 men—the former, with all their gear down to the last stone or elephant seal's tooth packed and labelled for home, are more than ever isolated from the latter, who have now unpacked and integrated themselves within the station. A man very soon becomes bound to the island and his work. Then, when the time comes for the station to be relieved, each man must sever a thousand spiritual and physical threads. Some men are very eager. Home, however it might have been despised in the past, suddenly seems the fairest Mecca.

I walked in the evening, sighting only eight of the 10 sheep and returning when heavy rain rolled over the Atlas Roads. The *Kista Dan* should reach Heard by Saturday night and, on account of water shortage, will call at Kerguelen.

Saturday 13 March 1954

A signal came in bearing to Len Welch the heavy grief of his mother's death. I felt sorry for Len missing his reunion by so little.

A furious sou'westerly, reaching little short of 100 miles per hour, scooped up the sea and raised great water spouts in the Atlas Roads. Whorls of spray reaching hundreds of feet into the air advanced on the lava cliffs and continued over the uplands for hundreds of yards, a truly magnificent sight.

Grahame and Lin set out with the Ferguson to empty the gash, everything well lashed down against the gale. I went by myself, leaning hard on the wind. A flock of dominicans took to the air from the edge of the cliffs and were instantly scattered like pieces of paper. I followed the edge of the cove, fighting my way along the beach and soon drenched with spray. At the far end had been washed some carcases of dogs, hideous now. Suddenly I was oppressed with the sight of wind-rubbed bones, of death and dissolution. The wind bombarded me with fragments of pumice and with spray. The white foam of the ocean's edge disappeared in the spindrift. Somewhere beyond an imaginary skyline rolled the Kista Dan, more lonely than an albatross in mid-ocean. I did not envy those afloat.

I climbed up beyond where the sooties nest to the edge of Cave Bay. Except crawling or prone, I couldn't reach the brink. I lay with my face in the stinging wind and watched the turbulence below. The cove was choked with spray which rose in the air and drifted in white clouds over the cliffs 200 feet above. No wonder no birds nest on the black island of the bay! Torrents of boiling surf ran down its sides.

I was blown back to the station in time for dinner and the news that the Kista Dan should be here tomorrow. She will not enter the Roads while this keeps up. For the last time I put out some beer for a Saturday ding. I played chess with Keith and we had some music from George Delahoy, but there seemed to be no focus to the evening. Late at night the wind held a restless whining note, as though still unsatisfied. I have seldom seen a blacker night, but in the north stretched a wide pale gash of light from the hidden moon.

Sunday 14 March 1954

Our ship sked was to be at 1.30 but I had a feeling that the Kista Dan might arrive before then. So I stirred up Jack and Lin and asked them to start the tractors. Then, quite suddenly, at about 11.30, there she was! Over the azorella, her masts rocking against the grey Olsen screes. By the time we had the dinghy dragged down into the sea, heavy squalls had sprung up. Several men wanted to go out to the ship but I chose Dick McNair and Grahame Budd, both of whom could row tolerably.

However, the outboard motor wouldn't start. Eventually the motor gave so much trouble that we decided to change it for one still crated. The three left with the motor chugging powerfully, but it stopped several times on the way out to the *Kista Dan* and I watched the heavy rowing from Wharf Point, when the dinghy made scarcely any headway. The motor eventually got her there.

Grahame Budd stayed on board but the dinghy soon returned with Jack, Dick and Danny Sweetensen. For the rest of the day there was intermittent rain with severe squalls. In the end Captain Petersen decided he must put to sea. All operations were suspended.

Danny Sweetensen was immediately very much at home. Soon Jack Walsh and Vic Cleland were down in the Bilge, with good Scotch whisky contributing a glow to the occasion. We heard a lot about the voyage and the establishment of Mawson. Danny is a good cook but he seems full of swagger and foul language, and not particularly intelligent. At the evening meal, when probably he was a little drunk, he voiced so much foulness and obscenity that finally, though it was probably my last night on the island, I told him quietly that we held different standards. I wandered down to the Bilge after dinner, half-intending to write for a while, but the place is no longer mine.

Monday 15 March 1954

Earlier than I expected the *Kista Dan* was back in Atlas Roads. Johnny Gore came in with a message shortly after seven that Phil required all men and gear on the beach as soon as possible. After yesterday's false starts men stuffed their blankets once more into their bags and loaded them on a trailer. As each man once again completed his packing, I sent him in to have breakfast. No boat came. Even after the radio announced that the boat had left, no craft detached itself from the *Kista Dan*. For a long time the unloading of certain crates continued at the ship's side.

Then, puffing black smoke through a long thin funnel, one of the ship's red lifeboats came chugging round Wharf Point. Once again our isolation was broken. I stepped down and welcomed Phillip Law, Arthur Gwynn—clean-shaven and almost unrecognizable—Jim Brooks and Dr Andre Migot, French observer at Mawson and late of Kerguelen. With delight I looked at them all. The *Kista Dan* might easily have been forced to winter in the ice—we might all easily have spent a parallel confinement on Heard.

With great pleasure I found the film projector, films and spares coming ashore. That, doubtless, was Grahame Budd's triumph. I am very glad indeed that for another year the rec room will know such fun as we experienced.

Keith Lodwick returned from West Bay with Leon. They had been over to collect four unfortunate gentoos for the Melbourne National Museum.

I discussed the matter of my successor on Heard Island with Phil; his decision was that Grahame Budd should be officer in charge with Murray Henderson, a stalwart-looking Met man who had been down to Mawson with the ship, as second in charge. In the rec room, after a brief lunch, Phil gathered all members of the 1954 party and myself. He announced the formal changeover and I shook hands with both Grahame and Murray Henderson. Phil wished the new party well. I knew just what they were all feeling; it would be good to be alone, to take stock of themselves and their charge.

Some of them wandered down to see us on our way. How hard to believe that we were homeward bound, that in a couple of weeks, after 13 months, we should see so many loved ones, trees, flowers and familiar rooms. One or two men wandered along the windy cliff to see us rejoin the ship. It seemed only a moment since I had done the same, when the little *Tottan* strained at her cables.

Here ends a personal
journal of more than
a year spent with
12 companions on
Heard Island.

Southern Ocean, about 120°E, 50°S
26th March 1954

It will not be long now, my dearest beloved. Further west in these latitudes I wrote the same words more than 500 pages ago in this long letter. Almost every day since then has added a page or more. For nearly 400 nights I have heard only the gathered voices of great winds sweeping half the globe, winds that always seemed voices of menace and power when they found our tiny frail settlement.

The loneliness and simplicity of life in the Antarctic has not refreshed my little love for the bright lights of cities. My utmost joy is in the thought of tranquillity at home, walking with you in the garden or in the country, playing with the children, digging earth, sitting at the kitchen table, reading a book or listening to music or talking with friends.

For the first time in more than a year, since we left the Atlas Roads, I have found no reason to record the passing days. I sit on my bunk now, with my little typewriter tied securely to a heavy box. After leaving Heard Island we ran out into a storm worse than anything the *Kista Dan* had experienced further south. Although this ship is a lot larger than the *Tottan*, 1200 tons seems very small amidst 45 foot waves.

We are now rolling along about a thousand miles south of the western end of the Bight. It is the roughest sea we have experienced since leaving Heard, except for the first day. This, beloved, is the end of my letter. I have no time for the past; I am impatient of the present. I shall watch the spray and the albatrosses.

We arrived in Melbourne on 31st of March, the last day of our charter. The temperature was around 80 degrees. The expedition evaporated (Fred Elliott, diary entry, 31 March 1954).

References

Primary Sources

Anon., Remarks on passage of Bark *Oriental*, MS227–28. Cambridge: Scott Polar Research Institute.

Béchervaise, John, Heard Island daybooks, Béchervaise Papers, February 1953–March 1954, National Library of Australia, MS7972, Boxes 5 and 6.

Bowden, Tim, ANARE oral history interview with John Béchervaise, 3 December 1987, Geelong.

Department of Defence, Antarctic (including Falkland Islands dispute), 1946–1948. National Archives of Australia: A5954, 2311/1.

Elliott, Fred, Heard Island diary, 1953–1954, Elliott Papers, National Library of Australia, MS9442.

Fitch, Stu, Activity report: marine debris survey and other matters, Heard Island 2000–2001, unpublished, in Stu Fitch's possession.

Fitch, Stu, Grit: a series of lighthearted newsletters from Heard Island 2000–2001, unpublished, in Stu Fitch's possession.

Gibbney, Leslie, Heard Island diaries 1950 and 1952, National Library of Australia, MS9392.

Paddick, Johnny, Heard Island diary, 1949, unpublished, in Tim Ealey's possession.

Phillips, Helen, oral history interview with John Béchervaise, 1976, Oral History Collection, National Library of Australia, TRC 430; plus transcription (initial interviewer Suzanne Lunney), re-recorded 10 June 1976, National Library of Australia, Canberra.

Secondary Sources

Anon., 'News Round-up', *Aurora*, vol.20, no.4, 2001: 31–2.

Australian Antarctic Division, *Atlas Cove, Heard Island Cultural Heritage Management Plan.* Kingston, Tasmania: Australian Antarctic Division, c.2001.

Australian Antarctic Division, *Preliminary Guide to the Flora and Fauna of Heard Island (for visitors).* Kingston, Tasmania: Australian Antarctic Division, 2002.

Australian Fisheries Management Authority, *Heard Island and McDonald Islands Fishery: Management Policy 1998 to 2000.* Canberra: Australian Fisheries Management Authority, 1998.

Australian National Antarctic Research Expedition, *Heard Island and Macquarie Island Operations Manual.* Melbourne: Antarctic Division, 1953.

Bergstrom, Dana and Paul Scott, 'Heard Island Uncovered: 2000–01 Summer ANARE', *Australian Antarctic Magazine*, vol.2, 2001: 30.

Bergstrom, D.M. and P.M. Selkirk, 'Terrestrial Vegetation and Environments on Heard Island', *Papers and Proceedings of the Royal Society of Tasmania*, vol.133, no.2, 2000: 33–46.

Bertrand, K.J., *Americans in Antarctica 1775–1948*, special publication 39. New York: American Geographical Society, 1971.

Bowden, Tim, *The Silence Calling: Australians in Antarctica 1947–97*. Sydney: Allen and Unwin, 1997.

Brown, K.G., 'The Leopard Seal at Heard Island, 1951–54', *ANARE Interim Report* 16. Melbourne: Antarctic Division, 1957.

Brown, Peter Lancaster, *Twelve Came Back*. London: Hale, 1957.

Budd, Grahame M., 'The ANARE 1963 Expedition to Heard Island', *ANARE Reports Series A*, vol.1, 1964.

Budd, Grahame M., 'Exploration of Heard Island between 1947 and 1971', *Antarctic and Southern Ocean Law and Policy Occasional Paper*, vol.10, 2006: 1–65.

Budd, Grahame M., 'Australian Exploration of Heard Island, 1947–1971', *Polar Record*, vol.43, no.225, 2007: 97–123.

Burton, Harry, '1987–88 Field Season at Heard Island', *ANARE News*, vol.54, 1988: 3.

Clark, Gerry, *The Totorore Voyage*. Auckland: Century Hutchinson, 1988.

Crowther, W.L. 'Heard Island', *Walkabout*, vol.17, no.9, 1951: 44, 46, 48.

Dalziel, Ken, *Penguin Road*. Sydney: Angus and Robertson, 1955.

Downes, Max, 'First Visitors to Heard Island', *ANARE Research Notes*, no.104, 2002.

Downes, Max and Elizabeth Downes, 'Sealing at Heard Island in the Nineteenth Century', in Ken Green and Eric Woehler (eds), *Heard Island: Southern Ocean Sentinel*. Sydney: Surrey Beatty and Sons, 2006.

Godley, E.J., 'Botany of the Southern Exploration Zone', *Tuatara*, vol.18, no.2, 1970: 49–93.

Green, Ken and Eric Woehler (eds), *Heard Island: Southern Ocean Sentinel*. Sydney: Surrey Beatty and Sons, 2006.

Gressitt, J.L. and Philip Temple, 'Introduction to Heard Island', *Subantarctic Entomology, Particularly of South Georgia and Heard Island*, Pacific Insects Monograph 23. Honolulu: Entomology Department, Bernice P. Bishop Museum, 1970: 17–30.

Haffey, Joseph C., 'The Metamorphosis of the Ship *Alert*, 1828–1862', *Log of Mystic Seaport*, vol.46, no.3, 1994: 66–75, 95–6.

Kiernan, Kevin and Anne McConnell, 'Management Considerations for the Heard Island Lava Tube Caves', *Papers and Proceedings of the Royal Society of Tasmania*, vol.133, no.2, 2000: 13–22.

Law, Phillip and John Béchervaise, *ANARE: Australia's Antarctic Outposts*. Melbourne: Oxford University Press, 1957.

Lazer, E. and A. McGowan, *Heard Island Archaeological Survey*, 2nd edn. Sydney: Department of Architectural and Design Science, University of Sydney, 1990.

Lied, Nils, 'Appendix: Narrative of the Atlas Cove Party', in Grahame M. Budd (ed.), 'The ANARE 1963 Expedition to Heard Island', *ANARE Reports Series A*, vol.1, 1964: 46–53.

Powell, William and Suzanne Y. O'Reilly, Nature and evolution of the lithospheric mantle beneath Heard Island: fieldwork and preliminary results, poster presented at Australian Antarctic Division workshop 'Heard and McDonald Islands', Hobart, 8–9 June 2002.

Quilty, Patrick G. and Graeme Wheller, 'Heard Island and the McDonald Islands: A Window into the Kerguelen Plateau', *Papers and Proceedings of the Royal Society of Tasmania*, vol.133, no.2, 2000: 1–12.

Roberts, Brian, 'Historical Notes on Heard and McDonald Islands', *Polar Record,* vol.5, no.40, 1950: 580–4.

Scholes, Arthur, *Fourteen Men.* Melbourne: F.W. Cheshire, 1949.

Shaughnessy, P.D. et al., 'Fur Seals at Heard Island: Recovery from Past Exploitation?', in M.L. Augee (ed.), *Marine Mammals of Australasia: Field Biology and Captive Management.* Sydney: Royal Zoological Society of New South Wales, 1988: 71–7.

Smith, Jeremy, *Specks in the Southern Ocean.* Armidale: University of New England, 1986.

Temple, Philip, *The Sea and the Snow: The South Indian Ocean Expedition to Heard Island.* Melbourne: Cassell Australia, 1966.

Thomson, Sir Wyville, *The Voyage of the 'Challenger'.* London: Macmillan and Co., 1877.

Thornton, M. (ed.), *Heard Island Expedition 1983.* Sydney: Spirit of Adventure Pty Ltd, 1983.

Truswell, Elizabeth M. et al., 'Late Miocene Vegetation and Palaeoenvironments of the Drygalski Formation, Heard Island, Indian Ocean: Evidence from Palynology', *Antarctic Science*, vol.17, no.3, 2005: 427–42.

Veenstra, C. et al., *Expedition to the Australian Territory of Heard Island and McDonald Islands 1980*, Technical Report no. 31. Canberra: Department of National Development and Energy, 1982.

Vincent, R. and A. Grinbergs, Isolation, ingenuity, innovation and experimentation: lessons for Antarctic expeditions from a ramshackle collection of old sheds, Atlas Cove, Heard Island Draft Cultural Heritage Management Plan, prepared for the Australian Antarctic Division, Kingston, Tasmania, 2002.

Williams, R., 'The Inshore Fishes of Heard and McDonald Islands, Southern Indian Ocean', *Journal of Fish Biology*, vol.23, 1983: 283–92.

Woehler, Eric J. et al., 'Long-term Population Increase of Black-browed Albatrosses at Heard Island, 1947/1948 – 2000/2001', *Polar Biology*, vol.25, 2002: 921–7.